Gliding Soles
Lessons from a Life on Water

Keith St. Onge

With Karen Putz

"I have been a barefoot water skier since age 16. I never learned the right way to do things, so I got Keith St. Onge to spend a week with me, my son, and some guys to show us how it's done and teach us some tricks. As my family and I spent time with Keith, getting to know him on and off the water, what really impressed me more than anything was this guy's character, his integrity and his relentless determination to succeed. I learned a lot from him, and you will too. This book is must read for anyone who wants to win in life."

Dave Ramsey, *New York Times best-selling author and nationally syndicated radio show host*

"Too many people walk away from their passion with the negative belief that pursuing it would be unrealistic. Keith skied right toward his passion and has a life of purpose and meaning as a result. A great example for all doubters and small thinkers."

Dan Miller, *Author and Life Coach (www.48Days.com)*

"Gliding Soles is a powerful book about life detailing the many steps, choices, and falls Keith St. Onge took on his way to becoming World Champion. I highly recommend it for everyone. Why? Because Keith's story is really your story. Life is tough and we all take some hard falls along the way. The key is getting up, making a better choice, and getting back on your feet. This book will encourage you to do just that no matter what your goals are in life."

Tom Ziglar, *Proud son of Zig Ziglar, President of Ziglar Inc.*

"Gliding Soles is much more than a book about barefooting, it really should be titled "Gliding Souls." This book touches on the many aspects of what it takes to succeed in life. Keith does a masterful job of taking you through the ups and downs of his life and even lets you into his soul...and that is where the true lessons are. This is a *must-read* for anyone looking to find the meaning to their life!"

Dan Leclerc, *credit union CEO and President*

"Every now and then, every sport has someone who is special—it may be through performance, contribution, or style. Whatever the reason--they stand out and are considered to be above all others. In the sport of barefoot water skiing, Keith St. Onge is one of those people and he achieved this through tremendous commitment to his life's goals and dreams.

I believe you should live an inspiring life both to yourself and to others, and Keith St. Onge has been an inspiration to me. Now others have the opportunity to experience this inspiration through *Gliding Soles*."

Glen Plake, *Ski and Snowboard Hall of Fame*

"Through hard work, imagination and an unyielding pursuit of his dreams, Keith St. Onge became a multi-time World Barefoot Champion. *Gliding Soles, Lessons from a Life on Water* takes readers of all ages on an inspiring journey through Keith's life, chronicling important lessons he learned along the way. I highly recommend this book if you are pursuing excellence in your life."

Scott N. Atkinson, *Editor, The Water Skier magazine*

"Years ago, when I took a shy, young boy out on the lake in New Hampshire, I had no idea I was teaching a future World Champion how to barefoot water ski. After I retired from competition I followed Keith's career and watched him climb the ranks all the way to the top. Just a few years ago, I learned the young boy I taught was Keith--I was blown away!

*Gliding Soles, Lessons from a Life on Wate*r is an excellent book. Keith shows people what it takes to be the best. Reading and learning to do more and more of what the Bible says has helped me thru my life far more than anything else. There are two books I recommend: the *Bible*... and *Gliding Soles*."

Mike Seipel, *Two-time World Barefoot Champion, owner of Barefoot International*

"Believe and you shall receive! In his first book, *Gliding Soles, Lessons from a Life on Water*, barefoot champion Keith St. Onge inspires positive thought, a strong ethic and the will to be your best no matter how daunting life's journey can be."

Todd Ristorcelli, *Editor, WaterSki magazine*

"If you're looking for a story of faith and courage, you'll find it in *Gliding Soles*. Those who know Keith probably envy his skiing skills, but sometimes they forget what it takes to get there. Keith shows what it takes to go through the highs and the lows to make it big: you gotta keep believing in yourself."

Patrick Wehner, *2002 Tricks Champion, French Barefoot Team*

"As an owner of multiple Fitness Centers in two countries, I understand the level of commitment and passion required to succeed at one's health and fitness goals. In the sport of barefoot water skiing, success can only come with incremental changes. I know of no other individual that has committed himself to a lifetime of incremental changes. Keith inspires me to be a better person because his success could not exist without a mountain of failures. What a book..."

Mike Betts, *Multi-Club Owner Anytime Fitness*

"I am not really a reader of many books, but when I got the opportunity to read Keith's book, I could not put it down. The story which unfolded in *Gliding Soles* really goes to show what a road it is to be a World Champion; a road that is filled with many obstacles and challenges. Keith shows what it takes to be one of the few--not one of the many."

Fred Groen, *Managing Director, Groenz Ltd*
World Senior Jump Champion, Iron Man and Ski Racer

"Keith's rise to World Champion and becoming one of the most-decorated barefoot water skiing athletes in history is no fluke. Keith had a plan and the desire to get to the top. From his early days of sleeping in vans at tournaments to being co-owner of the most successful barefoot water skiing school on the planet, his story is riveting. *Gliding Soles* is a must-read for anyone who has a quest to fulfill a dream."

Dave Miller, *Corporate Pilot for a major insurance company*

*It can take a lifetime to achieve
one small level of understanding.*

My father, Claude St. Onge

Table of Contents

My Life

As I settle into my aisle seat on the plane, there's a man sporting a three-piece business suit sitting in the seat next to me. He's clearly dressed for an important meeting and there's an agonized look on his face. No matter how much he fiddles with the knobs overhead, the weak stream of warm air only adds to his discomfort. I notice he is sweating through his suit and I can smell his Old Spice deodorant working overtime. I'm as comfortable as can be sitting in my board shorts, sandals, and a t-shirt with "World Barefoot Center" imprinted on the front. I feel sorry for him. After all it's 95 degrees on the tarmac and it feels like 85 degrees on the plane.

Yanking at his tie, he slumps back in the seat, and exhales a long sigh. "Hi, there, I'm Tom Rodrick." He extends his hand and I shake it. "I'm Keith St. Onge."

"I didn't quite catch that last name... did you say Orange?"

"Not quite," I grin. "Saint Onge, O-N-G-E. I get St. Orange all the time though."

"What's that, French or something?"

"French Canadian. My grandparents are from the Montreal area."

I learn that Tom is a senior lawyer for a large corporation and he's on his way to a meeting to handle business mergers. He's dreading the meeting and he doesn't like his job. The paperwork is overwhelming and the stress level is sky high. Tom pauses for a second. "So what brings you to Minneapolis, Keith? Are you heading home or traveling for business?"

"I'm going for business, but it's not like work to me, it's more like pleasure." His eyes widen. "Oh?"

I smile. "I'm a professional barefoot water skier, based in Winter Haven, Florida. I'm heading to Lake O'Dowd near Minneapolis for a week to teach barefoot water skiers proper techniques." Tom looks confused. It's a look I'm familiar with when I talk about my career.

"I barefoot water ski--with no skis on my feet," I explain. I reach into my bag and pull out the latest issue of WaterSki magazine featuring a cover photo of me with one foot in the air and the other gliding on the water.

"Wow...that's, uh, different!" he exclaims. "I've never heard of anything like that before. So, did you grow up skiing in Florida?"

"No, I grew up in Berlin, New Hampshire which is not far from Mount Washington."

"Do you ski at Sea World or any of those ski shows?"

I stifle a laugh. "I do get that question often! I've never skied at Sea World, but I've been in some water ski shows. I've actually won a few National and World titles."

"Isn't it awfully cold in New Hampshire more months than not?" he asks. "How do you get enough practice when the summers are so short?"

"Definitely short summers," I nod. "I started skiing in a ski show on Lake Umbagog, which is about an hour north of Berlin. From the age of ten, I was hooked on barefooting and skied every day I could. By the time I was thirteen, I knew I wanted to make a career out of it."

"You mean you can make a living with barefoot water skiing?" He shoots me an incredulous look.

"Yeah, I do. I co-own a ski school in Florida with the four-time World Champion, David Small. I also do traveling clinics like the one I'm heading to now and I own a wetsuit company. Barefoot tournaments don't pay the bills," I laugh. "But they take me all over the world."

"You're a lucky guy," says Tom. "I make great money as a lawyer, but I don't enjoy the stress that comes with it. At least you can make a living doing something you love!"

"You're right. Most days are great, but you know, some days sure do feel like work!"

"It sure doesn't sound like work to me," says Tom. "I mean, you travel and you're in the boat all day with different people each week--that sounds like a perpetual vacation!"

"Ah, think about those days when it's cold, one hundred degrees out, or raining-- it's not so much fun then!" I smile. "Every now and then, I'll have a customer who tells me how to do my job or one who whines all day. You know how it is...you can't make everyone happy. And the falls I take at 45 miles an hour--sometimes it feels like hitting concrete!"

"Man, that's gotta hurt!" Tom winces. "You've been doing this since you were a kid, what keeps you going?"

"This is what I've always wanted to do. Every time I put my feet on the water I feel incredibly free and I'm fulfilling my dream. It's just me and the water." I cross my fingers and hold them up. "You see, Jesus and I are like this," I wink. "We both walk on water."

Chapter 1: The Unknown Beginning

We can let circumstances rule us or we can take charge and rule our lives from within.

~Earl Nightingale

"Skiers, line up and get ready!" Swampy barked. Although only in his late-20s, Swampy's thick, booming voice made him seem much older. His balding head gleamed in the sun and his scraggly brown beard needed a trim. Gary "Swampy" Bouchard was the Lake Umbagog ski show director and he was a cousin on my mother's side of the family. The nickname was bestowed on him many years ago; it was a reference to being a little pest, just like a Swamp Owl.

"Keith, you're the first act, get on the kneeboard." Swampy directed me into the water. My first performance in the Lake Umbagog ski show was a simple one. All I had to do was ride on a kneeboard behind the boat and wave to the crowd. The show was held in front of our family cottage and featured water skiers riding around the lake doing pyramid formations, clown acts, tricks on skis, and barefoot skiing. Since we didn't have much room in our yard, the crowd for the show overflowed onto adjacent properties. Family, friends, and neighbors milled around, while the announcer stood on the roof of the cottage. My grandfather and his two brothers built the cottage many years ago from remnants of an old, blown-down farmhouse. The small cottage had three bedrooms with several bunk beds jammed together. We called it the "Bouchard Hotel," named after my mother's family.

I walked past the rows and rows of skis lined up against the concrete seawall. Wading in the shallow water, I climbed on the kneeboard. A show volunteer cinched the Velcro strap around my thighs, strapping me in tightly. A wave of anxiety washed over me. The deep waters of Lake Umbagog scared me. Ironically, the lake name comes from an Abenaki Indian word meaning, "shallow water." As long as I swam near the shore with my feet firmly on the bottom of the lake, I was fine--but the mere thought of my feet dangling in the water sent my heart racing. In my eight-year-old mind, I imagined a school of fish swimming under nearby lily pads just waiting to feast on my toes.

During the practice sessions before the show, I always kept the Velcro strap

1

loose. That way, if I fell, I could quickly scramble to the top of the kneeboard. I looked down uneasily at the strap as I prepared for the show run. I was not assertive enough to ask the volunteer to loosen it for me, even though she was my cousin. The rope grew taut as the boat abruptly moved forward. I tightened my grip on the ski handle, leaning back as I launched into the water. The boat gathered speed and began to make a turn.

"Coming up is eight-year-old Keith St. Onge on the kneeboard!" the announcer bellowed. Smiling and waving, I glided past our cottage and looked at the crowd watching from shore. The familiar faces of neighbors, aunts, uncles, and cousins flew by. My parents and my three-year-old sister, Kendra, watched with big smiles. They waved as I soared past them. I relaxed my grip on the handle as the crowd faded behind me and the boat began to turn.

Just ahead, a large boat crossed by sending a huge surge of waves in my direction. My eyes widened in panic. As I reached the top of the first wave the handle flew out of my hands. There was no time to think. I was flipped upside down and engulfed by the lake, trapped.

Wave after wave pummeled me. I tried to reach the surface. *I can't breathe! Help me! Help me--I'm drowning!* Frantically flailing my arms, I clawed at the strap around my legs, but the Velcro wouldn't budge. My nose and mouth filled with water. I gasped for air, screaming silently.

Oh my gosh, I'm going to die! I can't breathe!

A strong pair of arms reached down, ripped the strap off my legs, and pulled me to the surface. Uncle Clem pulled me into the boat. I coughed and gasped for breath. I hid my face in embarrassment.

My life didn't end that day but I learned something simple, yet profound: There would always be challenges in my life and I would have to learn to overcome them. My frightening incident as a youngster set in motion a series of experiences and life lessons that made me who I am today: a World Champion barefoot water skier.

Chapter 2: A Passion is Born

What we call the beginning is often the end. And to make an end is to make a beginning. The end is where we start from.

~T.S. Eliot

After the frightening incident, my Uncle Clem and Aunt Shirley tried many times to encourage me to ditch the kneeboard and learn how to water ski. One day, I finally agreed to give it a try. Uncle Clem strapped a pair of skis on my feet and gave me the handle. The heavy skis flopped from side to side. Uncle Clem idled his fishing boat slowly while shouting encouraging tips to coax me up. After several tries, I finally found myself zipping along Lake Umbagog on water skis. After a few weeks of gradual improvement I learned to ditch two skis for one.

"I'm going to put you in the show with your cousins this week," Swampy said after taking note of my new skills. I was thrilled. I wanted to do all of the same things that Ryan and Tim could do in the show. Ryan and I were a month apart in age and Tim was two years younger. "All right boys, I want the three of you to start off on two skis and drop one in front of the crowd," Swampy explained.

I was so psyched on the day of the show I could hardly contain my excitement. As the boat took off, the three of us stood up on skis at the same time. The boat towed us closer to the drop point. It was time. I kicked off the ski. Instantly, I wobbled from side-to-side and I fought to stay upright. I looked down. In the midst of my excitement, I had kicked off the wrong ski. I tumbled face first into the water.

Tim and Ryan showed off their skills as they skied away, while my empty ski handle skipped along the water. Embarrassment burned deep and I tried to hide it. I could feel a thousand eyes watching me as I swam to shore.

I climbed up on the dock and went directly to Swampy. "Can I have another chance? Please?" I begged him. "I want another chance! I just want to show everyone I can do this."

3

Swampy shook his head. "Sorry, buddy," he said. "You only get one chance, and when you fall, you have to smile, wave, and swim your butt to shore."

My pride was crushed. I walked off crying. Sure, I was just a kid and the crowd probably didn't even think twice about the fall, but in my own eyes I had failed. I knew one thing, though—there would be other shows and I would make sure I did not repeat the same mistake. I never wanted to face the long, embarrassing swim to shore again.

At the end of the summer, Swampy hired Mike Seipel, the World Barefoot Champion, to work with a group of barefooters on Lake Umbagog. The group performed on the Lake Umbagog Water Ski Show Team. Mike was a barefoot water ski legend who had just won his second World Championship title. He traveled around the country teaching the correct barefoot positions, tricks, and the latest techniques.

The group skied long and hard during the week of Mike's clinic and on the last day they were too tired to barefoot any more. Mike was looking for skiers to fill the boat, so he invited Tim, Ryan, and me to learn how to barefoot water ski. We climbed in the boat and gathered around him listening to the step-by-step instructions. "Don't kick off the ski until I let you know when you're in the perfect position," Mike explained. "Just put your feet on the water up to the arch of your foot. Push down more to keep the water edge under your foot."

He looked at the three of us. "All right, who is going first?" I looked at him and shook my head. It wasn't going to be me. I wanted to go last, because deep down, I was afraid I would fail. I didn't want to be the first to fall flat on my face.

The boat was outfitted with a metal bar called a "boom". The boom was a training aid which extended from the side of the boat and gave the skiers stability much like training wheels on a bike. After several tries, both Tim and Ryan held on to the boom and were able to skim the water for a short time. Soon, it was my turn. By this point, my competitive nature surfaced. I was determined to show my cousins up, even though my skiing skills weren't as developed as theirs.

"Don't do the kick off until I give you the okay," Mike reminded me. "Slowly put your foot in the water--no water above your toes. Transfer your weight, but keep the water under the arch and keep your foot flat. Sit low."

Placing one foot on the water, I kicked off the ski and put my other foot down. I was barefoot water skiing on the first try! I repeated it a second and third time to prove it wasn't a fluke. It was definitely no fluke. There I was, skimming across the water on my bare feet. I was a natural.

"Hey, great job, Keith!" Mike slapped me a high-five as I climbed into the boat. "So how do you like barefooting?"

"I really like it!" I said, grinning from ear to ear. From that moment on, I wanted to be on the water. I barefoot water skied every chance I could for the rest of the summer, gaining confidence along the way. Swampy waved to me while he was driving the boat and I waved back. Little did I know, he was teaching me to perform my very first barefoot trick. By the end of the summer, I learned to barefoot on one foot and moved from the boom to a 75-foot rope behind the boat.

I was hooked on the sport and I was hungry for more. I wanted to learn everything I could about barefooting. My parents, Claude and Jackie, were supportive right from the start. They encouraged me every step of the way and applauded every new skill I learned. During the summer I lived at the cottage with Swampy's family so I could train for tournaments. My dad worked long hours as a lineman for an electric company. When he finished work at three p.m. on Fridays, he picked up my mom and Kendra and made the 36-mile trip to Lake Umbagog. As soon as they arrived, Dad hopped in the boat and watched me practice until sundown. Meanwhile, Kendra slalom skied with her friends for hours on the other side of the lake.

Swampy worked various shifts at a local paper mill. When he wasn't at work, he spent his time with me. He quickly became my boat driver and coach. As soon as Swampy finished the graveyard shift at 7 a.m., he drove to the lake and pulled me on a few morning runs. I made sure everything was ready before Swampy arrived because I knew he was tired. "Did you eat breakfast?" he asked. "Is the boat gassed up? Are you ready to ski, buddy?" Most days my answer was the same: "Yes!" After the morning runs, Swampy grabbed some sleep while I hung out with my cousins. We did a couple more runs on the lake before he went back to work.

Every weekend, my dad joined us in the boat and offered his own tips on how to improve my skills. Between the two of them, I was more eager to do what Swampy asked me to do. I found it difficult to take instruction from my dad because he always was telling me what to do at home. *Take out the garbage! Make your bed! Clean your room!* On the water, I just wanted to have fun. Having my dad telling me what to do on the water seemed no different from home and I didn't want to listen. It was much easier taking instruction from Swampy.

Years later, I reflected on this and realized it must have been tough on my dad to see me leave the house with Swampy and go up to the lake to train without him. I know my dad wanted to be the one coaching me. My dad recognized the benefit of Swampy's coaching and stepped back without saying a word. In hindsight, having Swampy as my coach was the best thing for me. Although I missed my family during the week, Swampy became like a big brother to me.

Rena Gauvin, or Mrs. G. as we called her, lived right next door to us and quickly perceived that I was in need of a second mom. She was also known as Mother Umbagog because she watched out for everyone on the lake all year around. In the afternoon she provided a much-needed break from the grueling training. "You're my little prince!" she exclaimed. "Come inside, let's watch a movie."

Mrs. G. became my official videographer. She was the only person on the lake who even owned a video camera back then. Mrs. G. sat in the boat day after day videotaping my trick sequences with the heavy camera on her rail-thin shoulder. During one particularly difficult training day, Mrs. G. could not take any more of Swampy's yelling. Mrs. G. was uncomfortable with the sound of Swampy's booming voice as he instructed me. I had long ago learned to shrug off the sternness and just try harder on the water.

"Gary!" Her voice sounded like a mother scolding a child. She knocked Swampy on the arm. "You be nice to that boy! I think you're being too hard on Keith. You're giving him such a hard time and he's trying his best to do what you tell him to do. It breaks my heart when you talk to him like that!" Swampy motioned her to stop. He waited until my practice run was done and then he took Mrs. G. aside. "Rena, when I speak firmly to Keith, it's important that you don't say anything. I'm coaching him and teaching him when we're on the water." As hard as it was for Mrs. G. to refrain from interfering, she never spoke up again. Instead, she comforted me with plenty of her freshly-baked cheesecake.

After every taped session, we'd spend the afternoon at Mrs. G.'s house watching the videos. I was amazed at the truth captured in the videos--how the cold reality of the videos could differ greatly from how I experienced a run. I often thought I did a trick perfectly on the water and then later while reviewing the video, I would find many mistakes. Mrs. G.'s videos played a key role in helping me improve my performance.

The Video of Your Life

I was fortunate to see my mistakes directly in front of me on tape, even though while in the boat I would have sworn they did not happen. What I thought mentally and what I saw visually were complete opposites. Imagine how often this happens in everyday life. I encourage others to step back and watch video of their lives from another perspective so they can take the steps toward change.

I always find it helpful to surround myself with a team of people who can give me a different perspective on how I'm progressing through life. By doing this, I've learned to see my mistakes from another perspective and strive for improvement.

My First Tournament

I entered my first barefoot tournament in the Junior Division (ages 16 and under) when I was 10. The tournament was held on a private pond at a Girl Scout camp in Maine. I immediately stood out among the 25 competitors as I was the only one who brought a ski. "Hey! You're not skiing in a slalom ski tournament today," another skier laughed. "It's a barefoot tournament!" I shrugged and turned away. I didn't want him to see my red face.

The other skiers performed deep-water starts by starting in the water without a ski. Swampy approached one of the tournament officials, John Cornish, to ask what could be done. "John, we have a ten year old here and this is the only way he can barefoot by kicking off a ski," Swampy explained. "Do you think you can make an exception to the rule and next time we guarantee he will start without a ski?"

"You're in luck, the rule book allows a Junior to start with a ski," John said. "However, this rule will be eliminated next year, so he will have to learn the deep-water start."

Relieved, I trotted over to the starting dock with my ski in hand. Since it was my first tournament, I had no idea what to expect. I was the youngest competitor. I knew I had to do four runs; two slalom runs across the wake and two trick runs.

I quickly learned something about the barefoot community: they are a big family. Everyone pitched in to run the tournament. While some of the kids continued to make fun of me for bringing a ski, others helped familiarize me with the tournament process.

Swampy, Kendra, Mrs. G., and my parents were all with me and cheered after every run. I placed third in the Junior Division. I was pretty excited...a medal! I skied in my first ever tournament and won a medal! There was just one minor detail: only two other Juniors competed that day. I actually came in last place.

When we arrived back at Lake Umbagog after the tournament, Swampy made an announcement. "Today, we're learning the deep-water start." Swampy's instructions were simple: "All right, Keith, I want you to lie back in the water, cross your feet over the rope in front of the handle and let the boat glide you out of the water. Then sit up, put your feet in the water and stand up."

My first attempt was not pretty. As soon as the boat started moving, I let go of the handle. My hands and feet splayed in all directions. "I don't like getting water in my face!" I complained.

Swampy looked at me with an amused grin. "Keith, if you want to compete, you are going to have to learn this start. Now, try again."

For the entire summer I did everything I could to put off learning the start. I took my sweet time getting into the wetsuit and zipped it up ever so slowly. I took forever to ready myself on the rope before giving the signal to "hit it." As soon as the boat took off, I closed my eyes, scrunched up my face, and shook my head from side to side. I hated every second of the start. Every time the water hit my face, I let go of the handle. We repeated the same scenario over and over throughout the summer.

Nearly 100 attempts later, Swampy's patience wore thin. "Keith, if you don't keep your hands on the handle and ride out the spray, I'm going to duct-tape your hands to the handle!" Swampy bellowed.

I gritted my teeth and braced myself for the start. Swampy's duct-tape threat was enough to motivate me. I finally conquered the deep-water start and stood up on the water with a triumphant smile on my face.

When I look back at my barefooting career, I remember countless hours on the water with Swampy and my dad and not all of it was pleasant. We spent hours and hours under dark clouds and in rain and cold weather practicing the runs and learning new skills. Sometimes I wonder why I didn't quit. Throughout it all, Swampy and my dad displayed an unbelievable amount of patience with me as I developed my skills. Without a doubt, their endless patience was one of the primary reasons I was able to persevere.

The Virtue of Patience

Patience. It's a gift that I received from my dad and Swampy through the years. It is a gift I now give my students at the ski school. As a ski instructor, I've learned to have patience in taking each student through countless trials as they learn new skills. All of us start from the same place when it comes to learning new things; from writing your name to learning math to driving a car for the first time. Some of us advance more quickly than others. When students become frustrated at the slow pace in their improvement, I find that is when the skills of patience and persistence pay off big time.

The one place where my patience is often tested is at stoplights, especially if I hit several in a row. Sometimes I'll see people next to me become angry and start swearing. I try the opposite response. When I hit a red light I laugh and say, "Oh, the universe is testing my patience today. Not a problem!" If I hit another red light, I laugh once again and look up into the sky and say, "Good try, but you're not going to get me today--I have patience!"

Patience gives you opportunities to prove yourself. Many circumstances allow a second chance but most of the time people often run out of patience. They allow negative attitudes to get in the way before utilizing the second chance. I have found when I employ patience, most of the time opportunities present themselves.

Sometimes it's too easy to lose patience and give up in the middle of a journey toward a dream. Years ago, in response to a reporter who asked him how it felt to fail so many times before he invented the light bulb, Thomas Edison said, "I never failed once. It just happened to be a 2000-step process." Now, imagine if Thomas Edison had no patience after trying 1,999 times. Imagine if he had given up on his vision and resigned himself to the idea that it couldn't be done. Someone else would have come along later and achieved his dream.

Chapter 3: Early Guidance

My success was due to good luck, hard work, and support and advice from friends and mentors. But most importantly, it depended on me to keep trying after I had failed.

~Mark Warner

Swampy coached and trained several local barefooters in addition to me. Bruce Bunnell, Danny Leclerc, and Giles Frenette were the three I trained with often. They all performed in the Lake Umbagog ski show and they helped me develop my barefooting skills when I was just starting out.

Bruce was Swampy's best friend and a fun guy to hang out with. By the end of the summer, his red hair had turned blond from the sun and his face sported 100 more freckles than in the spring. Bruce often filled our days with laughter.

Once while driving to town for gas, Bruce pointed to a field and said "Hey, look!" I looked around, but I couldn't see anything to look at other than a very ordinary-looking field.

"What are you pointing at?" I said, puzzled.

"Don't you see?" he smirked. "There is 'hay' in the field!" I punched him one on the arm.

Bruce was known on Lake Umbagog for his endurance barefooting. One day he hung on to the rope and remained upright for almost four minutes around the lake.

"Hey, that's long enough!" he shouted, letting go of the rope. When he climbed into the boat, Bruce had a huge, red, ugly blister on his heel. He grimaced.

The next day, I decided to see how long I could endure a single barefoot run. As I looped around the lake, Bruce put a finger high in the air for one minute,

11

then two fingers for two minutes. At three minutes, his fingers went up somewhat haltingly. I knew his record was just under four minutes, so I held on until he put up four fingers; only then did I let go.

I climbed into the boat grinning from ear to ear. Bruce wasn't too pleased. "Do you have any idea how hard it was for me to go 3 minutes and 43 seconds?" he grumbled. "My feet are so sore! You beat my endurance record by 17 seconds and made it look easy!"

"Sorry" I said, with an apologetic smile. A few days later, Bruce's blister broke and he ended up with a quarter-sized hole in his foot. It took him nearly a year to get the feeling back in that foot. Today, he still has the scar as a reminder of his painful "feat."

Giles (pronounced Jill) was the star barefooter on Lake Umbagog--a very strong, athletic guy with a wellspring of natural talent. He was also a real ladies man—deeply tanned skin, dark curly hair and six-pack abs which made every girl look twice. Swampy called him Little Awesome. "Wow, he looks awesome out there!" He watched Giles power through the water, slaloming with ease. Giles was 14 years older and I looked up to him. Whatever tricks he worked on I wanted to work on too.

> When you strive to learn something new, seek out people who have the skills or accomplishments you're aiming for and have them mentor you.
>
> ~Keith St. Onge

Giles invented a crazy jump-start that he used in the ski show. He'd start off doing a pyramid on top of two guys on skis. He would jump off while the two guys pulled away, land on his rear end and then get up barefooting. That act always drew some "ooohs" and "ahhhs" from the crowd.

Swampy trained Giles and prepared him for tournaments. In his second year of competition, Giles placed first in the Eastern Regional tournament and went on to compete in the Nationals.

Danny Leclerc became the older brother I never had. Danny was four years older than me, but had learned to barefoot after I did. He earned the nickname, "Spray Danny," a take on a popular "Spray Daddy" wetsuit distributed by Mike Seipel. We called Danny "Spray" for short. There was another reason for his nickname: every time he got up on the boom he'd send showers of spray into the boat. Spray and I did a lot of boat driving for each other. On weekends we shared driving with Swampy and my dad, with each of us doing several sets throughout the day.

Spray had this huge, thick head of jet-black hair. He'd try to jam a hat on his head but it wouldn't stay put—the hat would spring back up. When he came out of the water, he'd shake his head, sending water rolling off like a duck.

Spray had a shy, reserved side, kind of like me. Over time, Swampy broke Spray of his shyness. In typical Swampy style, he would have a "pow-wow" with Spray and get him to open up and trust him. Swampy had a knack for building up not only self-confidence on the water, but muscles too. Spray started out pretty skinny and quickly developed bulky muscles.

Spray's large hands and feet would get him teased. "Look at the catcher's mitts on that guy!" Swampy teased. "Hey, Spray, when are you gonna kick off the skis?" Bruce razzed. "Oh wait, the skis are already off! My bad!"

Every once in a while, Spray and I had days when we would goof off. Before Swampy left for work he'd go over our training routine for the day and give us a list of tricks to practice. Our job was to ski twice a day while he was at work. Instead, Spray and I would do silly things like hang off the boom backwards or see how fast we could barefoot. (We achieved 50 miles per hour, if you're curious.)

One day, we thought it would be fun to jump out of the boat while it was moving. Soon we wanted to see how fast the boat had to go before we didn't dare to jump out anymore. We discovered that jumping out of the boat at 37 mph was quite painful and we left it at that. Although sometimes we got away with our goof-off days, it was hard to fool Swampy. The proof was in our skiing--if we didn't practice, it showed.

One day, Swampy arrived after a long day at work and began to grill us. "Ok, boys, did you work on your toe holds today?"

"Oh yeah, Swampy!" Spray said, with an extra dose of enthusiasm. "Keith nailed both toe holds today!" I tried not to laugh. We actually had spent the day joyriding and spinning the boat in circles.

"Is that right?" Swampy looked at both of us. "So, how come no one has seen you out there doing toe holds today? I have spies all around here watching you guys. I heard you were out running donuts with the boat."

I looked at Spray and then back at Swampy. We were caught red-handed. "If you boys continue pulling those stunts I'm not going to be able to trust you," he continued. "If I can't trust you, then there's no reason for me to make all these trips up to the cottage. I guess I can stop buying the gas and making payments on the boat. There's no need for me to waste my time training you two punks."

Talk about a guilt trip! We fessed up and learned something valuable that day: Trust was everything in Swampy's world. Once you break trust, you break a relationship. After that day, we had to earn back his trust. If we were honest, trustworthy, and open with him, Swampy always rewarded us. He would let us take his new truck on rutted dirt roads and his new snowmobiles into the woods. One lie, and all of his generosity and support would be thrown out the door--and we knew it.

Shyness

As a young kid, I was very shy and reserved. Barefoot water skiing served as the catalyst for breaking out of my shell, but it was a slow, sometimes painful process.

My extreme shyness held me back from asking to take a picture of one of the best barefooters around, John Martines.

"Why don't you go up and talk to him?" my dad coaxed. "I'll get a picture of the two of you together."

I shook my head. "Come on, Dad, please. Get a picture of him." I ran off and stood behind a car as I watched my Dad snap a photo of John.

Dad tried to help me with my shyness. He'd drag me next to him as we walked up to well-known barefoot water skiers and ask embarrassing questions like, "Have you met my son Keith before?" or "What do you think about the weather today?" I couldn't summon up a word, but standing close was all I needed! I wanted to be like them and it was a thrill just to stand within an arm's distance.

Today, the shoe is often on the other foot as I find myself surrounded by younger skiers who look up to me. I always go out of my way to ensure they're comfortable around me. I'm especially watchful for the kids who are shy and reserved, because I remember all too well what it was like for me to struggle and connect with my heroes. I work on being as approachable as possible to allow people to get close to me.

Chapter 4: My First Nationals

If you put in the work the results will come.

~Michael Jordan

I qualified for my first National Tournament in the Junior Division, and my dad and I flew to Piqua, Ohio, for the competition. The tournament attracted about 150 barefooters in 15 Divisions, including about 25 juniors. Prior to the competition, I stood in line to get autographs from the star barefooters at the tournament: Mike Seipel, Brian Fuchs, Rick Powell, his sister Lori, and a few others.

Although it was my first Nationals, I didn't feel any pressure. I was there primarily to learn and gain experience, not to win. I was nervous, of course, but my dad was even more nervous. His anxiety created a tension between us. I wanted to hang out on the dock with the other skiers and my dad made me stretch out and do this warm up jog I had never done before. Being a typical kid, I was embarrassed.

The tournament course required us to ski under a large bridge. When I wasn't on the water competing, my dad and I spent a lot of time on the bridge watching in awe as the best barefooters in the world skied by. At the end of the course was a buoy and the skiers were warned not to go past it. I was a bit scared; there was a small dam at the end of the course--and I had visions of being swept away if the boat didn't reach me in time. The whole experience was quite a bit to handle as a young kid. Despite coming in close to last place, I was filled with a tremendous desire to make it to the top.

"If you want to compete at the next level in the National Championships you're going to have to learn how to jump," said Swampy.

Lake Umbagog had no jump ramp for barefooters, so I never had the opportunity to learn. This was more than okay with me, because jumping off a ramp and landing on my bare feet seemed a bit more challenging than anything I had previously done on water.

Dad started shopping around for the standard 18-inch-high barefoot ramp. "Most

17

places want $2,600 for a jump!" he told us. "Heck, I think we can build one ourselves." My dad and grandfather were do-it-yourself kind of guys. They dove into the barefoot rulebook for the measurements, made some calls, and figured it out. My grandfather took off for the hardware store to buy the materials. Dad put me to work helping to build it and soon we had assembled a wooden frame. We used cardboard to cover the wooden frame and placed fiberglass on top. The fiberglass was difficult to put on and the stench of the resin made me nauseous.

"Are we having fun yet?" Swampy asked as he checked on our progress.

We continued to labor and put the finishing touches on the jump, painting the top a bright yellow. The resulting jump was six feet long, five feet wide, and floated 18 inches high above the surface of the water. We stood around the jump admiring our handiwork and exchanged high fives. We towed the jump out on the lake and anchored it in place.

Spray and I soon discovered the jump rocked from side to side—it was impossible to keep it anchored without moving. I stood on the front of the jump and it sank several inches into the water. I was pretty sure this didn't happen with professionally-made jumps, but at the time we didn't know any better.

"What about that curled lip on top?" I pointed out. "Won't that hurt my feet when I go over it?"

Dad shrugged. "Well, let's test it out."

I looked at Swampy, my dad, and Spray. "What are we supposed to do?" I asked.

Swampy turned to Spray and handed him the handle. "Take a ride over the jump and tell us what you think."

I breathed a sigh of relief. At least I wouldn't have to go first. My nerves were rattling inside, but I knew I had to learn how to jump in order to compete at higher levels in the sport.

Spray landed his first jump and actually made it look like a piece of cake. He took a few more turns and gave the handle to me.

Okay, well, if Spray can do it so can I.

I held onto the handle uncertainly as the boat took off and approached the jump. As soon as my feet hit the ramp, I panicked and immediately let go of the handle. I landed with a crash and a head-over-heels tumble. It wasn't too pretty—but hey, I lived through it and almost made the landing!

My juices were flowing: I wanted to do it again. As I neared the ramp on my second attempt, I tightened my grip on the handle and steadied my weight. My feet hit the ramp and I hung in the air for a second and nicely nailed the landing. I let out a huge sigh of relief. *Not too shabby, St. Onge! Not shabby at all!* Little did I know, barefoot jumping would become my toughest challenge in the years ahead.

In order to compete in the jump event at any tournament, I had to qualify by obtaining a jump rating from a tournament official. Paul Friel, an official from the Port Indian Ski Club in Pennsylvania, offered to watch me jump so I would receive my rating.

Dad, Swampy, and I drove ten hours in the pouring rain to get there and it was nearly midnight when we began searching for a hotel. There was a special event going on in the area and most of the hotels were booked. After searching for what seemed like hours, we finally found a room at a dinky hotel in a not-so-great neighborhood. Before we unloaded our bags, Swampy pulled back the covers on the bed and began to gag. The sheets had not been changed from the previous guests.

"We are leaving right now!" Swampy bellowed.

"But there are no other hotels with rooms available," Dad countered. "We're tired...and Keith has to jump in the morning!"

There was no arguing with Swampy. He made a beeline for the door and went back to the car. "Let's go," he said, tossing his bag in the trunk. Off we went, hunting for another hotel at one o'clock in the morning. By the time we found a cleaner hotel in a better neighborhood, it was close to three a.m.

The next morning, we met Paul at the river and we instantly knew there would be no barefooting that day. The river was moving at a furious rate, with logs and garbage floating downstream. It was the worst flooding the locals had seen in years.

My heart sank. There was no way I'd be jumping that morning and without a jump rating, I couldn't compete in the jump event at the Regional Tournament or National Championship.

Dad shook his head at the sight. "We just drove ten hours in the rain to do this test and the river floods out?" Dad filled Paul in on the details of our long trip culminating in the hotel fiasco. Without a word, Paul signed a piece of paper--the jump proficiency document--and held it out to me. I tried to take it, but he didn't let go at first.

He looked me in the eyes. "Here's your rating, Keith," he said. "And I fully expect you to land your first jump at Regionals!" Paul watched me barefoot in the preceding years and he knew I had solid skills. He smiled and let go of the paper.

At the Regional tournament, I landed my first jump smoothly with Paul watching from shore.

Dealing with Butterflies

Nerves can do funny things to people and learning to control them can be a tough task. I've been around people who cannot deal with competitions at all. Even after several years of competition, they have not figured out how to harness the nervous energy before a tournament. Turn the nerves into your strength. Learn to take deep breaths and visualize what you want to accomplish—this will help calm the nerves.

I was filled with butterflies before every tournament. "It's all right to have butterflies," Swampy would say. "Just get them to fly in formation." Swampy used that quote by Rob Gilbert (a sports psychologist) often when coaching. The first time I heard Swampy say it, I laughed out loud. The idea of butterflies in my stomach all flying in the same direction was, of course, pretty silly. Over time, I actually began to imagine a butterfly in the lead and the rest following along. Eventually the butterflies in my head became Canadian geese instead, but it worked--I just followed their lead: forward!

Chapter 5: Passion Wins Out

Follow your passion, and success will follow you.

~Arthur Buddhold

On a bright, warm Sunday morning Swampy came up to me and said, "Let's go for a ride."

Swampy and I took rides quite often and they usually involved a "powwow," an open, honest discussion about something to do with barefoot skiing or life. I happily obliged for I enjoyed long talks about my favorite sport. To say barefooting had become an obsession at that point in my life was pretty accurate; I was willing to talk about it from morning until night to anyone who would listen.

Our ride that Sunday went innocently enough, with Swampy talking about the importance of commitment and staying dedicated to the sport. I wasn't prepared for what came after we got back to the cottage. Swampy led me straight to the kitchen. My mom and dad sat next to each other on one side of the table, which was odd. Clearly something was up. I felt a ripple of apprehension in my stomach. Swampy sat down opposite my parents and I took a chair between. He looked expectantly at my parents, who nodded for him to begin.

"Keith," he said, leaning forward. "We know how much you love barefooting and that's great, but we're at a point where we have to make some decisions about where you want to go with it." He turned out his palms. "The sport is taking up a lot of time and money. A lot. If you are serious about this and want to continue to compete, then we need you to make a decision about how committed you want to be. In other words, we need to know.... Keith, are you in this for fun, or are you in it to win it?"

Before I could answer, my dad chimed in. "If you're doing this just for fun, we will probably end up selling the barefoot boat and keep the other boat." The other boat was my mother's cruiser, which she used most weekend afternoons. "But if you want to continue to do all the tournaments and traveling, then that

21

means you'll be responsible for taking care of the barefoot boat—washing it, maintaining it, and gassing it up." He cleared his throat. "It also means you'll have to be completely committed to practicing. Completely. Even on the days you don't want to get out of bed!"

I pondered the ultimatum they laid before me. I was 13 and my skills in barefooting were emerging fast, but to take it to the next level required a serious commitment of time and money. Money was a tough one--my parents simply didn't have enough of it for me to go pro on their dime. Swampy had been helping out, paying for half of the boat payments and gas, and for most of my equipment. Swampy and my parents reassured me that if I wanted to chase my dream, they would find a way to make the funding happen. All they were asking of me was a solid commitment.

> Ultimatums can be a good thing or a bad thing. Either way— they force growth.
>
> ~Keith St. Onge

"Your parents are willing to give you full support if you decide you want to take this sport seriously," Swampy continued. "You can do this for fun or if you want to go to the Regionals and Nationals and all the others, you have to work for it. So...do you want to barefoot just for fun or do you want to work hard and go all the way?"

I didn't have to think long. That day, I fully recognized my passion for barefooting. The Merriam-Webster Dictionary defines passion as "a strong liking or desire for or devotion to some activity, object, or concept." To me, passion is when you love something so much that explaining why you love it is irrelevant, you just do. There was simply no way I could walk away from the competitive aspect of it and do it only for pleasure. I was driven by a fierce desire inside to become the best barefooter the sport had ever seen. I knew the answer, because the passion--the fire for the sport--had been growing steadily inside of me since the first day I placed my bare feet on the water: I was committed to barefooting. I wanted to be a World Champion.

My answer was "yes".

On Passion

Passion is something that means a lot to you, it feeds a belief inside of you. Passion sparks something deep inside of your soul and you have to have courage to follow your passion.

Passion is your joy. It is who you are. You have to unwrap it and find it. Some people find it easier than others. Passion is finding the essence of who you are. The body and the mind and the soul become one when you find your passion. Passion comes naturally to a person. It's like running water, turn on the tap and it flows.

~Jackie St. Onge

Chapter 6: Life Lessons At An Early Age

If you really want to do something, you'll find a way. If you don't, you'll find an excuse.

~Jim Rohn

The White Mountains of northern New England became my winter playground. I spent the winter snow skiing, ice skating, and snowmobiling with my cousin Nathan. Nathan was three years younger than me, but the two of us were extremely competitive. He was more daring and had more raw talent on snow than water. A few times a year, the two of us would get up at 5:30 a.m., hop on our snowmobiles and ride through the woods to high school. The trip could be quite intense, since the weather was below zero on most mornings. The route wound through the backside of Mount Forest, the largest mountain in Berlin. At the top of this mountain, was an incredible view of the city.

Fir trees lined both sides of the narrow trail with branches straining from the weight of the snow. The noise from our snowmobiles reverberated through the forest causing a shower of snow to rain down as we drove past. Every now and then, I stood up, grabbed hold of a tree branch, pulled it forward and then let it loose, sending it straight back into Nathan's face. When we arrived at school, the two of us reveled in the attention we received as we navigated our snowmobiles into the parking lot.

In the off season, my parents and Swampy began planning and setting up fundraisers to raise money for the boat gas, travel, tournaments and the ski shows. We held most of the fundraisers during the winter.

One year, Swampy came up with a creative way to raise funds. He went to the local police station and arranged to borrow a radar gun. "We're going to clear a track on the lake and have people run their snowmobiles as fast as they can and we'll clock 'em," Swampy announced. Initially we all thought it was a harebrained idea. I mean, who would pay just to clock their snowmobile against a radar gun?

The "Radar Runs" turned out to be one of our most popular and successful fundraisers each winter. The day before the event, I went out on the lake and plowed a track for the run. People came in from several local towns--some coming from as far away as Massachusetts. A few people tricked out their snowmobiles with nitrous oxide and pipes to make them go faster just for the event. There would be 20 to 30 snowmobiles lined up on the bank and each driver paid three dollars to run their machine against the radar gun. Mrs. G., my mom, my grandmother, and Swampy's mom, Estelle, dished out food from the back of a parked truck. My dad made a shelter in the bed of his pick-up truck to help the women stay warm as they sold food, hot cocoa, and coffee.

The fundraisers paid for the ski show, the costumes, and the gas. Mrs. G. scoured the local businesses for sponsorships and one year she convinced Budweiser to sponsor the ski show. It was an amazing amount of work to put together the fundraisers and sponsorships for my own training, but my parents, friends and extended family never wavered in their dedication and commitment to helping me achieve my dream.

> Are you holding back from pursuing your passion because you "don't have the money?"
>
> Lack of money is often the number one reason cited as a barrier to pursuing a passion. That's where you'll have to become creative about bringing money into your life. Dave Ramsey, author of *Total Money Makeover and EntreLeadership*, has a quote that he uses often: "If you live like no one else, later you get to live like no one else." Quite simply, it means that you will have to make sacrifices in your life now to get where you want to go in the future. Save money like no one else--so you can live like no one else. Develop a plan to save until you have the money needed to achieve your dreams.

Barefoot water ski season began as soon as the ice disappeared from the lake. Nothing happened fast in the mountains of New Hampshire—except the storms which rolled in from nowhere. The spring thaw was excruciatingly slow. The mountains cast an early shadow on the lakes and ponds so we were always the last skiers in the Eastern Region on the water every spring. Most days after school I passed by Nay Pond at the base of the mountains to see if the ice was gone. At the boat launch, I scoured the ground for a medium-size stone and I launched the stone as far as I could onto the black ice. If it bounced on the ice, it would be more than a week before we could ski. If the rock went through the ice, we had less than a week to go before getting back on the water. As soon as the rock broke the ice, the boat came out of storage and I gave her a good waxing. This was not one of my favorite chores, but I was always eager to get the barefooting season started.

Early in the spring season, we wore specialized dry suits with rubber seals around the hands and feet to keep us warm and dry when we barefooted. Only our feet, hands, and head were exposed to the cold temperatures. I wore sweat pants and a sweatshirt under the suit to keep the cold water from pushing the suit up against my skin. Swampy and my dad bundled up in winter coats, hats, and gloves; hunching over to keep warm as they drove the boat. Meanwhile, Spray and I were freezing out on the water. After every set, we climbed into the boat and plunged our hands and feet in a bucket of hot water to thaw out.

On most cold mornings, Spray and I argued about who had to go first into the frigid water. Both of us were reluctant to be the first one on the water because it meant sitting in the boat cold and wet after a few runs. The two of us often argued until Swampy picked one of us to go first.

One morning, we were getting ready to practice some jumps and we thought it would be fun to turn the tables on Swampy.

"I want to go first!" Spray announced. He shoved me out of the way. Swampy turned in surprise and raised an eyebrow.

"No, I wanna go first!" I insisted, shoving him back. We started wrestling each other. Swampy had just finished a long shift at work and was in no mood for our antics.

"I don't care who goes first," he barked. "Shut up and get in the water!"

We both jumped at the same time, forgetting one detail: our dry suits weren't zipped in back. The icy water instantly flooded the suits, pulling us underwater. We struggled to kick our way back up to the surface.

Oh my gosh, we are in trouble now! When I hit the surface, I took one look at Spray and he had the same *oh-my-gosh* expression on his face. We burst out laughing. The joke was on us; we climbed back into the boat, soaking wet and shivering. On the way back to the dock, our teeth chattered between laughs. Swampy was not amused. He had just finished a graveyard shift and was operating on no sleep. He hauled us back on the water and drilled us until we worked up a sweat under our dry suits.

> From the Boston Globe, 1988:
>
> Keith St. Onge, who competes in the pumped-up version of water-skiing called barefoot jumping, has been practicing for years on the lakes of northern New Hampshire. When he starts training in May, he sometimes has to ski around chunks of ice. His feet get so cold; his father has to keep a bucket of hot water in the boat to thaw them out. "He does it for the love of the sport," says Claude St. Onge.

A Test of Character

Swampy, my dad, and I drove to the Illinois Fairgrounds Lake in DuQuion, Illinois, for my second Nationals tournament. DuQuion is a small southern Illinois town between Carbondale and St. Louis. In the glory days, it was once home to the Hambletonian horse races. Other than that, it's just a Midwest town in the middle of nowhere.

I skied in the Junior Division in slalom and tricks. Since the tournament was a week long, we planned to leave for St. Louis to visit some family after I competed and to return at the end of the week for the awards and the banquet.

As I readied myself for the slalom competition I felt confident I would do well. The moment I crossed the very first wake, I caught a toe and landed face first in the water. I was mortified. Just like that, I was done with the slalom part of the tournament. No matter how well I did on my second pass, my combined score wouldn't be good enough for a medal. I did, in fact, have a really great second run, which made me feel slightly better.

In the tricks competition, every skier has 15 seconds to complete a trick run and each trick has a weighted score. I was determined to make up for my disappointing slalom by going all out with my tricks. I had to complete my tricks with rapid speed, so one trick blurred into the next. Everything clicked, and at the end of my run I knew I had scored well.

The competition came down to me and another skier, Jim Aberly. The two of us waited around anxiously for the scores. Soon the announcement came: I won the gold! My very first medal! Only a few points separated my score from Jim's, which was an unusually close margin in competition. Swampy, my dad, and I went crazy, celebrating the win with high-fives and excited phone calls to family members to share the good news. After things settled down, we piled into the van and drove towards St. Louis to spend the next few days with relatives.

When we returned to the tournament site at the end of the week, another skier came running up. "Where have you guys been?" he asked, wide-eyed. "They took your medal away!"

"Huh?" I said. "What are you talking about?"

"They took your medal away. Seriously!"

I looked at Swampy and my dad with an uncertain look. They were puzzled too.

"Let me see what's going on," Swampy said. He walked off to talk with the tournament officials at the check-in trailer.

> "You are only as strong as your weakest link."
>
> ~Swampy Bouchard

Swampy learned that Jim's brother had videotaped the trick runs from the shore. The tape showed that I had done two tumble turns (a turn done on the back as a half or full turn) in the same direction, which comprised only one trick and should have brought in a lower score than what the judges had given me. To receive the higher score, the tumble turns had to be in different directions. Jim's brother brought the video to the judges and after viewing the tape; they lowered my score and awarded Jim the first place medal.

I thought back to my trick run and the more I thought about it the more I realized I did do two tumble turns in the same direction. Reverse tumble turns were one of my weaknesses back then; I never liked doing them and I didn't practice them much during training. In the competition, I had gone through my run so fast--not only did I not catch myself doing the turns in one direction; I fooled the judges as well.

"Keith, did you do the tricks in the same direction?" Swampy asked. With a sigh, I admitted I was pretty sure I had.

"If you skied the way you did, what would your score be?"

"A lot lower," I mumbled.

Dad chimed in. "Okay, then we have two choices, we can go to the officials and say, 'You guys got that information illegally,' and protest, or we can accept the fact that you didn't really earn the gold."

"What do you want to do?" Swampy looked at me.

As much as I really wanted that gold medal, I knew I didn't earn it. Video replay wasn't allowed at the time and several other skiers encouraged me to fight it on that basis, but I accepted the silver medal.

Giving up what would have been my first gold was tough to do, but it was a lesson that has served me well in life. Dishonest glory will hurt you in the long run and the burden of guilt is always a heavy one to bear. Guilt will stay with you your whole life. Unknown to me at the time, I had earned respect from fellow barefooters because I did not protest the use of an unofficial video that changed the results of the tournament—I chose honesty over notoriety. Swampy and my dad taught me well.

I also learned that I am only as strong as my weakness. I avoided practicing the reverse tumble turn because I was not skilled at it and couldn't do it well. My inadequate practice cost me my first gold medal. Today, at my ski school, I encourage my students to work on their weaknesses over their strengths. It is important to be balanced and diverse by improving the skills that are the weakest link.

I encourage my students to identify their weakness in barefooting and have them focus on this first. If a student is strong on their left foot, I make them stand on their right foot three to five times more than the left. There is no benefit to having a weak side become weaker and a strong side become stronger! You want to make each side in each skill as equal to the other as possible.

Work your weaknesses in life as much as you can. It will make you a stronger and more balanced individual and along the way you will learn things about yourself you may never have discovered otherwise.

There is a flip side to this: understand your limits. It's possible your weaknesses will never become as strong as your strengths. This is the point that you will have to turn to others for help. For example, I'm terrible at math. No matter how hard I try, the right side of my brain just won't cooperate. As the ski school grew, I was in over my head with the taxes. I casually mentioned this to a friend and discovered his wife was an expert in taxes. She got involved and helped me figure things out.

I find most people are afraid to admit the areas where they are weak. Instead of getting help, they find ways to avoid their weakness and end up making excuses instead. I encourage you to find help and tap into other people's expertise.

31

Chapter 7: Growing into the Sport

Everything worthwhile is a risk. To play it safe is to miss the point of the game. Certainly, risk brings with it the possibility of pain, but there is a more profound pain that comes from the emptiness of never having risked at all.

~Leo Buscaglia

Dad and I spent a lot of time together traveling to tournaments. Every summer, we made trips to the Port Indian Ski Club near Valley Forge in Pennsylvania. The ten-hour drive became our bonding time as Dad would regale me with stories about growing up. On Fridays, we would leave at noon and search for a motel at ten o'clock at night. At first, we had no idea every tournament site had an "official" hotel until someone asked us why we weren't at the host hotel.

During one trip, Dad and I arrived late at night and tried to find a hotel. "Let's sleep in the van," I suggested. "It'll be like having our own fort and camping out!" Back home in the mountains, my parents would let me host sleepovers in the nearby forest. My friends and I would build forts from leftover wood my dad had lying around. Sometimes we would cut down trees to use them as framework for the structures we built. We would cook small meals on a camping stove and explore trails. My sister, Kendra, would do the same with her friends at a camp my dad built.

Sometimes Kendra and I would hang out together. One day, we shared a scary moment out in the woods. I hooked up a dog sled to a snowmobile and we set out for a ride with Kendra standing on the dog sled holding onto a cross bar. I raced over some large bumps at a relatively fast speed and the sled came unhooked. The long hitch rammed into the snow and Kendra jettisoned into the air, flying over the handle bar. She landed deep into the snow with a thud. I ran to her quickly. She wasn't moving. *What if she broke her neck? Maybe she broke an arm? I hope she is alive!*

I heard her laughing through the packed snow. I pulled her out and wrapped her in bear hug. We bubbled over with hysterical laughter. Fortunately, she was wearing a helmet, which protected her from any serious injury. She escaped with only a few bruises, but for one heart-stopping moment, I learned how much I could love someone. I still give a prayer of thanks at the memory.

Dad parked the van in the parking lot of a hotel and we proceeded to hunker down for the night. We found that we couldn't sleep with the parking lot lights beaming down on us, so we hung up t-shirts in the windows, slipping the top of the t-shirt over the window and rolling it up. Dad opened the cooler and brought out some cookies. My mom always packed us a cooler filled with homemade snacks and drinks. We rolled out the sleeping bags and tried to sleep. It was hot and humid in the van, despite leaving some of the windows open.

Suddenly, there was a rap on the window. Dad motioned me to be quiet. We sat there holding our breath trying not to move or make a sound. I was scared, but I tried not to show it. A flashlight shone in the window; the light partially blocked by the t-shirts that were hung up. We watched as the light moved around the van and then disappeared. We heard a car door slam and then Dad peeked out and saw a police car drive off. We laughed and spent a few more hours talking. It was just too hot to sleep. The next morning, we arrived at the tournament, bleary-eyed. That was the one and only time we camped out in the van.

Later that fall, we headed back to Pennsylvania for another tournament. We borrowed Swampy's new Chevy Blazer for the trip. On Sunday night I was one of the last skiers in the tournament, so it was late by the time we started driving home. Dad found himself getting sleepy at the wheel. He nudged me. "Keith, can you take over and drive for me for a while?"

"Are you joking?" I looked at him in surprise. I knew 13-year-olds were not allowed to drive, but I had driven from the lake to Swampy's house many times so I had some driving experience under my belt. Toss in the snowplows, the snowmobiles and the boat--and I was no stranger to driving motor vehicles. This would be my first time driving on the highway and it was nighttime, which made it more challenging. But heck, what kid would turn down an opportunity to drive? Dad pulled over and we switched places. He grabbed the map and outlined where he wanted me to go. "Remember, watch your speed limit!" he reminded me as I pulled onto the highway. We talked a bit as I drove under his watchful eye, and then he fell asleep. A half hour later, he woke up. "How's it going?" he inquired.

"I'm doing fine," I said. He went back to sleep. I drove for three hours until Dad woke up and switched places with me. It was now my turn to sleep. Since I had school the next day and Dad had to work, the rotating shifts became our routine on long trips. By the time I received my license, driving was a piece of cake.

Learning a Lesson on Blame

At a tournament in Vermont at the age of 13, I told the boat driver to give me a Fast-Fast-Fast start during my second trick pass which was a backward start. This commanded the driver to take off as fast as possible through three different stages of the start. The judge in the boat looked concerned. "Keith, you don't want to call that start because it will be much too fast."

"That's what we always do back home where I ski," I insisted. I gripped the handle and readied myself for the start. The judge shook his head and settled in his seat.

As the boat pulled away I began to porpoise like a dolphin. Before I could catch my breath, the handle popped out of my hands and I slid to a halt. I sat there in the water, stunned. There was nothing I could do but head back to shore. There would be no points for that run.

As I walked off the dock, Swampy walked over to me with a puzzled look on his face. "What happened?" he asked. "You never miss a start!"

"I don't know," I shrugged. "The driver went too fast. It wasn't my fault!" I stole a glance at Swampy--he was fuming.

"So you're saying that it's the driver's fault that you messed up? You know, Keith, blaming someone else for your lack of performance is only an excuse!" He glared at me.

"What do you mean? I gave the driver the same orders for my start as back home and it was totally different than the way you drive the boat," I whined. "We have an old, crappy boat that doesn't take off as fast as this one did and ours has a big roller that I always have to ride over. We need new equipment...and a new boat."

That did it. Swampy blew a gasket. He grabbed my arm and pulled me aside. "You are ungrateful!" He shook his finger at me. "I cannot believe you are complaining. You should be happy for what we have rather than tearing it apart!" Swampy's voice grew louder. I cringed, hoping no one was overhearing us. "There are kids your age that would do anything to be in your shoes. That's fine though, if you are not happy we will sell everything!"

Sell everything? Stop barefooting? I didn't want that to happen!

"Something was different about that start," I slowly explained. "I know I'm not supposed to blame others for my mistakes and I was wrong for saying that. I am lucky for all the support and equipment we have. I'm sorry...I'm just...frustrated." I hung my head.

Swampy softened. "Ok then, let's talk about it and figure out what went wrong." He put his arm around me. If there was one thing about Swampy-- and he is a master at this--it was his openness with communication. He helped me learn to talk about problems and challenges instead of stuffing them inside. He taught me how to be open, and to release fears and doubt. I could talk to Swampy about anything and this allowed me to find myself and understand what I wanted in life.

I meet many people who are closed about who they are. I can see and feel they are holding onto something in their past or they're not being who they truly are. Even when they have the opportunity to let it out, they hold onto it. All types of relationships fall apart because of this. Being open with another person shows your trust in them and vice versa. When a trusted person confides in you, that is a perfect time to be open and discuss problems or issues you may have. It allows the individual to let go and move on. The past is just that, the past. There's a quote by Jan Glidewell that comes to mind: "You can clutch the past so tightly to your chest that it leaves your arms too full to embrace the present."

When we arrived home after the tournament and for the rest of the summer, Swampy dragged me through all kinds of starts. Slow starts, medium starts and endless fast starts. I never, ever blamed a driver again and I never had to worry about making the wrong call. I could handle whatever the boat driver gave me!

One morning during our practice runs at the lake I told Spray to start fast for

36

all my runs. After an entire morning of fast starts, Spray nudged me as I climbed in the boat. "Hey, what's the deal with the fast starts?"

I looked at him with a sheepish grin. "My butt hurts--and if you take off fast, I can stand up quickly."

"Your butt hurts? From what? What did you do?"

"I don't know. I've got these, um, bumps that developed. It hurts when I'm sitting on the water or heck, sitting *anywhere*, for that matter."

"Bumps? What do you mean?" Spray looked confused. Then he let out a roar and started laughing. "You mean...hemorrhoids?"

"What are those?" Now I was confused. I had never even heard of the word, much less understood what it was. So Spray gave me a complete run down on hemorrhoids and I learned more than I ever wanted to know. "You'll need to slap some Preparation H down there," he chuckled. It wasn't until years later I could look back at the memory and laugh. Thankfully, that was the one and only time in my life that I experienced the painful need for a fast start.

Professional Conduct

At every tournament I studied the other barefooters intently, watching how they performed on the water. Swampy and my dad would point out new tricks and techniques that they observed and took mental notes. We would always find Swampy talking to others trying to gain as much knowledge as he could before leaving the tournament. Occasionally they would point out unprofessional behavior among some of the skiers. "People who behave unprofessionally will most likely not succeed in the long run and people remember that," Dad remarked.

During one tournament, Brody, a young barefoot skier, had been oust by his competitor and sat on the shore, crying. His performance on the water was impressive and several people came up to congratulate him. Yet, Brody shrugged everyone off and did not say a word to them. He didn't utter thanks or even make eye contact.

Brody's father stepped in and turned it into a teachable moment. "Everybody is happy when they win, but people will judge you at your lowest moment," he told Brody. "This is when you must truly shine! You must keep your head up, say thank you, and show you are a good sport."

Brody has come a long way since that lesson his father taught him. He conducts himself very professionally as a young boy and people take notice.

Working Through Fear

"We're going to work on the front-to-back today," Swampy announced one morning as he roused me out of bed. Swampy was in a cranky mood--he had been up all night and was functioning without sleep. He had just arrived from the graveyard shift at the paper mill and it was eight in the morning. Spray hopped in the driver's seat and Swampy grilled me on the turn technique as we idled out on the lake. I slipped into the water with reluctance. The front-to-back is one of the most mentally challenging turns because the skier starts barefooting forward, rotates on the surface of the water, and ends up barefooting backwards. As simple as it sounds, it is a tough trick to master. I wasn't looking forward to practicing it.

As I connected the short rope to the boom, I tried to mentally prepare myself to visualize the trick. The front-to-back scared me. I was trying to psych myself up to summon the courage to take the turn. Spray gunned the throttle and I got up on my feet. I crunched down and back up, trying to get ready for the turn. I continued to crouch down and back up again and again, chickening out on the turn every time. I could not make myself go through with it. I let go of the handle and sank into the water.

"Get back out there and try it again," Swampy commanded. With a sigh, I got up and steadied myself once again. Gripping and ungripping the handle, I squatted. I spit over my shoulder to stall for time. *Come on, you can do this, just turn!* I went through the sequence again: squat, pop up, squat again, pop up...

I couldn't make myself go through with the turn.

Deep down, fear simmered under the surface, paralyzing me. It was the fear of the unknown, of dealing with an unfamiliar outcome.

Swampy hollered again, trying to convince me to go through with it once more. I tried over and over, up and down the lake, mile after mile, ending with the same result: no turn. The fear won. I couldn't gather the courage to follow through with the turn. I let go of the handle and glided to a stop. Spray cut the throttle and idled back toward me. I watched Swampy gesturing animatedly and I could tell he was not pleased. Swampy was all worked up, but I couldn't hear what he was saying. As the boat came to a stop, Swampy stood up and angrily threw his keys down on the floor of the boat.

The keys bounced overboard and landed in the water with a splash.

For an eerie moment, there was only silence. Swampy's keys sank to the bottom of Lake Umbagog. The key ring contained his work keys, house keys and car keys. I thought Swampy was pretty worked up before, but it was nothing compared to the moment the keys sank. The stream of foul language which ensued was enough to make a sailor blush. I didn't know whether to laugh, cry, or begin swimming home.

"We must have burned a friggin' half tank of gas going up and down the lake waiting for you to make your move!" Swampy growled. "Stop being such a candy ass! You need to complete the turn on the third up-weight. Now get out there and turn around! And--if you aren't going to turn around, we might as well quit, because you're wasting my time!"

Spray and I looked at each other in disbelief. We had never seen Swampy so rip-roaring mad. I high-tailed it back on the water and I finally worked through the fear. I made myself go through the turn and I fell on every single attempt. I didn't accomplish the front-to-back turn that day but it sure wasn't from lack of trying. A few weeks later I successfully completed my first turn.

By then, Swampy had replaced all of his keys and kept them on shore.

When Fear Holds You Back

In the sport of barefooting, fear is usually something that everyone faces at one time or another. If a maneuver is done improperly, the end result is usually a fall. When I work with students, I know the process of overcoming fears will take time. No one should be forced into an uncomfortable situation, but at the same time, fears must be faced and overcome within a timely manner. The longer one puts off facing a fear, the harder it is to work through it.

Usually fear stems from a weakness, a lack of skill, lack of experience or the unknown. The first way to face fear is to acknowledge your weakness, accept it, and then go boldly into the fear.

For example: I hate snakes. I don't like the way they look, move, or feel. One day, I saw a three-foot green and black snake. It did not have a diamond head, so I knew it was not poisonous. I knew I had to face my fear. I grabbed a long stick in the yard and decided to catch the snake. I needed to understand this animal better. As I cornered the slithering creature, I studied its movements. Quickly, I pounced and grabbed the snake by its neck. I picked up the snake and held it while it quivered. The feel of its skin disgusted me. The smell was like something rotting and I later learned it was a chemical the snake puts off when in danger. I held it high in the air, studying it and suddenly, I smiled. I was no longer afraid of this creature. The fear was gone.

The Reason I'm Still Tricking at the Top Today

After the key-throwing incident, Swampy knew he needed to bring in more expertise for me to advance with my turns. The only way for me to advance my skills on the water was to seek out more experienced skiers and another skier recommended that we call Scott Gray. Scott won the Nationals in the Men's I Division in 1987 and he was known for teaching a specific method of surface turns on the water. Hiring Scott turned out to be a smart move, for he is the reason I'm still setting records today.

Scott was a southern boy from Georgia and he had never traveled to a northeastern state before. When he arrived at the lake, Scott put one foot in the water and immediately retracted it. "Damn! That's cold!" he whistled. "And it's in the middle of July!"

"You think that's cold?" I retorted. "You ought to come here in the spring right after the ice thaws. We have to ski around chunks of ice. Now *that's* cold!"

Scott soon discovered that we had no running hot water in the cottage and no shower. The tiny, single bathroom was outfitted with just a sink and a toilet. "What do you do for a shower?" Scott inquired.

"We take a bar of soap and some shampoo out to the lake," I explained. The cottage was basically just a step up from camping. "There's no way of escaping that water now, Scott!" I grinned.

Giles, Spray, Swampy and I gathered around Scott when he began explaining his technique on the first day of the training clinic. "The four surface turns are the basic foundation for all advanced tricks," he began. "You will begin your turn with your weight on one foot, which will be your axis point. Keep your eyes focused on the direction you're turning in. Step over the spray during the turn, not through it!" Scott had us videotape him doing the turns correctly and incorrectly so we could see and understand the difference. Once I saw Scott perform the "step over" turn, I quietly visualized myself doing them just as he did.

The three of us worked on turns all week, putting the new technique in motion. A few days later, I felt quite comfortable turning on the water wearing shoe skis. Shoe skis are shoes with little platforms just slightly larger than the foot. The shoes make learning turns much easier because there is more surface to use and the boat speed is much slower.

> Success means being able to walk away from what you love, content. It means you have no regrets about the time you spent doing whatever you love... and you knew you gave it your all.
> ~Scott Gray

Late in the week, we moved to the nearby river in search of some calm water. I begged Scott to hop in and show us some tricks but he was reluctant to get in the cold water. "I'll tell you what," he said. "If you can get out there and show me a couple of turns, I'll jump in and do a backwards deep-water start. And I'll do it in my underwear."

"Oh yeah, right!" I laughed. "With no wetsuit? Isn't that going to hurt?"

"Well, get out there and show me the turns and I'll show you a back deep without a wetsuit," he challenged. I was all for it. After a few tries, I triumphantly completed my turns and climbed in the boat. "It's your turn!" I announced. "Let's see what kind of underwear you have on!" Scott, being a man of his word, took off his shirt and pulled down his shorts, revealing a tiny scrap of Speedo-type underwear in dark, navy blue. We all took one look and burst out laughing.

Laughter turned to awe as we watched Scott plant his feet and gracefully glide up on the water backward. The people on shore received an eyeful as Scott barefooted up and down the river with his rear end leading the way.

Surface turns continued to strike fear in my heart, especially when I advanced to the toe turn. The toe turn was the most difficult trick I ever had to learn, mentally and physically. The trick required me to put one foot into a strap in the handle, let go with both hands, and turn 180-degrees on the water. Many skiers were hurting their knees doing this trick and I was petrified of getting hurt. Over and over, my foot caught water half way around and I landed on the water in a split. I lay in the water screaming until the torturous pain in my hips subsided I could not hold the required position nor employ proper technique. Years later, I cleaned up my form and began to do the trick right. The toe turn was one of the scariest and most painful tricks for me to learn in barefoot water skiing.

Training with Swampy was excruciating at times. He pushed me to do run after run until I couldn't hold onto the handle. Since we made the forty-five minute drive to the lake almost every day, we were going to make the best of it while on the water. Lake Umbagog had very protected shorelines and we could usually find calm glassy water. We usually skied in one perfect spot behind Big Island, but on some days we encountered white-capping waves. On those days, we headed out to a local river. I hated the river. The water was about 60 degrees and icy cold, even in the summer. Driftwood was scattered along the river—the floating debris became landmines for our feet. We spent a great deal of time cleaning up the river before putting our feet on the water. I dreaded going to the river because it meant facing a long boat ride through massive waves and hours of skiing.

My grandfather was a wise man. "Always see the next step before you get there. Always stay one step ahead," my grandfather taught my dad. "If you see me working on something, bring me the tool that I will need next. This will make the project go smoothly and it will teach you what I am doing at the same time."

Taking the easy way out or short cuts in life will often hurt you in the long run. Always plan for the future in all that you do today.

~Keith St. Onge

Swampy would pound all of us on the water until we couldn't handle any more. During every pass, he critiqued our positions and urged us to improve. The countless hours blurred into one another as I took fall after fall on the water. Yet, Swampy motivated me and kept the fire lit under my butt. I kept my dreams and my goals ahead of me. The grueling process was a requirement to become a champion in the sport.

Pushing Ahead

As my skills started to advance, I found myself beating my own personal scores at every tournament. Spray was doing the same. Swampy's training was working! Swampy put together the same basic run for every tournament and then he would add a new trick for each tournament to bump up the score. Whenever we faltered at completing a new trick, Swampy would make us go back to the basics again to build up a good foundation before trying it again.

I was getting to the point where my scores were slowly building up, yet I had not won a gold medal in my division at the National Championship. Swampy brought up the idea of breaking into the Open Division and competing with the pros.

"Keith, you need 2600 points in tricks to break into the Open Division," Swampy calculated. "You're getting close to that score in tournaments. I think you should go all out and try to break that."

I hesitated at the idea. Skiing in the Open Division meant I would have to face the older, more experienced skiers who were all professionals and I would be even less likely to win a gold medal. It also meant that at the age of 15, I would be the youngest skier in the Open/Professional Division. Some of the Boy Division skiers would actually stop skiing as soon as they reached a score high enough to bring in first place--but just shy of pushing them into the Open Division.

Swampy didn't want me to hold back. "You should strive to be the best you can be and always aim to beat your own personal best score. Think about it Keith, let's say you had the opportunity to play for my favorite NHL team, the Boston Bruins--would you grab the opportunity to play with them or would you be satisfied playing on a farm league?"

We called those skiers "Sandbaggers." They held their talent back at local tournaments, keeping them from breaking into a professional division.

> Don't bother just to be better than your contemporaries or predecessors. Try to be better than yourself.
> ~William Faulkner

"I have seen 90% of sandbaggers lose a championship because they trained to hold back. When it's time to turn it up a notch, their nerves get in the way and they can't reach their goals," Swampy continued. "It never pays to sandbag because it means you are holding yourself back. If you hold back you may never see what you can accomplish! Wouldn't you rather go all out and know what you are capable of?"

Swampy also put it in another perspective for me. If I were to "sandbag" it was not fair for my competitors in my age bracket. It was time for me to move on with the skills and strive to do my best. I made a decision: I would go all out for the Open Division.

After six years of only three months per year of actual skiing, I thought I had a chance to break into the Open Division at our first tournament of the year in Port Indian, Pennsylvania. Swampy had a trick run planned out for me. He knew the exact amount I needed and we worked on the runs over and over to near perfection for several weeks before the competition.

My dad picked me up early Friday afternoon after just a half day of school. The nine-hour trip was a long one, but I saw it as an adventure. With every trip, I enjoyed my dad's stories, although sometimes I had to remind him, "Dad, you've already told me that one before."

On the way to the tournament I could feel the nerves stirring up inside and my heart began to hammer. Once I stepped out of the car, the pounding diminished and my stomach settled down. We greeted everyone, signed the necessary paper work and I took off to the starting dock to ready myself for my two tournament passes. The slalom event was first and I was thankful for that. Though I was much better in slalom than tricks, it was much more difficult to break into Open in slalom. I put a decent score on the board and prepared for the trick event next.

I sat on the dock waiting my turn. "Breakfast of champions, I see!" A skier motioned at the Mountain Dew in my hand. I was munching on a fudge-round with the other. I sheepishly shrugged.

"Keith St. Onge!" The judge called out my name. I grabbed the rope and jumped into the water. The nerves had settled down to a mere rumble. I ran over the trick routines quickly in my head. I was ready. The countless hours on the water were about to be tested. From the corner of my eye, I could see my dad pacing the shore.

I ran through the run effortlessly, my body knew the motions systematically. The second pass was a little more challenging but I was filled with confidence. I thought of my dad and Swampy. They had put so much time, money and effort into training me and I wanted to make them proud. Half way through my second pass, I started to celebrate too soon. *Just three more tricks and I will be in the professional division!* Just as that thought ran through my head, I bobbled in the middle of my trick.

Oh crap! Focus! I caught myself just in time and steadied my feet. I snapped back to the task and finished off the three tricks. I had to reach 2600 points to qualify and I scored 2690. *I did it!* My fist shot up. I was going to ski with the pros!

During the National tournament in 1994 at the age of 15, I found myself competing head-to-head with the two-time World Barefoot Champion, Mike Seipel, in the Open Division. I looked up to him and I wanted to be just like him. He won several National titles and held numerous records. I was fortunate he gave me my first barefoot lesson—his early influence is what set everything in motion for me.

Now I was facing him in the same tournament. It all came down to one final run. Mike decided to take an optional re-ride, in which he had to do his start over. During the re-ride, he fell on his start. Right then and there, I had a moment of glory: I beat my idol on the water! For one brief moment I felt bad that he fell, but in the next moment I was celebrating inside—dreams do come true!

After outscoring Mike, I began striving for more. I wanted to win the Overall in a National tournament. It was one step closer to becoming a World Champion.

Why Role Models Are Important

During my journey in life, I found it beneficial to always have someone to look up to. I strove to go beyond my idols and to do even more. At first, I thought, "I'll never be better than my idol, they're so far ahead!" Thinking of the impossible was fun and energizing. After awhile, I began to tell myself, it is possible!"

The first time I set a new world record in tricks, I scored 6,790. If someone had told me I would one day double that score, I would have scoffed and said, "That's impossible!" It's too easy to look at a goal and become overwhelmed at the impossibility of achieving it.

Fast forward many years later, I have actually accomplished many goals. When you build a good foundation around your goal and approach it in baby steps, you can achieve what you once thought was impossible. Everyone has 24 hours in a day. Adjust your day to devote time to your goal. If you do this day in and day out, you will move closer and closer to your dream.

The first time I said, "That was unbelievable!" my dad gave me a different perspective. "That was believable!" he would say. "It was believable because it just happened in front of our eyes!"

I believe we have so much more potential than what we initially think we're capable of achieving. I learned to aim higher, and to go beyond my idols. Never stop-- never rest--never be content. Keep on pushing. I learned to keep the dream ahead of me, to keep my vision steady and my focus intense.

The natural instinct of a human is to always want more. Even when we achieve our goals we set higher goals. When we reach the higher goal we're still not content with ourselves. Having a role model helped me strive for more. This gave me direction and kept me moving forward.

Today, my skills on the water are better than that of my idols. When I was younger, I could not imagine being as great as them, but today, I tell others: "Do not sell yourself short." As my skills progressed, my confidence did too. When I competed against my idols, I began to realize I had the chance to beat one of them. Once that thought ran through my head, there was no stopping me. I sought out others to motivate me. I had Swampy telling me I could do it, which excited me and kept me believing I could improve.

I took the opportunity to work on overcoming my shyness and introduce myself to some of the barefooters who I looked up to. The first person I scoped out was Brian Fuchs. Brian was known for his excellent slalom skills and he was the first child to barefoot backwards at the age of six. He could cross the wake at lightning speed and with great form.

Waiting for the right moment, I went up to him. "Hi, Brian, my name is Keith St. Onge. I'm skiing the Open Division for the first time and I wanted to introduce myself." Brian responded in a positive way and I gained some confidence from that encounter.

Brian Fuchs held the world record for slalom which he set in 1994. I set a new record in 2006.

I went up to another competitor and started out with the same introduction, "Hi, my name is Keith…." I noticed he had some earphones around his neck and was getting ready to listen to some music. He took one look at me, put his earphones over his ears, rolled his eyes… and walked off. Here I was, a 15-year-old kid competing for the first time on a new level, trying to overcome my shyness and I was dissed by a guy who I revered. I was crushed.

The two of us later skied on a World Team together and there was no trace of the same attitude by then. We shared a room together, but I hadn't yet drummed up the courage to talk to him about the incident.

A few years ago, I ran into him and I brought up the incident. I told him bluntly how I felt about his reaction to my introduction. To my surprise, I learned he didn't intentionally plan to be rude-- he was simply protecting himself from getting close to other barefooters so he could concentrate on his performance on the water. "I didn't want to talk to anyone--so no one could get into my head. I wanted to stay focused on competing," he explained.

My encounter was a fateful one and it became a lesson for me. I was left with a mixture of emotions after that meeting. I knew I didn't want anyone else to feel the same way when meeting me for the first time, so I make sure I reach out in a positive way. As I became well known in the barefooting world, I understood the value of first impressions, especially for the younger athletes who were new to the sport and meeting their idols for the first time. A positive, engaging first impression will be remembered for years.

In the winter of 1994, Spray and I took off for Florida to spend two weeks at Ron Scarpa's Ski School. I was trying out for a place on the U.S. team to compete at the World Championships. Ron was a well-known barefooting legend, and he was considered one of the best. Ron was one of my idols and I couldn't wait to spend time with him.

Ron was in all the magazines and he was a big name in the sport. He won Nationals and continually set new world trick records. My dream at the time was to get as close as possible to his tournament scores. I couldn't envision beating him because he was so talented. Nobody could beat him!

I was so shy, I kept quiet at the beginning of the training. "How old are you?" Ron asked. I explained I was 16. "What grade are you in?"

"I'm in ninth grade, uh, a freshman."

"Oh, you stayed back a year?"

I hung my head in embarrassment, engulfed in self-pity. "Yeah, my parents held me back in first grade, due to my birthday."

"I was held back too," he smiled. I couldn't believe it—Ron had gone through the same thing! Instantly, I felt better.

It was a huge honor to be invited to try out for the team. I wasn't picked for the team, but this was a trip to gain experience and get closer to my goal of being a U.S. Team member one day.

49

Chapter 8: Staying Committed and Dedicated

Procrastination is opportunity's natural assassin.

~Victor Kiam

In my junior year of high school, a petite blond beauty named Jan popped into my life. I took one look into her hazel eyes and I was smitten. At that point, I was well known in the barefooting world and Jan initially accepted it as part of the package. At this point of my life, barefooting started to take a bit of a back seat because I found myself wanting to spend more and more time with Jan.

Around this same time, I picked up the nasty habit of smoking. The first time I lit a cigarette, I could hear Swampy lecturing me in my head. *Don't smoke, don't do drugs. You don't want to mess up your life or the dreams you have ahead of you.* I put Swampy out of my mind and took a drag. The first cigarette led to another and then another. Before long, the cancer sticks were a part of my life. Smoking is one of the most immature things I have ever done in my life and something I am not proud of.

> **Looking Back**
> As much as I wanted to buck the system when I thought I was a know-it-all teenager, I look back and notice my dad was right 99.9% of the time. It just took me until I was thirty to notice.

When my dad caught me smoking and lectured me about quitting his lecture only fueled me to continue. I saw it as an attempt to control me and I didn't want to be controlled. The challenge of hiding my smoking habit became a bit of a game and I ended up smoking more just to see if I could get away with it. Anytime someone tried to get me to quit, it made me want to light up another cigarette. I didn't want anyone telling me what to do or controlling my life. Being the typical teenager, I thought I knew it all.

I knew I had to hide the smoking because of my image as a competitive athlete. I couldn't smoke at the tournaments nor did I want anyone to know. I picked up the habit of chewing tobacco to substitute for the cigarettes. I figured it couldn't be as bad as smoking and it was much easier to hide. During breaks from my training runs, I'd head to the back for a bathroom break and secretly put a pinch of tobacco into my lip. It was easy enough to get away with it because it was a normal thing to see guys spit. The tobacco was becoming a growing problem and the only time I was not dipping was when I was eating or sleeping.

Rolling the Dice

The teen years can be a tough time in life. Making foolish decisions like smoking will not get you anywhere. Most teens are picking up cigarettes for the wrong reasons: to feed the rebel inside, to appear cool or simply to mirror their friends. The moment you pick up a cigarette, you are hurting your body and overall health. When I look back, I cringe at how I played Russian Roulette with my own life.

When you are seen with a cigarette in your hand, people will think you don't care about yourself, and in fact, that's the truth--you don't care about yourself.

It was challenging to wean myself off of cigarettes and chewing tobacco. There was no easy way around the cravings. That's why today, if I have the opportunity to influence someone to steer clear of the nasty habit or to stop, I do everything I can to support them down a healthier path.

You may not feel the side effects at a young age but they will catch up to you. The same goes with drinking alcohol. Don't drink at all or keep it to a limit--or your life will be limited.

As my junior year wore on, I found myself wanting to spend time doing the things that all teens do, especially hanging out with my friends and my girlfriend. I was often torn in two different directions because barefooting took up so much time. "You act as if your barefoot water skiing is more important than me!" Jan said. I had given up so much in the previous years: time away from my family, summers away from my school friends and I wasn't able to pursue any school sports like track or hockey. I played two years of soccer in high school but the sport took a toll on my barefoot water ski training. I had to make a choice: I gave up soccer.

Alcohol was another vice I picked up in high school. I was spending more and more time hanging with my buddies and tossing back a few. Barefooting was starting to take a back seat to life. The lack of motivation was catching up to me. There were some mornings I had absolutely no motivation to get out on the water. The more I wanted to hang with Jan or my friends, the harder it was to get myself up to go out and practice. Swampy was never up before me because of the graveyard hours so on the days I wanted to sleep longer I learned how to fib my way out of practice. "There are big waves out there making whitecaps," I said one morning. "Alright, go back to bed and check on it in an hour," Swampy mumbled. It was pure bliss to head back into bed.

I tried another excuse one morning. "There's too much fog on the water this morning so we'll just have to wait until it lifts," I said. This worked well until one day Swampy got up and caught a different reality outside the window. The water was dead calm and the sun was rising. He jostled me awake. "Get something to eat, stretch out and get the boat ready. We're going out in 20 minutes." I protested and dove deeper under the warm covers but Swampy wouldn't relent. He threw the covers back. With a sigh, I dragged myself out of bed and went for the wetsuit. All I could think about was spending the day with Jan or hanging with the guys from school.

Swampy was becoming concerned with the change in my attitude and my lackluster devotion at that point. It wasn't that I stopped working hard—once I was on the water I gave it my all. I just found that I wanted to spend a little less time on the water and more time being a typical high school teen. Swampy and my parents had sacrificed so much to push me far into the sport and I was losing my focus.

Swampy enlisted the help of Bruce to talk some sense into me. He hoped a pep talk from someone else would do the trick. Bruce and I took a ride around Big Island and just sat in the boat with no distractions around. "Keith, buddy," he nudged me. "You have two years of school left and it will go by in the blink of an eye. This is a tough time as a teenager. I know you want to party and be with your friends and I understand that. I know you feel like you're missing out on the stuff that all of your friends are doing." I sat there in uncomfortable silence. "Here's the thing," Bruce continued. "You can explode as a professional barefoot water skier. You have a career ahead of you. Swampy sees you as a professional, he's not just telling you that. You have the talent. Don't throw it all away drinking and partying with your friends. High school is one big party—then the party is over—what will you do then if you toss this away?"

I took it all in, but inside, I was annoyed. Here was Bruce, along with my parents, my girlfriend, and Swampy--all of them telling me what to do, what not to do, and how to live my life. "I'm not tossing this away," I insisted. "I just want to have a break and some time to do fun things with my friends and my girlfriend. She wants to spend more time with me and she's not happy about all the time I'm spending on the water."

"As far as your girlfriend goes, don't let her get to you," Bruce said. "There's plenty of time to get serious with her or other girlfriends later. You're going to have to figure out how to deal with the peer pressure. These next two years will either make or break your skiing career. Your choices will factor in how the next two years progress." In the distance, the yodeling call of a loon pierced the air. Bruce spoke up again. "There are two kinds of people who graduate from high school. One has a plan in life, the other will say, 'What do I do now?' You know, Keith, Berlin used to be known as the hockey capitol of the North East. Many talented young high school students signed contracts with semi-pro teams in Canada but their drinking and partying got the best of them. They enjoyed it so much they lost the opportunity they had. As for you Keith, you've got a plan and you have to keep that plan in front of you."

"Yeah."

"You know Mount Washington, Keith?" I nodded. "Someday you're going to reach the top in this sport. Your life is going to be like standing on the peak of that mountain."

Building a Team Around You:

I was fortunate to be surrounded by a team to help me get where I wanted to go. I was around people who agreed with the direction of my dreams when I was younger--they liked my vision and supported it. They also kept me going during the times when my own dedication began to falter. They helped me keep my goals, dreams and vision in front of me and guided me during the times I lost direction.

Over the years, I've learned to find the people who light me up inside and I learned to stay away from those who bring me down.

As I've grown older, I've learned to evaluate the choices I make in my life. I discovered I made poor choices whenever I wanted to blend in with a crowd or wanted to fit in. With every choice, I was either getting closer to my goals and dreams or I was wasting time with the decisions I made.

I've come to understand the people who stand out are those who differ from the norm and they are those who come up with new and innovative ways to do things in a different way.

In the Shadow of a Spotlight

As the spotlight grew brighter and brighter for me, there was someone else who was getting lost in the shadows: my sister, Kendra. Even though I was absent from home so much, the two of us were still close. Kendra looked up to me and I protected her. The spotlight was always on me, especially in our small town. Kendra held in her thoughts and feelings so we were completely unaware of what was going on inside. Kendra felt like she was in the back seat all the time. It wasn't until years later I learned she had a tough time dealing with the attention people showered on me.

Kendra really didn't have much of a choice in how she spent her time—she was five years younger than me and we dragged her from tournament to tournament in the first few years. In the later years, she attended the tournaments willingly to support me. One winter night, we held a fundraiser at a local restaurant for an upcoming tournament and the whole family was helping out. Kendra broke her foot the night before while ice-skating. She was clearly in a lot of pain, but she kept a smile on her face and cheerfully talked with everyone as she helped sell 50-50 raffle tickets. When I look back on that night, I'm filled with admiration for my sister and always thankful for the love and support she gave me throughout the years.

For a short period of time, Kendra and I bonded over barefooting when she picked up the skill at the age of 13. Her interest didn't last long. She quickly discovered she didn't enjoy the falls that came with the sport and she felt as if she was being pushed into it. She turned to water skiing and quickly learned show acts. Years later, my dad did the unthinkable and bought a tube. Tubing quickly became the hot ticket with her friends around the lake and she employed me as her boat driver. I dubbed her the "Tubing Queen" because she could hang on through the tightest whips and largest waves on the lake.

When Kendra turned 16, she sought out counseling so she could have someone to talk to about everything she was going through. Kendra learned to find her own way to shine. She joined a hockey team during middle school and fine-tuned her talent on the ice, holding her own against the guys. In high school, she joined the first girl's hockey team and played for two years. For the last nine years, she's been playing broomball on a local team and she can really whip that broomstick on the ice. I always say that broomball is just like barefooting, except the water is frozen!

In high school, Kendra discovered a passion for styling hair. She enjoyed working with her friends' hair, creating new styles and giving haircuts. She went to cosmetology school to learn how to cut and style hair. Whenever I know I'm heading home, I let my hair grow long so I can cop a free haircut from my sister. I do try to tip her, but she never lets me. Kendra is so popular in town she has to turn clients down because her schedule is full.

Individual Passion

Everyone has something they enjoy or something they are passionate about. You don't have to do what everyone else is doing to be accepted. My sister thought by learning to barefoot she could have the same attention that I was getting but she quickly realized it was not for her. If you do not enjoy the activity or career then it is simply not worth it. It is important to unwrap the passion that you have inside of you and own it--it is uniquely yours. Passion will push you above and beyond in anything you do.

For any professional athlete, the time devoted to a sport usually means time taken away from family. As I progressed in the sport we began to spend more time apart as a family. Dad and I were traveling from tournament to tournament, leaving behind my mom and Kendra. My mom didn't take it well. The years were flying by fast and she felt like I was drifting away from her. In her mind, Swampy was to blame. The two of them would occasionally battle over the use of my time. "You have Keith for eight months out of the year," Swampy would remind my mom. "Let me have him for the other four months." He would sweet-talk her every time and each time she would put her feelings aside and support me.

It was hard to find time for the family vacations my mom dreamed of taking because we were always off in different directions and so much time was devoted to the sport. One day, my mom had enough. "We are going to the beach," she announced. Swampy and I both protested but she stood firm. "I need some time with my family and we're taking the day off." Once I hit the beach with Kendra, I relaxed. I needed the break and the precious time with my family.

Conquering Fear Once Again

After the break, I was ready to learn more. For me to advance in the sport of barefoot water skiing I had to learn the inverted style of jumping. Picture a "Superman" pose off the jump with legs flying back in the air--that's inverted jumping. Swampy searched around for someone to teach me and he found Jon Kretchman who was an expert in inverted jumping. Jon grew up in Fergus Falls, Minnesota--a blue- eyed, blonde-haired, tough-as-nails football player.

Short, but extremely stocky, with legs like tree trunks--he had a neck that never seemed to get sore even from the roughest barefoot falls. Jon walked with an air of confidence and determination as if he was on his way to kick someone's butt.

Swampy organized the training and I took off to Fergus Falls, Minnesota for one month to work with Jon. My first attempts at inverted jumping were on the boom off the side of the boat. I felt pretty confident as I racked up jump after jump. Jumping on the long line behind the boat was a whole other story. For three weeks, I made mistake after mistake on the jump. I floated in the water after every crash, playing mind games to try and psych myself up to jump better. Jon was teaching me a very different way to jump and the technique did not seem to suit me well. There was also something else weighing heavily on my mind: fear.

I thought back to the previous year's tournament in Connecticut. Only a few competitors were jumping inverted. The rest of us stuck to the old-fashioned, straight up and down jumping style. Hank Butler was one of several competitors in the beginning stages of learning the inverted jump. Everyone liked Hank, he was the guy with a big heart for the sport. He would pull up his RV at every tournament and serve margaritas at the end of the day to anyone who walked by. Hank was not shy with his wallet and he contributed a lot of time and money to the sport.

Swampy was working as the Safety Director. His job was to make sure that the tournament operated in a safe manner and to oversee any first aid that was needed. He had to wear a life jacket during the entire tournament just in case he had to pull an injured skier out of the water.

Swampy, my dad, and I were standing on the shore, watching jump after jump and taking notes. It was a very hot day and the water was glass calm. I was suited up and getting ready for my turn on the jump. I watched intently as Hank approached the jump. I wanted to study his form as I was learning everything I could about jumping.

Just before Hank reached the jump he caught a toe and slammed head first into the jump. Hank cart wheeled over and landed face-first into the water. He wasn't moving. "Get out there! Get out there! He's out!" one of the skiers screamed. Swampy and another skier rushed out to Hank and carefully flipped him over, holding his head steady as they removed the helmet. Hank's face was turning blue. They brought him to shore quickly so they could administer CPR.

"Call 911!" someone screamed.

"Go get some towels!" yelled someone else. I grabbed my towel nearby and ran over. As I handed it over, I caught a glimpse of Hank and stepped back. Blood was pouring out of his ear and down his face. He wasn't moving and he wasn't breathing. I took it all in with shock. I closed my eyes and recalled Hank laughing just a few minutes earlier. I couldn't believe he was lying on the ground fighting for his life. The sound of a helicopter grew louder as it landed in a nearby field. The medical crew secured an airway and loaded Hank into the helicopter. Hank was breathing when they took off for the hospital.

At the tournament site, the mood was somber as we took it all in. One by one, we each went out on the water and finished our runs. We sat around and waited for updates about Hank. The next morning we learned Hank passed away. The news reverberated through the barefoot ski community as a huge shock. Hank's death hit me hard. Suddenly I realized the sport I loved so much could actually claim a life.

I had Hank in the back of my mind as I listened to Jon's instructions preparing me for the inverted jumps. I approached every jump with fear bubbling inside of me. I could not will my body to get into the inverted position. I was terrified.

Come on Keith, shift your thinking to something positive or you'll never get through this. My thoughts drifted to a girl back home, a female barefooter. I had a crush on this girl and I wanted her to notice me. *If she could just see me jumping inverted she will think I'm so cool and she'll like me,* I thought to myself. Suddenly, I was filled with a sense of bravado. *I'm going to do this! I don't care what happens. I'm going to go out there and launch myself in the air. I don't give a crap if I fall or hurt myself.* As I approached the jump, I was determined to go all out. I leaped off the jump and hurled through the air with my legs lifting out from behind me. I flew higher than I ever had before and in mid-air I found myself turning upside down. Frantically, I tried to right myself and get my feet down. I crashed into the water near Jon's eighty-foot buoy, landing on my neck. The zipper on my wetsuit burst open and my helmet flew off.

Time suddenly stood still. I floated motionless for a few minutes, struggling to breathe. The wind was completely knocked out of me. There was a flurry of commotion on shore as people ran towards the edge of the water. "Keith! Keith! Are you all right? Are you ok?" Several voices overlapped at once.

Everything hurt all over. I let out a gasp of air. "Yeah, I am ok," I rasped. I was shaken. The padding from my helmet was strewn around me. Slowly, I moved upright in the water. I swam over to my helmet and collected the floating pieces. Jon drove up. "Are you ok?" I wasn't sure. I reached for the boat platform and slowly crawled back into the boat. My neck was throbbing. I was just glad to have finally taken the inverted jump behind the boat and survived. I didn't relish the thought of having to do it again. "All right Jon, I did it. I'm done!" I started to peel the wetsuit off.

"Get the padding back in your helmet and put it on," Jon ordered. "You're going again." I stared at him in disbelief. "I'm not going again. I'm all beat up here!" I was mangled from the landing and wasn't in any shape physically or mentally to tackle another jump. The weeks of mind games, the fear of inverted jumping, and the loss of Hank--all of that had put me over the edge. Every ounce of confidence had gone down in the crash.

Jon shrugged. "Too bad, Keith! You're going again and you're going again *now.*"

I reached for my helmet and stuffed the padding back in. I was not about to question the reasoning behind his order. Jon had his arms folded and his muscles bulged under his shirt. I didn't want to debate him any further. Either way, I would lose.

Slamming the helmet on my head, I cinched the strap and got back in the water. "Hit it!" I snapped as I leaned back for the start. I got back up on my feet and aimed for the jump. My hands felt as if they were actually sweating. I tightened my grip on the handle and braced myself. I launched off the jump with my feet dangling in the air behind me and I could see the water coming up fast. My feet came down in front of me and I landed on my butt. The handle snapped out of my hands and I skidded to a stop. *Hey--that wasn't too bad. I did it!* By the time the next jump set came around, I was finally landing the jumps on my feet.

In hindsight, I'm glad Jon pushed me to jump again. It goes back to that old saying of "get back on the horse after you get bucked off." If he hadn't pushed me when he did, it is possible that I would have let the fall get to me in a negative way and it would have been quite difficult to face the fear of jumping inverted after that. I might have continued to play those mind games with myself and allowed the fear to escalate to a new height. Sometimes the only way to work through the fear of failing is to get out in life and practice over and over the very thing that brings out the fear. What I learned that day, I apply to my life every day. When I fail, I don't give up. I don't walk away. I go for it again. Determination and persistence will always give results.

Pressure

Pressure can be a good thing. The more you put yourself in an uncomfortable position, the better you become at handling it. Sometimes the only way to learn a new skill or move toward a dream is to gain experience through trying and practice. Experience gives you several opportunities to improve. When you are in an uncomfortable position you get to practice what works and learn what doesn't.

A Tough Tournament

In 1995, we were back in DuQuion, Illinois for the Nationals at the very same place where I had almost tasted gold a few years back. I wanted to put those memories behind me and do well. I was flying high that summer, racking up the trophies and medals at the local tournaments. I amassed a collection of newspaper articles and magazine articles describing my accomplishments. People from all over recognized me and approached me at tournaments. Inside, I was filled with pride and I tried not to show it, but my head was pretty swelled up. As the youngest kid to ski in the Open Division and the youngest one who could jump inverted, I was getting a lot of attention and I loved it.

When I arrived at the starting dock at the Nationals I didn't have my own rope with me. I used the tournament rope, a rope I was not familiar with. In tournaments, skiers can use a personal handle and rope if they don't want to use the tournament line and handle. I decided to use my personal handle and attach it to the supplied tournament line.

I felt pretty confident, with just a few butterflies rolling around inside of me. Swampy taught me to welcome a few nerves as a good thing and to use them to my advantage. Excessive nervousness made me weak in the knees. It would take time and experience to learn how to control them. I learned to breathe slowly and deeply before each competitive run.

"Ok!" I leaned back and prepared myself for a "Toe Up," which is a start on one foot with the other foot gripping a strap attached to the handle. I stood up on one foot and showed my hands to the judges in the boat to ensure the points. The start gave me 300 points. I went to retrieve the handle and out of nowhere--as if someone just slapped me up-side the head--I caught a toe and slammed into the water. My face was flaming red when I tumbled to a stop. Disgruntled, I climbed on the Jet Ski which would take me to the other end for my second pass. I slammed myself down on the seat. I was mad as hell and frustrated with myself. How could I make such a simple mistake? It was one thing to fall during a complicated trick but it was a total embarrassment to fall by simply taking my hands off the handle.

I readied myself for my second pass, but inside, my emotions were flip-flopping all over the place. I hooked my foot on the rope and turned over to execute a backwards start. I rose out of the water quickly and started to push myself outside of the boat wake. The boat was only going twenty-five or thirty miles per hour when I attempted to turn to the front. I hit the water backwards with a splash. This time, I didn't bother wiping the scowl off my face as I bobbed in the water. I climbed on the Jet Ski and slammed myself down once again. Hanging my head, I slumped over. Over and over, I reviewed my starts to figure out what went wrong.

"Keith, keep your head up and wave to the crowd!" My dad was on shore hollering a lesson at me but I didn't hear him over the roar of the engine, nor did I care. My ego which was soaring high earlier that morning had come crashing straight down, just as I had done on the water. I scored just 440 points for those two runs. In previous tournaments I was averaging over 4,000 points.

> Winning is not everything.
> Wanting to win is.
> ~Catfish Hunter

I climbed off the starting dock and walked toward shore with my head down. My dad walked toward me. I took one look at him and I couldn't hold back the emotions. I started to cry. "I'm sorry...," we both said at the same time. I wasn't even sure what I was sorry about at that moment. My dad and Swampy put so much time and energy into my training and I felt like I let them and myself down. I tried to deal with all the emotions I had internalized for so long but I just couldn't stop the tears. My dad started crying too and there was no holding back. He reached out and hugged me tightly. I felt something powerful between us at that moment. All the long practices, the time, the money, the traveling--everything came together at once. We were both learning that sometimes despite immense effort there'll be times when you hit some less-than-desirable outcomes. I had rode such an incredible high for so long that it was truly humbling to literally be brought to my knees on the water.

My dad brought my head up with his hands and looked straight at me. "Never hang your head down in front of the crowd, son. That is a sign of bad character. Wave to the crowd and hold your head high even after falling. People want to see a good sport and you must control your emotions."

"I understand...I won't do that again." I replied. Dad handed me my sandals and we walked toward the stands. Ron Scarpa came up to me. "Come here, I want to show you something," he motioned. He took his own ski rope and tied it to a telephone pole. He instructed me to lean back and pull on it. He then tied the tournament rope to the same telephone pole and said, "Pull on this one. Look how stretchy this rope is," he explained. "You are not used to skiing with this rope and it will not give you a consistent pull. You know how your own rope performs. Next time, you need to bring your personal rope to the dock and use that. Don't be shy about asking the boat crew to switch to your rope."

I thanked Ron and then went off to the grandstand. Brian Fuchs came up to me. He was another idol of mine--a guy who held the World Record for slalom for twelve years. "Do you have a difficult time staying in the backwards skiing position for a long period of time?" he asked.

"Yes, exactly...how did you know?"

"I have the same problem and it's a tough habit to break!" he explained. "You've got to be patient and wait for the boat to get up to speed before you make your turn. That's why you fell, the boat wasn't fast enough at that point." I was grateful for Brian's advice and he made me feel like I wasn't the only one with this problem. I learned how to control my backwards skiing several years later. Yeah, it took that long!

> Surround yourself with people who are more skilled than you because you'll learn at a much quicker pace from their experience and doing this will keep you motivated.
>
> ~Keith St. Onge

Chapter 9: Taking a Leap Toward a Dream

The only thing that will stop you from fulfilling your dream, is you.

~Tom Bradley

"I think I found the perfect, private lake for you!" my dad announced after work one day. "It's about 300 feet wide and looks to be about 1800 feet long. It seems to be an abandoned property," he explained. Dad had been working on an electrical line high up on a telephone pole in the town of Lancaster when he noticed a sparkle of light coming from a sand pit filled with water. "Let's take the boat over there and see if it's deep enough. This could actually be a great place to host our own future tournaments!"

Swampy joined us, and on the ride over we talked about all the possibilities that the private lake could hold for us. "If we can make this lake work for us it would be a great way to bring people to the Northeast and showcase the sport to more people in our area," Swampy mused. "We probably would have to expand the lake more, but we could even host the Eastern Regionals," Dad said. "Jackie and the girls could do the cooking during tournaments. We could use this site for fundraising as well." We were all hyped up on the ride over, dreaming of jump tournaments at night, of houses around the site, and of opening a ski school.

It was around six p.m. when we arrived at the lake. The sand pit looked like something a child would dig in the middle of a beach and fill with water. The glass calm water glistened with a tint of green but on further inspection the water seemed clear. Small, gray rocks dotted the shoreline and the lake was surrounded by trees. Dad walked around the site taking measurements to make sure it was long enough for a run. Dad stopped and pointed to Mount Washington jutting out among the White Mountains which dotted the terrain at the north end of the lake. "Look at that view! The view alone is enough to draw people to this site!"

Dad backed the boat into the water and tied a rock to the end of a rope to measure the depth. There was no depth gage on the boat so we trolled up and down slowly, measuring the depth by dragging the rock on the bottom. We wanted to make sure that the water was deep enough throughout the pit. At the very minimum we needed at least four feet of water and enough distance to complete a 15 second trick run. "It looks like it's plenty deep. I think it's good to go," said Dad. "Let's try timing a run." He turned the boat around near the bank. As Dad throttled the boat down the middle, Swampy called out the seconds. "13... 14... 15... It's long enough to do a trick run!" He pumped his fist in the air. "Ok, Keith, jump in and let's give this a try," Dad said. It took me a few minutes to don a dry suit. Jumping overboard, I sank into the water. Excitement was bubbling up inside of me. I couldn't wipe the grin off my face. This was going to be a slice of heaven to have an *entire* lake to myself.

"Hit it!" I yelled. Dad throttled the boat and I put my feet on the water. I stood up, adjusted my grip, and prepared myself to do a few tricks. *Bang!* The boat came to a sudden stop. Swampy and Dad jolted forward. The rope went slack. I let go of the handle and sank into the cold water. "What the hell was that?" Swampy said.

"What happened?" I called out.

"I think we hit something!" Dad said. I swam to the handle floating a few feet away and Dad started pulling me in with the rope. We gathered around the outboard engine to survey the damage. There was complete silence as Dad raised the motor out of the water. Then the swearing began in earnest and it wasn't pretty. The lower half of the engine was mangled. The bolts holding the motor to the boat were bent and protruding. The propeller looked as if someone had taken a hammer to it. Dad leaned on the pylon and let out a deep sigh. "We must have hit a big rock or sand bar."

"I didn't think there would be rocks down the middle," Swampy said. "What the hell were they thinking when they dug this pit?"

"It's going to cost us a couple of grand to get it fixed," Dad said. "How are we going to explain this to the ski club? And what are we going to do for a boat in the meantime?" As the two of them chattered, I was lost in my own thoughts. *It took a long time to get in this dry suit and now I have to take it off!* My mind was not on the chopped up motor. As a teen, you think of the stupidest things. "We've gotta paddle this to shore," Swampy's voice snapped me back into reality. Swampy grabbed an oar and I used a shoe ski to paddle back to shore. The mood was somber as we contemplated how to come up with the funds for a repair. Fifty two hundred dollars and three weeks later, we had a boat again but our dreams for the site slipped away.

Trying Out for the World Team

The World tournaments were held every two years and I wanted to try out for the Elite team. The team trials were approaching quickly but I still didn't have any practice time on the water. Swampy started making some calls to barefooters and coaches in Florida. He connected with Richard Gray who trained one of the legends of barefooting. During his conversation with Richard, Swampy was describing my skills on the water and telling Richard a bit about me. "I think Keith has a good shot at making the team. He skis quite well," Swampy explained.

"I don't know why you're wasting your time," Richard said. "The kid doesn't stand a chance of making the team." Swampy hung up the phone and relayed what Richard told him. I was infuriated. Nothing spurred me on more than someone doubting my ability to accomplish something. Swampy knew this and he knew I would be driven even more to work my tail off just to prove Richard wrong. There was some truth to what Richard shared and the chances were slim for me to make the team. Swampy wanted me to be prepared for this.

Swampy got back on the phone and made a couple more calls to find me a place to practice. He located a coach, Calvin Bramlitt, from Jacksonville, Florida. His son, Wade, was a National Champion in the Junior Division. We competed against each other in previous years and he kicked my butt in every tournament. Calvin agreed to give me two weeks of coaching and practice time at his site on the Black River.

A few days after arriving I developed an ear infection, a completely new experience for me. The piercing pain radiated down my neck and I tossed and turned all night. During the day, I couldn't concentrate on my skiing. I consider myself a pretty tough guy, but that day, I found myself turning into a crybaby from the pain. Calvin brought me to a local doctor. The doc took one look into my ear and then reached for a plastic cup. "Here, hold this next to your ear," he said. He filled a plastic syringe with water and proceeded to flood my ear. The debris that came out was some of the nastiest stuff I had ever seen. I had no idea gunk that large could find a home in my ear. I have a strong stomach, but I left the doctor's office feeling a little woozy.

Just a week before the team trials and shortly after recovering from the ear infection I encountered another challenge. I was walking down the dock that led to the river and I felt a sudden, sharp pain in my right heel. *Please don't let it be a cut! This will ruin me!* Peering closer, I examined my heel. *Damn!* I stared at it in shock. Lodged deep into my heel was a splinter. Not just a little sliver of a splinter, but a huge piece of wood. *Great. Just what I needed! A cut on the foot one week before the team trials!*

I hobbled over to a nearby chair and suddenly a crowd of skiers swarmed around me. Calvin took one look at the wound and shook his head. The parent of another skier examined my heel. "Hang tight," he said. "Let me get some needle-nosed pliers." He returned with the pliers and grasped at the sliver but the pliers kept slipping off each time he yanked at it. His arms were shaking when he painfully pulled the three-quarter-inch piece of wood out of my heel. Thankfully, the whole thing came out at once. I stared at the gaping hole. How the heck was I going to get through the next five days skiing with a hole in my foot? That was my introduction to...Super Glue. That's right, I super-glued the wide-open cut. I had to experiment with several different brands of glue before I discovered Wizard Super Glue was the best brand to keep the cut closed. For the next five days, I skied with shoe skis to guard against infection. When I began skiing on my feet I coated Super Glue over the cut. Every three runs, I would get back into the boat, reapply the glue, and hop back out on the water.

During the two days of team trials, I blocked out the cut out of my mind and focused on my performance on the water. I was determined to go all out and secure my place on the team. The selection committee was made up of eight people and for two days they dished out feedback as we completed three rounds of slalom, tricks and jumping.

I had a great time with the other skiers during the trials, especially Paul Stokes. I met Paul in 1993 at the Nationals and we instantly hit it off. "Stokes" was a pro barefooter who taught clinics all over the U.S. He could do front flips perfectly along with many other technical maneuvers. He was extremely fit. His wide, flat feet probably resulted from all the years that he worked at Sea World as a show skier because he shouldered the girls in pyramids up to four levels high. As a barefooter, the wide feet worked to Paul's advantage.

By the end of the second day, I still wasn't sure if I stood a chance of making the team. I had slalomed well and I knew the team needed someone with strong slalom skills. I had some nice jumps and performed my tricks well, but

I didn't know if that was enough to put me on the team. One by one, the committee announced the team members. "Ron Scarpa, John Kretchman, William Farrell, Don Mixon Jr., Lane Bowers, Jennifer Harris, Jennifer Calleri..." There was only one spot left and I held my breath. "Keith St. Onge." My legs went numb. I tried not to wobble as I took my place next to the World Barefoot Team.

Today, Richard Gray is the chairman of the World Barefoot Council and we are great friends. Every now and then, I like to rub it in and razz him about making the U.S. Team despite his predicted odds.

> When other people doubt you, never doubt yourself and never under-estimate your opponent; because he's trying not to doubt himself too.
>
> ~Keith St. Onge

Struggling on the Water

Even though Paul didn't make the team he offered to train with me at his place. Paul was taking college courses, but he was off for the summer so he invited me to ski with him in preparation for the World Championships. I flew to Houston, Texas and hung out with Paul for three weeks. Spending time with Paul was nothing but fun, fun and more fun. We didn't have a care in the world and no responsibilities.

"We're going to start on Clear Lake and work our way up to Barefoot Alley," Paul explained. "Make sure you watch out for the white buoys-- those are the crab traps. You don't want to get tangled in those!" As we powered down the lake, I was in awe of the massive houses and mansions that dotted the shoreline. Clear Lake sat on the west shoreline of Galveston Bay near Houston. I thought back to Lake Umbagog and my grandfather's cottage-- we had no hot water, shower or a TV-- and here, the residents were doing comfortably well.

As soon as I dove into the water, I was left with a brackish taste in my mouth. "Why does this water taste so nasty?"

"That's just the Texas water. Suck it up!" he laughed. He always loved calling me by a nickname I can't repeat here. The only way to get rid of the salty taste was to munch on crackers or candy. Clear Lake connected to the ocean and the water level was tidal which meant we had to be aware of the low spots at times. We made our way down the lake going under several bridges along the way. As we got closer to Barefoot Alley, the bridges became narrower and lower. There was one railroad bridge that was so low we had to lower the bimini top and push the boat down so the ski pylon could clear the bridge. "Why do you go through all this trouble to get to Barefoot Alley?" I asked. "Just wait. You'll see," Paul grinned.

As it turned out, Barefoot Alley was a skier's paradise. Gazing down the long stretch of alley, I whistled. The shores were banked up high, with a thick blanket of trees on each side. The water was protected from the wind and right in front of us was a long stretch of glass calm water. It was narrow enough so other boat traffic wouldn't interfere. It was definitely worth all the work it took to get there. We followed the same routine every day. The days were blissful. We got up late, practiced all morning, and then came in for lunch. We rested a bit and then headed back out again.

Paul was an expert at the one trick I could not do: the front flip. He would skim along on his feet at 45 mph, flip head-over-heels and get up skiing again. It was a popular trick at the time, a "bread and butter" trick that a lot of footers were adding to their trick routines. Every time I tried the trick, I would bail out half way and land on my ribs and bounce away. I could do turns on my feet but I couldn't land a flip. Back home at the lake, Swampy would always egg me on. "What's the matter? Spray can do the front flip with no problem! It's just a simple flip. You're not as strong, so you probably can't do it." Swampy always knew how to wind me up! I would grit my teeth and hurl myself over, only to twist myself in mid-air and crash once again onto my ribs.

"Come on, let's practice in the pool," Paul suggested one afternoon. He grabbed the ski rope and we took off for the pool in the back of his apartment complex. Paul tied the rope to a nearby tree and grabbed the handle. "All right, Keith, now watch me. Roll forward, tuck your head down, and your body will follow." He gracefully completed a flip and landed in the water on his butt and feet. I took the handle from him and gripped my toes at the edge of the pool. Taking a deep breath, I hurled myself forward. In mid-air, I could feel my legs swinging sideways and I splashed into the water. Paul slapped his thigh and doubled over with laughter. "I don't get it. You can do all kinds of other tricks on the water. You can do some of the hardest tricks that other skiers can't do but you can't... do... a simple flip!"

"I don't know why I can't do this stupid trick," I complained. "I'm all messed up when I'm upside down! My aerial perception is crap!" I tried over and over that afternoon much to the amusement of Paul and his girlfriend, Heather, who sat at the edge of the pool. The two of them tried to fine-tune my aerial movements between fits of laughter. I left Texas with the realization that I probably never would add that trick to my routine.

> ** Two years later, I finally accomplished the front flip with the help of two other barefooters, Robert Teurezbacher and Jason Lee. Robert would whip me out by turning the boat sharply and I was able to flip over and land on my feet using shoe skis. I kept practicing the flip and I finally could do it with some consistency. I landed a flip successfully during a jump tournament in Rhode Island. It was the one and only time I did a flip during a competition.
>
> A couple of years later, I threw out my back during a practice flip and couldn't ski for two weeks. It was just three weeks before the National tournament. I could only walk slowly up and down the road--for two weeks-- it was so locked up. I went to see a massage therapist and was able to move once again

My skiing was on target for the rest of the summer and I was feeling good about my skill development and my performance in the tournaments. I was starting to become more recognized at the competitions but I had yet to win a gold medal or even place in the top three at the Nationals. After all of the training I did with Paul I was feeling pumped up to perform well at the upcoming Nationals, but it was Paul who performed exceptionally well. He landed in the top three, taking third in the Overall. I congratulated Paul and I could see how proud he was to be among the best. He worked hard to make his name known as one of the greatest barefoot water skiers from the United States. We headed to the banquet for the awards ceremony to celebrate. I was bummed and disappointed with myself, especially because others had higher expectations for me. I had an awesome year with my skiing, but I just could not put it together at the National tournament.

As the award ceremony progressed, "Banana George" Blair walked up to the stage in his classic yellow suit. Banana George is probably *the* most well known barefooter of all time and the oldest person to barefoot water ski. He was born in 1915 and took up barefooting in 1961 when he was 46 years old. He first attended barefoot tournaments as a spectator, handing out his favorite fruit, Chiquita bananas. The company sent him boxes and boxes of bananas for every tournament he attended. Surprisingly, Banana George didn't enter his first competition until he was 64 years old. The moment he started competing he was unstoppable. He won the Nationals in the Senior Division and set a jump record at 34 feet. He's the only guy to barefoot water ski in all seven continents and 69 countries.

I wasn't paying much attention to Banana George as I was deep in conversation with my friends. He described the Banana George award and the barefooter to whom he was about to award it to. The bits and pieces I heard appeared to make the young man look well-behaved and well-liked throughout the barefoot community. The next thing I heard the Banana man say, "And the Banana George award goes to... Keith St. Onge!" My mouth fell open in surprise. I didn't have a clue I was going to receive the award. Several others knew and they had kept it to themselves. As I walked to the podium the other footers started chanting, "Speech! Speech! Speech!"

I wasn't prepared. I had never spoken in front of an audience before and I wasn't sure what to say. I scanned the audience. My heart was pounding and my breathing was labored, but words still came out somewhat smoothly. I kept it simple and to the point, thanking everyone, especially Banana George, for the award. It was an honor to stand next to a legend and receive his prestigious plaque.

After the Nationals, I headed up to Fergus Falls, Minnesota for the World Championship. I was thrilled to be on a team with many of my idols, but I was disappointed that my very first Worlds tournament wasn't going to be held out of the country. The tournament site was set on the Otter Tail River, the same site where I learned inverted jumping the year before. Jon Kretchman and the local organizing committee did a phenomenal job putting together the tournament and gathering local sponsors. It was a tournament like I had never experienced before, with TVs rigged all over the site to play back runs of the skiers. The team was also assigned to do many autograph sessions and that was a first for me. I skied well and was able to take seventh place overall--very respectable for an eighteen-year-old in his first World Championship tournament.

The awards banquet was a lively one. Barefoot water skiers are a boisterous group and anytime you mix people from all over the world into a common sport, things are bound to happen. My first taste of the "wild lot" came from the Italian skiers on the dance floor. I noticed the Italians going around and ripping the shirts off people on the dance floor. "Better take your jacket and shirt off," Jon, advised me. "We rented those tuxes and they can't get ruined." I was grateful for his advice because a few minutes later, one of my teammates lost their shirt to an overzealous Italian who ripped the shirt right off his back.

Leaving Berlin Behind

The summer after my high school graduation was an explosive summer. My life started taking some crazy turns. Just before the end of the school year I called Ron Scarpa, who was the current World Champion and one of the most revered barefooters in the history of the sport. Ron was very intimidating and he could easily rattle the nerves of inexperienced skiers. I always thought he should have been nicknamed "The Intimidator," just like Dale Earnhardt Sr., the NASCAR driver. Picture a short, wide bull, mixed with a WWE wrestler-- and you have Ron. He was extremely quick-witted and had a sarcastic comeback line for everything. No one could outwit Ron. His fans were attracted to his outgoing personality. Ron always intimidated me on the dock so the only thing I could do was keep quiet and let whatever he was saying go in one ear and out the other. There were times when I felt two feet tall next to Ron when he started trash-talking or playing mind games. He was shorter than most barefooters but he had a massive attitude and personality. To hear Ron on the phone, one would think he was over six-feet tall!

If a skier was on the dock with Ron they were likely going to choke or fall short of their potential because he would subtly psych them out. "There's a little back wash off the sea wall over there so be sure to watch out for that," he would casually say. "Remember that trick you were struggling on? It may get you here." Some skiers trained under Ron for many years but once they became a competitor on his level, all bets were off. Next to Mike Seipel, Ron was my biggest idol. Ron was "the man" from 1990-1996 and he set several trick records. He always kept himself a little ahead of all his competitors. He was one of the most well known names in the sport and everyone wanted to be associated with him.

Now that high school was behind me, it was time to go to work and I wanted to work for Ron. I looked up to him. I knew it would be a great honor to work for him and he could take my skiing to the next level. I was hoping for a barter agreement where I could teach the students at his ski school and in return, I'd have a place to live and barefoot. When I picked up the phone to call Ron, my heart was pounding like a drum. I rehearsed what I would say many times and I knew in my heart I wanted this.

"Hi, this is Ron, what can I do for you?" I was so excited to be able to speak with the World Champion and hear his voice. I explained why I wanted to come down and how I could be of assistance. "I'll tell you what, send me a letter outlining this request and tell me what you can do for me," he said. "Explain in detail what you will be able to do at the ski school."

"I will do just that and I'll send it out as soon as possible." I replied. I sat down and wrote a one-page letter detailing how I could be an asset to his business. I was determined to get down to Florida.

At first, I didn't hear back from him. When I called Ron to follow up, he explained that he already had others working there so he had no need for me. There was one option: I could pay my own way to ski and live there. The price was high and I didn't have the money to afford that option.

I tried another competitor's ski school. "Sure, you can come on down here. It will cost you $850 a month for food and training." It was a great deal, but I only had one thousand dollars in savings and my parents couldn't fork up that amount each month. "Keith should go to college and get a degree," the competitor advised my dad and Swampy. "He can still do clinics and compete, but an education will give him more options in life."

In hindsight, I'm thankful it worked out the way it did because it paved the way for me to start my own ski school. If I had gone to work for one of my competitors, I might still be working for one of them today. I might not have ever had the courage to start my own business. It turned out to be a blessing in disguise, like so many things in life. A line from a Garth Brooks song reminds me of this: "Some of God's greatest gifts are unanswered prayers."

All throughout high school, Swampy had made it clear that he would coach me until I graduated. He had plans to move to Montana and start up a new mortgage business with Spray. I was like a son to Swampy, and even though he wanted to move to Montana before I graduated, he was willing to stay and train me until I was ready to go out on my own. It was a commitment that helped shape my life and future skiing.

Before he took off to Montana, Swampy talked to Brian Heeney, another well-known competitor, and asked if I could train on his site. Brian's site was located on a private lake just three and a half hours south of where Swampy lived in Whitefish, Montana. So even though Swampy was no longer training me, he was close enough to call on him when I needed support. I wanted to take my skiing to the next level and I needed a place to stay and someone to drive me. Brian and his wife, Linda, took me into their home and Brian began training me.

If there ever was a nerd on water, it was Brian. He would even admit it. I love this guy. His intense blue eyes have scoured every single line in the rulebook and he's quick to spit out the rules at every tournament. On the water, I was in awe of him-- watching him churn out smooth and graceful surface turns.

When Brian wasn't available, his neighbor, Tim Bailey, drove for me. Tim was in his 40's and had three kids, so he enjoyed getting out in the boat to rip up and down the lake. Tim didn't have a full-time job that summer, so we had a lot of time to hang out together. We talked about life while I smoked cigarettes, and from time to time, Tim fed me a couple of beers.

One day, during an intense training session with Brian, I accidentally discovered a new trick that was going to change history in the sport. It was one of those amazing, beautiful Montana days where the lake was glassy calm. The reflection from the mountains glistened everywhere on the water. I was practicing a 180-turn while stepping over the ski line and unintentionally continued to fall over the opposite way while bringing my other foot over the line again.

"Hey--the 'line-step 360'--I think that trick just might be in the rule book," Brian said as he idled the boat past me. "Why don't you try it again? This time, complete the whole turn as you step over the line."

"I'm not sure I want to try that again. If the top footers aren't doing it, maybe it's not in the rule book." I was a bit hesitant about that trick. It was no easy feat to step over the rope in mid-turn. But if the trick was in the rulebook it would give me the incentive to try it again.

"Okay, then let's take a break and head back to the house. I'll check the rule book and we'll see if it's in there," Brian suggested.

Sure enough, Brian found the line-step 360 in the rulebook. We wolfed down a quick lunch and went back out on the water. I practiced the turn on the water and by the end of the afternoon I had completed several turns. I worked on the trick the entire week, doing three sets per day. By the time we headed to a small tournament in Helena, I decided to add the trick to my run. Brian and I were excited at the thought of showing off a brand new trick--that is--if I could pull it off. Sure enough, by the end of the tournament, I had accomplished the very first line-step 360. I also racked up 6790 points--a new World Record.

I now had two new tricks to bring to the Nationals; I could do a line step 360 in one direction and then go the other way for a reverse turn. At that moment, I had a feeling that the line-step 360 was going to be my ticket to a new title.

But first, I would have to face Ron Scarpa in the Canadian Nationals. The Canadian Nationals was a very low-key tournament and the Americans were skiing in the International Division of the tournament. The tournament was held in Edmonton on a man-made lake surrounded by a steep bluff. It was great for the spectators, but tough to ski on because the runs had to be completed quickly. As soon as the boat took off, I had to get up and get my feet on the water immediately to be able to finish my runs before the boat shut down. The end of the course came rapidly on the small, two-thousand-foot lake.

I was fired up and feeling pretty good at the start of the tournament. I didn't care if I won or not, because I was using the tournament as a warm up for the U.S. Nationals. There were just three of us in the International Division--Brett Sands, Ron and I. I was aiming to kick Ron's butt for the first time and this was a good place for practice.

I was leading in the first round when we took a break to have some fun. There was a jousting tournament set up and I donned a helmet and grabbed a joust. I found myself facing Ron during one of the bouts. At first, the jousting started out as some friendly fun. Ron knocked me off with a swift blow. I laughed as I sat up from the cushions I landed on and began to climb back up on the pillar. I had almost reached the top of the pillar and was on my knees attempting to stand when Ron's joust slammed into my helmet. The helmet spun on my head as I tumbled back down. I gingerly rubbed my sore neck. I could hear laughter all around as I climbed back up on the pillar.

By this time, a crowd had gathered around us, watching every move. It was payback time. I gripped the joust and we battled again. Securing my footing, I waited for just the right moment. A quick slam on his arm knocked him off balance. I jabbed him in the helmet and watched him tumble off. I stood there with a grin as he landed with a thud. I wasn't finished with him though. If Ron wasn't going to play fair in this game, then I wasn't going to either. I aimed right for his helmet as he stood up on the pillar, landing a solid blow that nearly sent him tumbling again.

We went back to the business of skiing, and for the first time in my career, I outscored my idol. I walked away with the first place International Overall title at the Canadian Nationals.

At the U. S. Nationals a few weeks later, I faced Ron again in the Men's Open Division in Houston, Texas. Ron was the reigning Nationals champion and he held the title for the previous seven years. I had never won a gold at the Nationals, but I had a feeling that things were about to change. I had prepared myself properly in the previous weeks and this time, I was filled with confidence. I knew if I nailed my trick sequence with the line-step 360's I would also set a new world record with the points. No one had accomplished the line-step 360's at a National tournament. Excitement was bubbling inside of me.

As I readied myself for the trick run, I thought back to the training that I did before this tournament. It was like a dream, so surreal. I didn't ski long sets at all. Sometimes I'd take two runs down the lake and back, nail every trick and then go back in the house. If I accomplished the tricks perfectly the first time, there was no need to do them again. My routines that summer consisted of quality sets instead of quantity. This was a change from my previous routines. For years, I aimed for quantity over quality during my runs. All of the long hours that I had previously spent on the water were about to pay off. I now had a chance to ski with brains, instead of the "do-it-until-I'm-worn-out" approach.

I still had to face the challenge of dealing with the trash talking that other competitors dished out. In previous tournaments, I would sometimes let the mental games get to me, but at this tournament I learned to tune it out. I took the trash talk and stuck it where it mattered: in my feet.

I was determined to get out there and walk on water like no one had ever done before. Somehow, I simply knew I was not going to fall. I just knew it! Call it arrogance if you want, but I look back and call it pure instinct. My training evolved perfectly going into that tournament. I was filled with more confidence than I had ever experienced in the past. I made sure no one was going to psyche me out; none of my competitors would be able to crack me this time.

A warm sense of calm and confidence enveloped me as I got ready for my run. My practice runs at the tournament had gone well. I was buoyed and excited at the idea of showing something new to the crowd. The moment the boat took off, I was "in the zone." I could almost feel the crowd gasp as I completed the line-step 360's in my routine. When the 15th second passed, I knew I had kicked some serious butt on the water with a new trick world record. My fist flew up in the air--there was no containing the excitement I felt inside. *A world record!* It would still have to be reviewed by the World Barefoot Council before it could be officially declared a record, but inside I was celebrating.

After the trick run, Ron pulled me aside and we walked down the side of the lake. "I want to talk to you about something," he said. I thought he was going to congratulate me. Instead, he pointed to the trick handle that I was holding in my hand. "Why is my name missing from this handle?"

I hung my head.

During the previous summer, I asked Ron to sponsor me with one of his signature series trick handles. He sent me a free handle in the mail. At first, I was ecstatic to be using it. A handle from my idol! I had used the handle so much it began to fray. By that point, the competition between the two of us started to heat up. Every time I grabbed the handle to ski, I was staring at his name. It was frustrating to see his name there every time I went out to ski. So I decided to do away with his name...I cut off his signature on the handle.

I admitted to cutting it off. I was embarrassed at the fact he noticed it was missing. I knew what I did was wrong. It's pretty simple: when someone sponsors an athlete, there should be appreciation in return. I had disrespected and dishonored him by removing his name from the handle. Ron was my idol for so many years but I was at a turning point--I wanted to swipe the Overall title from him. It was at that tournament I began to see him as a rival instead of an idol. Yet, there was no excuse for defacing something he had given me as a gift with good intentions. I apologized for cutting off his name and thanked him for the sponsored handle.

> When you prepare yourself properly and fill yourself with confidence, you can accomplish your goal.
> ~Keith St. Onge

The rest of the competition was intense, but I was feeling energized. I placed first in slalom with ease and I came off the water on a natural high. The tournament was moving along well but I still had a tough challenge ahead: the jumping. I knew I had to land one out of three of my jumps and gain some reasonable distance to take the Overall trophy. I just needed to place in the top five to win, but jumping was always my weakest event--the one that always played mind games with me. I landed my first jump between 65 to 69 feet. I was embarrassed to jump so short, but I wanted to put a positive score on the board. I got up for my second jump and approached the ramp.

No need to go big, just land it.

I missed the landing. On my third jump, I decided to aim for more distance. As soon as my feet hit the water and I skied away, I knew the Overall trophy was mine. It was a jump in the low- to mid-seventies, and I knew that would be far enough to secure my first Overall win at the U.S. Nationals as a professional skier. What a feeling!

The countless hours of practice had paid off. I walked away with a new World Record and an Overall medal. If you find a dusty copy of the 1997 Guinness Book of World Records at a garage sale, you'll find my name printed in it as the World Barefoot Water-Ski Trick Record Holder. At the award ceremony, I received a standing ovation as I stepped up to the stage to receive my Overall medal.

The X-Games on ESPN

For the first time in history, barefoot water skiing was added to the X-Games in 1995. In the summer of 1997, I was thrilled to find myself among the sixteen skiers invited to compete in the games. We were all aiming for the $10,000 1st prize, which would certainly provide a lot of gas for future barefoot runs. The event was held in San Diego, California on Mission Bay with full ESPN coverage. It was an exciting time for the sport—the third consecutive year of being featured in the X-Games.

To get myself ready for the event, my dad brought in a bucket truck from work. We put a piece of plywood over the open bucket and lifted it as high as it would go. I practiced jumping off and skiing away. It wasn't as high as the X-games tower, but it gave me some idea of what to expect.

Brian and Linda were responsible for setting up and maintaining the video jump system, which records the distance for the barefoot ski jumping at the X-Games. The three of us flew out together.

The X-Games were unlike anything I had ever experienced before. Our helmets were outfitted with mini-cameras and the ESPN crew followed us everywhere we went. We were required to leap from a 15-foot tower, execute a round of tricks and then complete the run with a jump off the ramp. It was the first time that I had skied in sea water, and I wasn't prepared for the mouthful of salt I encountered during a practice run. It was much worse than the brackish water I encountered in Texas. My eyes burned and my nose ran constantly. I was used to fresh water lakes. At the end of the practice runs, I felt like I had walked across the desert. My mouth was parched and felt as if it was full of sand. I noticed some guys chewing Skittles and they offered me one. I ate one and it was like a magical fruit--colorful rain from heaven! I munched on a bag of Skittles to take away the nasty taste of salt water after every run. Looking back, I shudder to think how much sugar I consumed at the X-Games.

The venue was pretty tough because we only had a two-hour window for our event each day, and that window was when the tide came up. This was bad news for us because when the tide came up, so did the wind. The course was rough and many skiers had to hold back on doing certain tricks because no one wanted to take a chance at falling before the jump. It was survival just to get to the ramp--let alone doing tricks! I was worried about catching a toe in front of the ramp. I thought back to Hank, but I immediately pushed him out of my mind. I could not let fear take over.

I was the youngest skier there and I was surrounded by my idols everywhere. The ESPN cameraman stood with us on the 15-foot tower. Two of us at a time were crammed on this platform and there was no room to spare. From the top, you could see all of Mission Bay, San Diego.

I was up next. The boat crew launched the handle up to me. I quickly scanned the cove of Mission Bay and took it all in. I saw snow boarders going down the snow hill, half pipe riders and in-line skaters hitting kickers on the open course. *I'm at the X-Games, with an ESPN camera in my face and I'm about to jump off a tower!* I gripped and re-gripped the handle. As soon as the rope tightened, it was my turn to leap. "Ok!" The boat took off and I plummeted down with my feet on the rope. I braced myself as my back and shoulders smacked the water. I was being broken in the hard way...with red marks and bruises on the back of my arms. It didn't matter. I was a freshly graduated high school student with the world as my jungle gym--and I was exactly where I wanted to be: at the X-Games.

From a Salon.com article by Joyce Millman on the X-Games:

"Shoeless kamikaze skiers break the sanity barrier racing toward a slick ramp at over 40 mph, flying inverted 90 to 100 feet and landing upright," trumpets the X Games' blurb for barefoot water-ski jumping. A report on last year's X Games reads like a casualty list. One barefoot water skier used Crazy Glue to close a cut on his foot so he could stay in the competition.

The boat pulled me onto my feet and I began a conservative trick routine that I knew was safe. I did a couple mid-grade maneuvers that gave me some decent points. I concentrated on making it to the jump in one piece. My feet almost slid out from under me as I rattled over the water like a car on a bumpy road. I approached the jump and caught it quite well. I flew through the air like Superman with my feet suspended behind me. I instantly knew I had to hold on and my hands were not letting go. Like an osprey catching a fish in the water, I brought my feet down for the landing. My feet hit the water first and my head snapped back. The force of the landing ripped my helmet right off. I held on, refusing to let go of the handle. I bounced off my butt, but I managed to ski away from the jump. Pumping my fist in the air, I was filled with unbridled happiness—this was my first X-Games appearance and I landed my jump. I scanned the TV in excitement and there it was: *Keith St. Onge, seventh place!* It was a great place to be for my first X-Games!

I flew back to Berlin. Summer was over and I spent some time trying to figure out what I wanted to do next. I took a job raking leaves. Fall in New Hampshire was an enjoyable time of the year. I was outside day after day by myself, raking the never-ending autumn leaves. I looked at the sensational view of mountain ranges splattered with yellow, red, and orange and thought of how lucky I was to live in such a beautiful area of the world.

Where was I going to go next?

The crisp smell of the northern winds blew down from Canada and filled my lungs with the familiar cool air. I was taking a much-needed break from barefoot water skiing and I was enjoying every moment, but I was filled with questions about the future. Winter was just a few months away and I knew I didn't want to spend it in New Hampshire anymore.

Blisters started to form under my gloves and I took a break. I looked down at the massive pile of leaves. There were six piles left and they all had to go in bags. I really didn't want to do this kind of work the rest of my life. I began to pray. I asked for guidance. I wanted to own my own ski school and I wanted to become the World Champion. What would it take to make it happen? It was a suitable place to pray and think about my future--because I happened to be raking the grounds of a church.

Out of the blue, my parents received a call from the Channel Nine News station in southern New Hampshire. The reporters wanted to do a piece on me after winning the Nationals. I was fired up and ready for whatever they wanted me to do. "We're going to send a helicopter to take video from it while you are barefoot skiing," they explained. A helicopter! I could hardly contain my excitement. Nothing like that had ever been done on Lake Umbagog before. I prayed for great conditions because for the past few days, the northern winds were blowing hard.

The next day, we made our way up to the lake. We turned the final corner and the lake was a sheet of glass. Not a breath of wind was in the air. We scouted a landing pad for the helicopter and waited for their arrival. The boat was ready, the lake sat still, and the anticipation excited me!

"Do you hear it?" I nudged my dad. The chop of the blades grew closer. "There it is! I can't believe we're shooting a video with a helicopter. This is awesome!"

As the crew landed and introduced themselves, they decided to do the interview first. I struggled with the decision because we had perfect barefoot skiing conditions and when you have perfect conditions, you have to seize the opportunity. The interview seemed to go on forever, but my excitement carried me through.

Finally, it was time to hit the water. I suited up, got the boat ready and the camera crew piled in. The crew shot video from the boat for nearly an hour and then climbed in the helicopter. It was going to be a learning situation for both parties, but I was young and enthusiastic enough to ski all day! The lake continued to have glassy conditions with no wind. The helicopter flew over me while I performed my tricks on the water. I skied harder and longer that day than I ever had before. Four hours of skiing went by instantly as they aimed for one perfect shot after another. As I jumped off the barefoot ramp, the chopper hovered overhead and captured shots that had rarely been seen before.

At the end of the day, the crew was very pleased with the footage. We spread the word through the whole town, urging everyone to watch the news. When it came on TV, I was blown away. The video was spectacular, the interviews were perfect, and the lake looked different than it ever had before. This was my playground, my training ground, the place where I put so much time and effort into working toward my dream, and it was a thrill to see it on TV. I was able to view my skiing on Lake Umbagog from overhead, a view that I had never seen. It seemed like everyone in the small town of Berlin saw the news coverage and everyone complimented me for several weeks afterward.

Later that year, the Channel Nine News station won an award for the video.

Chapter 10: Putting the Dream in Action

Anything worth doing is worth doing poorly— until you can learn to do it well.

~Zig Ziglar

From the time I was 13, I knew I would end up in Florida someday. All of the top-level competitors ended up there. My dream was to run my own ski school, but first, I still had to gain some experience of my own at an existing ski school. Swampy called The Skiing Center in Florida to see if he could work out a deal for me. I was looking for a barter agreement where I could teach students in exchange for free room and board and ski time. The World championships were coming up in January and I needed some serious practice time on the water. Back in New Hampshire, there was four feet of ice on our lakes, making Florida a logical choice. The owners gave me an offer I couldn't refuse: I agreed to teach students and in exchange, I could live there for free and get practice time on the water.

The school hosted a lot of international students mostly from Europe. Hanging out with the students was a new cultural experience for me and it was challenging to decipher their languages. I quickly learned how to say "faceplant" in Finnish, Swedish, and Dutch. Christian Antos, a student from Austria, came to stay at the ski school during the winter and we quickly became great friends. Tall, lanky, and good-looking, he was a chick magnet. The girls were drawn to his long, blond locks and lazy grin. He could slip in and out of several languages at once as he was fluent in Italian, French, German, and some Russian. Like most of the Europeans I knew, Christian was loud and boisterous. Every once in a while, I would have to walk away and take a break from his endless energy, which flowed like water from a wide-open tap. Christian was a few years older than me but from the first day we met it felt like we had known each other for years. We built an instant bond based on trust and we quickly became like brothers.

We both shared a talent and love for the slalom event, so we spent a lot of time on the water working to improve our speed and form. In fact, slalom was the only event Christian was incredibly motivated and driven to succeed in. I tried to get him motivated in the other two events but he rarely wanted to work on tricks and hardly ever jumped. "You only like slalom because it's the easiest event!" I teased him. As much as I teased him, he never gave in to my pressure to work the other events. That was one thing I came to love about the Europeans I hung out with; many of them said what they wanted to say, with no hard feelings, and got right to the point with no remorse. They sported an "if you don't like it, then I don't care" attitude. I wished I had a little more of that in me at times!

At the ski school, we ate a lot of pasta, smoked a lot of cigarettes, and drank a lot of beer. Pasta was cheap so we filled up on the white stuff at every dinner. During the day, I taught students the skills they needed to learn. I kept busy doing odd jobs, but I also found myself with a lot of idle time. The ski school wasn't nearly as busy as it had been in previous years so I was able to train anytime I wanted.

On the weekends, I hooked up with members of a local show ski team called "Desires." On Saturdays, we would do "river runs," a caravan of boats pulling skiers all day long up the 25-mile stretch of the St. John's River. I became friends with Dusty Vines, one of the show skiers. Dusty was the tough guy on the bottom of the water ski pyramids. He shouldered the girls up to three tiers above him. Dusty was built like a bulldog: short and stocky, with a square face and receding hairline. He was ten years older than me. He always sported a golf-ball-sized of "Golden Blend" chewing tobacco in his cheek. He had a heart of pure gold. "Keith if you ever move to Florida and you need some wheels, I will take care of you," he often told me.

Dusty wasn't much of a drinker, but we shared a spring day on the St. John River that is forever burned into my memory. A caravan of skiers, wakeboarders and footers gathered at the bank of the river. Some of them were students from nearby colleges and a couple of older ones that skied on the Desires team. The plan was to ski all day long, kicking back every so often to swim or eat. At the end of the day, we landed at Silver Glen Springs, a beautiful area with crystal clear water. The area looked like the Caribbean, but the water was not salty. Everywhere we looked, we could see fish swimming just under the surface. The water never went below 72 degrees.

Once we arrived there would be a chain of boats hooked up to each other with everyone partying together. It was a scene right out of the song, "Red Neck Yacht Club:"

I'm meeting my buddies out on the lake
We're headin out to a special place
We love, that just a few folks know
There's no signing up, no monthly dues
Take your Johnson, your Mercury or your Evinrude and fire it up
Meet us out at party cove
Come on in' the waters fine
Just idle on over and toss us a line

It was my kind of crowd! I fit right in, except for the New Hampshire accent everyone teased me about. Partying was the great equalizer. Most of the guys were five to ten years older than me but the age difference didn't matter as long as the beer flowed.

It was a typical sunny Florida day when we unloaded the boats into the river and one by one we skied. Every boat was outfitted with coolers filled with beer and there was hardly any room for the ice. Up the river we went--taking turns driving and skiing. Dusty did most of the driving, which was a blessing when I look back on those days. We spent the whole day going up the river to the spring and at the end of the day, we would drive 25 miles by boat back to the boat ramp. As the day wore on we emptied the coolers and the ice turned to water. At that point, I was a goner. I had one too many beers and I was feeling good.

"I'm gonna do a front-to-back!" I announced.

Dusty laughed. "Watch yourself out there, buddy! You are pretty drunk!"

"That's ok," I slurred. "I'm gonna put my shoe skis on. I can do *any* trick I want on my shoe skis!" It was a bit of a struggle to get the shoe skis on as I had difficulty coordinating my movements. I jumped in. The water was spinning around me and I tried to steady myself with the handle. As soon as the boat reached enough speed, I managed to get up on the water with shaky legs. I was drunk and I knew it. Nothing else mattered at that moment. I was on the water with friends on a hot day--barreling up the river on my shoe skis.

I flipped my feet around and my right foot plowed into the water. I snapped backwards and tumbled to a painful halt. I was too out of my mind to care. I threw my head back and laughed. Through my drunken haze, I saw everyone in the nearby boats looking at me.

"I gotta go again!" I announced as Dusty idled the boat toward me.

"You've had enough, Keith. Get in the boat," he said. "You're going to hurt yourself or someone else. You gotta know when to stop." I climbed into the boat and sank to the floor. The next day, recovery was hell. The pain in my neck lasted for weeks.

The Price of Choices

Looking back on that, I can only shake my head and ask myself— "What was I thinking?" I put everything at risk-- my business, my career, and my future-- all for drinking and partying. I was a professional athlete, but I was engaging in behavior that could have had detrimental outcomes. And in many ways I paid a price. I drank most of my career away at the time.

In our lives, we can choose to follow, or choose to lead. Back then I made the choice to follow the crowd instead of focusing on responsibilities and my business. If I could do it all over again, I would have made better, more responsible choices. My career would have likely been totally different in all the good ways.

Competing in Australia

I was excited about the upcoming World Championship in Liverpool, a suburb of Sydney, Australia. I had always wanted to see this "down under" part of the world. I was on the same team with the other barefoot powerhouses. Our training site was just down the road from our accommodations, so the team piled into a couple vans and headed down the road to check out the river. The site took my breath away. The river lay in a deep ravine with lush greenery all around. The sides of the river were high, which meant great wind barriers and calm water. There was only one boat available for practice runs so we had to split the team up into shifts. I opted to join the second crew so I could sleep in a bit. I wasn't much of a morning person at that point.

"You've got to check out the upper branch of the river," the first crew told us when they arrived back. "The water is flat like a mirror!" As we approached the ravine, the view was simply stunning. Steep rock walls 200 to 300 feet high jutted out from the banks. Here and there, trees sprouted out from the occasional grassy oasis surrounded completely by water. Goats and wallabies were grazing on a nearby hill. Fog lingered on top of the water, giving the whole place a mystical look. The presence of fog meant the water was colder than the air and the air was pretty darn chilly at that point. It took every ounce of energy to get in the water for our practice runs. One of my teammates and I started yelling, "Cold is power!" just before jumping into the water. It was the only way to get our blood pumping and our minds ready to brace for the cold landing.

The whole U.S. Team churned out great practice runs but we were concerned because there was no jump to practice on. The Australian hosts had promised us a jump, but all of our inquiries fell on deaf ears. The competition was fierce between the U.S. and Australian teams in the years past and the jump competition brought in massive points--which could turn a competition one way or another. We began to wonder if they were holding out on us. Two days went by and we still had no jump to practice on.

By the end of the second day, we began to realize that we had to take matters in our own hands and locate a jump if we were going to get some practice time in. The emotions ran high and several of us became upset with the inaction from the host team. We had a couple good Aussie friends who directed us to a jump at one end of the water ski cable park. Years ago, the cable park used the jump for cable barefoot jump tournaments, but in recent years, it was used for kneeboard and wakeboard ramps. We had no choice but to make do with the scratched-up jump they provided us with.

The next day, Dad and I decided to take off on a train and explore downtown Sydney. We figured, "Hey, we are here in Australia, let's take advantage of it!" The team captains did not tell us when practice was the next day, but we knew we were not skiing in the morning. Taking an hour train ride to Sydney sounded like a pretty fun idea! As we walked toward the train station, we had no idea that we had to look the opposite way for oncoming traffic. Unlike the States, we should have been looking to the right--but of course it was not ingrained in us after only being in Oz for four days. As we stepped out into the street, a motorcycle whizzed by us with inches to spare. It was an incredibly close call and I was a bit shaken up. A collision would have definitely put me out of commission for the tournament. Note to self: when in

Australia, always look "right" before crossing the street! Looking left will only get you killed.

My dad and I arrived in downtown Sydney late morning and we decided to head to the Sydney Opera house, the big, white building with a crazy design sitting at the edge of the harbor. I was always amazed at how that building shimmered every time I saw it on TV and I wondered what the interlocking shell structure would look like up close. I figured it was constructed with concrete and covered with white paint.

As we walked closer, a square-like pattern emerged. *That's strange*, I thought. *The building looks so smooth on TV*. I could not believe my eyes. The material used on the side of the Sydney Opera house was white tile. Ordinary white tile! I was stunned. I could not believe that's all it was! Unfortunately, the opera house was being prepared for an event and we were unable to see the inside. As we headed towards downtown, a thought hit us: *What time should we head back?* "Well Keith," my dad said. "We already bought our train tickets for the rest of the day and here we are-- standing in downtown Sydney, Australia--so we might as well make the best of it!" He had a huge smile on his face and I'm sure I had the same look. "Who cares what time we get back!" I said. "Let's see what else there is down here and decide later."

Darkness descended when we finally boarded the train and headed back to the hotel. As soon as we walked in we were met by the team captain, Jon Kretchman and the team coach, Don Mixon, Sr. One look at Jon's stern face told me something was wrong. "We need to have a meeting with you, Keith," he said. I caught my breath and looked at my dad then back at Jon and Don. I didn't know what to say. Dad had the same speechless expression on his face. We had no clue what was going down. "Keith, meet us in the coaches' room in five minutes," Jon glared at me.

My heart was racing when I walked into the coaches' room. "Where were you?" Don Mixon, Sr. tilted his head and looked at me with squinty brown eyes. I could see he meant business by his tightened jaw. "We had no clue where you were all day!" he continued. "Were you aware that we had team practice today? We also spent the day working on the jump and getting it ready--and we couldn't find you."

"Team practice? I--I didn't think we were practicing today," I stammered. "I didn't know we were creating a problem by leaving. I didn't hear from anyone, so I figured we might have a day off and...and...and my dad and I went to Sydney since we were only here for a few days and we lost track of time--"

"What you did was wrong," Jon cut in. His eyes bore right into me with his eyebrows knit together. "You can't just take off. You have a responsibility to the team. There's no 'I' in team--you can't be thinking about yourself. The team has to come first. We flew out here as a team, we practice as a team, and *you* are here to represent your country. Don't you take pride in your country?"

I didn't know how to answer him. I could only nod my head. I had so many thoughts swirling through my mind. He had pushed my buttons perfectly. *I ski for my country*, I wanted to say. *Of course I take pride in my country!* I was too afraid to open my mouth. I knew deep down how proud I was to represent my country but I just couldn't express it.

At this point there were no right answers and I knew it. The American Barefoot Club was funding this trip and I was off gallivanting around. The two of them kept hammering at me and it took every ounce of energy not to cry. Yes, that's right, I felt like crying inside. These were the guys I respected and looked up to and I had let them down. When they finally finished drilling me I turned to leave the room and tried to keep it together until I passed the door. Suddenly, I heard laughter behind me.

What the heck? I turned around to find Jon and Don Sr. grinning at me. "All right, don't worry about this," Don said. "We had to go hard on you to teach you a lesson. You worked hard in practice yesterday and I like what I saw. You have a lot of potential!" Don Sr. did not hand out compliments very often so when he said I had potential he must have truly meant it.

As the tournament drew closer we moved our practice runs to the tournament site. The site was very unique—it was a rare site which offered perfectly smooth water conditions. Standing in the middle of the site I could see a small river that carved through a ravine. To the left was a large bridge that required us to ski underneath it for each pass. Just beyond the bridge was the starting dock which was barely visible behind the bridge pillar. The jump ramp was parked in front of the grassy knoll where the spectators could get a perfect view of the jumping but just beyond the jump, I noticed a large willow tree. The massive tree completely blocked the view. There was no way to see if a skier finished their run. Just a few days later to our surprise, the Aussies brought in a large JumboTron TV and installed it on the shore across the river. The skiers were showcased on the screen as the camera followed them through the course. This site turned out to be one of the top-notch sites for both the skiers and spectators.

The U.S. team was comprised of powerhouse barefooters, but the Aussies specialized in jumping. In the last nine years, the U.S. team won the gold in every World Championship as a team. If the Aussies did well in the jump event they could finally steal the Overall title from us.

As the last event of the five-day tournament came under way, the fans began to crowd the shoreline to watch the jumping. Over the announcements, we learned that one of the female barefooters on the Australian team was the first female to jump inverted. It was rumored that she hadn't yet landed an inverted jump and she would attempt to do that in the tournament. The announcement rattled us. If she landed just one inverted jump, the Aussies would be within a few points of our overall position and could even sweep it away from us.

I stood with my teammates as we watched the young gal leap off the jump. She flew through the air inverted but she quickly lost control and landed in the water with a splash. She did the same for her next two jumps--falling short once again of a positive score. The U.S. Team breathed a sigh of relief. The threat was behind us.

The men's jump event started and I was one of the first to jump. I had just barely made the cut into the second round and was seeded in the middle of the pack. The team coach, Don, came up to me. "You have been skiing great this tournament, Keith," he said. "I'm now asking you to jump better than you have ever jumped before. We need a specific distance from you to lock in our overall team championship and it is almost three feet further than you have ever jumped before. So, that being said, you must jump as big as you can to help the team."

Just before I stepped into the boat, my dad ran up to me. Many of my teammates were also there wishing me well. I was the first U.S. skier to jump and we all knew we each had to jump our best to hold off the Aussies. I was feeling the pressure to jump well. A poor jump result would only put more stress on the rest of the team to close the gap.

The site exhibited perfect conditions and mentally I felt ready to go. I jumped off the back of the boat and concentrated on taking slow, deep breaths as the boat moved ahead. I watched the rope unfurl in the water. Glancing up at the massive bridge overhead I could see people lined up--waiting and watching. I told the boat crew to go and we took off towards the bright yellow ramp. Crouching low, I cut outside the boat wake to line myself up. Out of the corner of my eye, I could see people crammed onto a small dock on the shore. I knew my dad was watching and it gave me confidence knowing he was there.

I came off the jump with perfect focus. Everything felt great. *My air time is longer than usual,* I thought to myself. I came down for the landing bearing down on the handle with a tight grip. The boat pulled hard and in one quick bounce I stood up. I landed a great jump! The people on the crowded dock flew by me in a blur and they exploded in applause. The entire U.S. team cheered from the dock and the shoreline. As we idled down the river to set up for my second jump, I patiently waited for my jump distance to be announced.

I heard the distance come over the microphone--it was exactly what the U.S. Team needed to capture the Overall title! I whipped my fists in the air. What a great feeling to know I had taken some of the pressure off the team. It wasn't quite over yet, as the Aussie's had a massive jumper that could disappoint us in the very end and we still had to have great follow up jumps. The U.S. Team continued to land great jumps. The Aussie's had a couple of chances at stealing the title as they went far enough to beat us in distance, but they did not land their jumps. The U.S. team celebrated their tenth consecutive Overall win.

After the World tournament, I was invited to participate in the 1998 X-Games and for the second time, I hopped on a plane to San Diego. This time, my parents, Kendra, Kendra's friend, and my girlfriend, Jan, were with me.

With the cameras recording every move, I failed big time. I didn't land a single jump, putting me in the *second-to-last* position. Back home, my friends were watching ESPN expecting me to perform well. I got caught up in the moment of being an X-Games athlete with my special badge and credentials and I didn't put enough focus on my performance.

For all the highs that I experienced with the growth of my skiing, the X-Games humbled me and brought me back down to earth. I had to deal with failure in a very public way and learn to move on from it.

A Moment of Unexpected Glory

When I arrived in Houston, Texas a week before the 1998 Nationals I was looking forward to making a splash on the tournament scene. I wanted a repeat of last year's first place. I was also riding high on the fact that I had made the U.S. Team for the World Championship. I met up with my wetsuit sponsor at Lake Terre-Mara, the site of two private lakes that he co-owned with another partner. The tournament was sponsored by a local Ford dealership and I was presented with a very nice Ford Explorer to use for the week.

ESPN was slated to film the U.S. Open tournament following the Nationals and we scheduled several radio interviews around town to bring attention to the tournaments. Several local radio stations came out to the Nationals site and interviewed me live. The hype was unbelievable-- it was nothing like I had ever experienced before. I was selected to do the interviews and announcements for the radio spots around town. I had no experience doing radio spots before, so I was both nervous and excited. "Come on out and have a good time and make sure to attend the Nationals being filmed by ESPN this weekend!" I managed to squeak out.

Throughout the week, I found it difficult to concentrate on skiing. My practice runs on the water were up and down--some runs were good and other runs were completely off. My mind wasn't on the water--I was having too much of a good time going from one activity to the next. There was a bit of pressure on my shoulders; I had to rack up enough points to ski in the U.S. Open. ESPN was filming it--I didn't want to miss another chance to be on TV! I was also defending my National title from the previous year which was a new experience for me.

Just as I had struggled with my practice runs, I struggled on the water during my slalom and trick runs. When I finished my runs, I knew the Overall trophy was out of reach. I did not ski to my potential and did not put up a respectable fight as a defending National champion. I beat myself up mentally after my two strongest events were a bust. My weakest event was coming up and I was not looking forward to it. I needed to land my jumps to make it into the U.S. Open.

I couldn't shake off the antsy feeling that was washing over me as I prepared myself for the first of three jumps. There was no question I had to jump big by my standards just to get into the next round of the tournament.

94

I missed the landing on the first jump. I had two more chances and I had to nail one of them to guarantee a place in the U.S. Open. I tried to go higher and longer on the second jump but my timing was off. I found myself turning a bit in mid-air and I didn't square the landing up in time. The handle ripped from my hands and bounced away. My second chance went right out the window. I had just one chance left. I was dealing with a piss-poor attitude at this point. Nothing was going right at this tournament.

All right, go easy and get one on the board. Don't try to go big. Just ease off the jump, keep it smooth and stick the landing. At this point, who cares...nothing could get any worse so there's nothing to lose.

I hit the jump and launched into the air much higher than I anticipated. I mean, I went huge--and I went high. Everything was almost in slow motion.

Whatever you do, don't let go! You gotta land this to get in the U.S. Open! I squeezed the handle hard as I brought my feet forward for the landing. *Don't let go--don't let go!* The moment my feet touched the water, I could feel my left foot dig under the surface. *Oh God, I'm going to catch my foot and fall!* I rolled a bit to the left, sliding on my hip and my back. The leg of my wetsuit skidded all the way up to my hips. The face-guard on my helmet caught the water, twisting at a 90-degree angle. Suddenly, I couldn't see anything. Instinct took over. I straightened myself out, pulled up on the handle and found myself skiing away. *I landed it! I could not believe it! I landed it! Holy cow--that was one of the highest jumps I have ever felt-- I could see the floor of the boat--I was so high!* I knew the distance was definitely a personal best. I let go of the handle, straightened out my helmet and let out a scream. I was cheering because I knew I made it into the next round and this guaranteed me a spot in the U.S. Open--as well as a chance to be filmed by ESPN.

Finally, something good came out of this tournament!

Over the loudspeaker, I heard the announcement. "What a jump! We think it may be a world record!"

A world record? I couldn't believe what I was hearing. A few minutes later the judges confirmed it. Eighty-six-point-five feet! I had just set a new world record in jumping! The previous record was held by Brett New from Australia. What started out as a lousy tournament had turned into a shining moment of glory. It was one of the sweetest world records I ever set because I did not expect to break it. Jump was my weakest event and I was having one of the worst tournaments of my life, but the jump record made my day and week. The barefoot community exploded with congratulations. The nicest one of all came from Jon Kretchman. All of the weeks of inverted jumping with his instruction had just paid off with that jump.

The U.S. Open was a new, head-to-head format with the top eight qualifiers being matched up against each other--one against eight, two against seven, and so on. I fought my way through the brackets to finally face Jon. Not only was he the guy who taught me to jump inverted style, but he was also one of my idols and a tough competitor. He was gearing up for his run when a crazy storm blew in. The tournament officials asked him if he still wanted to ski in the pouring rain. "If the driver can see, I will ski!" Jon said.

Well, if Jon was going to ski in the rain, then I was determined to do the same. Jon took off in the rain and we soon lost sight of him. The boat was barely visible when it reached the other end and ESPN was still filming. I was nervous as heck because I knew I would hardly be able to see anything in the rain. I stood in the rain holding my handle and rope, straining to see Jon as he skied back. He turned out a sensational run and that put some pressure on me.

As the boat drew near, the rain began to soften and the sun peeked through the clouds. Jon's plan to ski in the rain seemed to backfire on him and I now had perfect conditions. I managed to edge him out that round and faced Ron next. I ended up taking second place at my first U.S. Open.

Florida Bound

I had one thousand dollars I had saved, but I still had not figured out how to move to Florida to pursue my dream career. Out of the blue, I received an email from Mike Holt. Mike was a short, well-built guy from Cuba who came into barefooting later in life. I had met him a few times at tournaments, but I did not know much about him. "I heard you are planning to move to Florida," Mike wrote. "I have a guest house where you can stay and in exchange, you can teach me new barefoot waterskiing maneuvers."

> Follow your bliss and the universe will open doors for you where there were only walls.
> ~Joseph Campbell

That's a sign, I thought. *That's my ticket to Florida!* I sat there in amazement at how the plans were coming together. Mike's generosity set everything in motion. I was getting closer and closer to making my dream of owning a ski school a reality.

Now that I had a place to live, I called Dusty to take up his offer of lending me some wheels. True to his word, he said he would supply me with a Chevy truck.

I accepted Mike's offer, packed my bags and flew down to Orlando. Dusty picked me up at the airport and we drove out to his apartment, which sat above a residential garage. We drove up a narrow, sandy road through a wooded area. The area was pretty isolated, but I trusted Dusty with my life and I knew he wouldn't put me in a situation that wasn't safe. I hauled my big suitcase up the narrow stairs. I was expecting to see a typical, messy bachelor pad, but to my surprise it was actually pretty clean and had been remodeled. "Here, you can have my bed-- I'll park myself on the couch this week," Dusty offered. I tried to protest, but he wouldn't hear of it.

The next morning Dusty brought me outside to check out the wheels he was letting me borrow. "To call it a truck is a bit of a stretch." Dusty said. "*Rustbucket* is a more appropriate term and it's a good thing it's brown--the rust is less noticeable."

"Does it run?" I laughed.

"It will get you around town." Dusty reassured. "Keep some gas in it and it's always good to go. Hop in and let me show you a few things." As I slid over the cracked vinyl seat, the first thing that caught my eye was the Bud Ice draft handle in place of the stick shift. "Is that really a tap?" I laughed.

"Sure is!" He grinned. "Every once in a while, the engine overheats. When that happens, just pull over, turn off the AC and turn on the heater. That helps the engine cool down. After about ten minutes, you should be good to go again." Dusty pushed a couple of buttons and the truck began to belt out Red Hot Chili Pepper's "Get on Top" He cranked it up even louder. The truck began to vibrate.

"I souped it up with some sub woofers!" Dusty shouted. He pointed to the speakers right behind him. They were positioned right behind the driver's seat.

"You ain't seen nothing yet!" Another turn of the knob and my whole body began to pound along with the bass. I was sure half of Lake County could hear it.

I looked around the truck. *I can toss out the trash and give it a little cleaning--heck, as long as this thing moves, I should be okay*, I thought to myself. I was just thankful for Dusty's generosity because I was starting out with nothing and he was my only true friend in Florida at the time.

A little over a week later, I headed out to the Holt's and met up with Mike and Linda. The first time I set eyes on the guesthouse, it was not quite what I expected; it was basically a shed with a large barn-type door in the back--a shed that looked more like home for a lawnmower instead of a bed. As I walked inside I noticed a small TV on the left and on the right there was a futon. On one end of the room there was a small sink along with a two-burner propane stove. Indoor/outdoor carpeting covered the wide-open space. One door led to a narrow bathroom. The other door led to Mike's office where he worked on his books. "The water heater is on a timer," Mike explained as he showed me around the place. "You'll have to turn it on ten minutes before a shower to give it time to heat up the water." It may have been a shed, but it was a roof over my head and a place to stay. I was grateful for it.

Now that I had a place to live and a way to get around, the next challenge was to find a job and earn money to pay for my gas and food. I turned to Mike Salber, a six-foot paramedic who I met at the 1994 Nationals and asked him if he had any leads on a job. "I've got a friend who owns a start-up company called 'Ice Magic.'" he said. "He may need someone to help set up ice displays and take them down. I'll see if he can use you."

I started working for Ice Magic right away and I liked the job. The ice sculptures they created were amazing, with objects embedded inside of them. The job took me to various hotels and resorts around Orlando, including Disney, Universal and Sea World. Once the tables, lights and sculptures were set up, I had time to walk around and see the sights. The hours were long, as most events did not finish until late into the night. There were some mornings I arrived home at two a.m. Little did I know--my late nights were upsetting Linda. As a mom of five kids, she felt personally responsible for me. She had even promised my mom that she would look out for me. So when I didn't come home at a timely hour, she began to worry I might be lying in a ditch somewhere. During phone calls to my mom, Linda would tell her that everything was okay, but in reality, I was out partying somewhere or getting back late from work.

Linda invited me to join the family on Thanksgiving and I agreed to attend. When Thanksgiving morning rolled around, I decided to head out to Dusty's place and hang with him a bit. We sat around and watched football and tossed back a couple of drinks. The next thing I knew, it was getting late and I had to sober up to drive home. It never occurred to me to call the Holts and let them know I wasn't going to show up for dinner. My lack of consideration had put a big damper on the Holt's Thanksgiving celebration. They had been terribly worried.

The next morning, I woke up to a loud pounding. I rubbed my aching head. It took me a few minutes to realize that someone was at the door. With a groan, I forced myself upright and headed for the door. I opened it and looked into the eyes of a very angry Mrs. Holt. "You ruined Thanksgiving!" she ranted. "The next time you decide not to show up, you *call* me! I promised your mother I would be responsible for you! I was worried about you all night. Don't do this to me again. How am I supposed to know you're not lying in a ditch somewhere, dying? What if something happened to you, how would I be able to tell your mom?"

I stumbled out an apology and instantly felt like a jerk. Linda walked off in a huff. I definitely forgot to count my blessings and be thankful for the Holt's incredible generosity and the roof over my head. I thought I was a free man with only me to worry about. It wasn't until years later I could reflect back on this and realize the ungratefulness I had shown that day.

As I was approaching the third month of living at the Holt's, I started to realize I needed to find a place near a lake so I could establish my ski school. Dusty agreed to rent a house with me, so I scoured the area for affordable rentals. I also needed to find sponsors. From the time I was fourteen, I was able to obtain wetsuits from sponsors. My very first one was from a company called Heat Wave. They approached me at an Eastern Regional tournament and asked me to ski in their suits for the rest of a season. I happily agreed-- I was proud to strut around in a sponsored wetsuit and I didn't care that the wetsuit was too big on me. That was my first experience with a sponsor.

A friend arranged for another wetsuit company to sponsor me. I was thrilled—the company produced a popular wetsuit everyone wanted and now

I would be skiing in a sponsored suit. I couldn't wait to see which wetsuit they would send. What's more, I couldn't wait to get out on the water in front of my friends, showing off my free suit. When the box arrived, I tore it open with great anticipation.

Now let me tell you, there's only one color in the world I absolutely detested at the time: the color purple. The wetsuit was black, teal, and...purple.

Purple! I can't believe they sent me a purple wetsuit! How am I going to ski in this thing? I tried it on and it was a perfect fit. I had to look beyond the color-- after all, I was now among the elite skiers who were sponsored by the hottest wetsuit on the market. I was psyched!

Chapter 11: A Ski School is Born

Don't be afraid if things seem difficult in the beginning. That's only the initial impression. The important thing is not to retreat; you have to master yourself.

~Olga Korbut

The holidays were approaching and I booked a ticket to fly home for Christmas. I was looking forward to celebrating my 21st birthday with my family and friends. I hadn't seen my parents since the beginning of summer and I was truly homesick. Besides, my mom would have never let me hear the end of it if I didn't get home for the holidays.

After a few months at the Holt's, I knew I was wearing out my welcome and I needed a place of my own. I was also itching to get started on formally setting up my ski school. I continued looking for a house to rent. One evening, I drove into Clermont for some groceries and I came upon a hill where you could see for miles in all directions. I spotted a lake in the distance and I made a mental note to come back and explore it more. I bought a map of the area and pinpointed Lake Minneola and headed back out there. Lake Minneola connected to eight other lakes via a series of canals. It was a prime spot for the ski school because it was easy to find calm water on one of the lakes.

Waterfront rentals were hard to come by, so it took several trips out to the area before I found anything. After several days of driving around, I finally spotted a "For Rent" sign. The 1950's era house was on five acres of land surrounded by massive oak trees. Spanish moss was hanging from the branches of the oaks and palm trees, just the way I had pictured Florida as a New Hampshire boy. I headed to the back door and carefully stepped on the porch. The wood was rotted through in several places. The house was white with red trim around the windows and paint was peeling off. The green metal roof spotted with rust. Before I could knock, the door swung open. "Are you here for the rental?" The owner invited me inside.

The two-bedroom, one bath cottage instantly transported me back to Lake

Umbagog -- I felt as if I were back in my grandfather's camp. The oak trees shaded the interior, giving it a dark feel. The rent was cheap, yet steep for me, so Dusty offered to pay the first two months of rent until I could get the ski school rolling. With Dusty's help and my side job, I figured I could manage well enough. I signed my first lease with some trepidation mixed with excitement. I now had my first home rental and still no guarantee of a steady income. I was starting off on shaky ground, but confident I could make it work. Directly after signing the lease, I flew home for Christmas to be with my family.

I didn't realize how much I missed home until the moment I walked in the door. A familiar scent greeted me, a mixture of fabric softener mingling with the musty antiques which dotted the rooms. The fragrance sat deep down in my memory. I took in a deep breath. It was the smell of home.

I walked over to the snack cupboard to see what goodies Mom had stocked up on. I was in search of my favorite snack, Funny Bones, a peanut-butter-filled cake with chocolate icing. I lived off those as a kid! As soon as I opened the cupboard doors I stopped short. I stared at the health food snacks which lined the shelves. "Mom! What happened to all the good stuff?"

"Sorry, Keith!" she laughed. "You're never here and we don't eat those things anymore. Besides, we're eating much healthier now." I reluctantly helped myself to a jar of nuts.

Swampy came in from Montana and I couldn't wait to see him. I missed the big guy. We had spent day after day together in the boat for years and now our visits were short bursts here and there. Swampy was always a hugger and I was long overdue for a bear hug from him.

After Christmas, Swampy finally arrived at the house and wrapped me in a hug. My dad and I sat down at the dining room table. Swampy announced that it was time for a "powwow." I rolled my eyes because I knew what was in store. I was either in for a life lesson, a lecture, or I was in trouble.

"I want to talk to you about something," Swampy began.

His voice turned serious. I felt like I was 13 all over again and I had a feeling that another decision was coming up regarding my future in barefoot water skiing. As usual, Swampy had the floor and the two of us listened to see what crazy idea he came up with this time. Swampy was always creative in preparing for the future. His mortgage business with Spray was going well and he had a new business that was generating income. Swampy explained to us that he was involved in some investments, giving him a great return on a monthly basis. My dad was aware of the investments and had gone in on a few with Swampy.

"I would like to help you get your ski school established, Keith," Swampy said. "I'd like to put some money into an investment which will help you pay some bills."

"Really?" My eyes grew wide. "I'm all ears."

"This would be a great way for you to establish a good foundation for a business," Swamp continued. "Part of this monthly income can pay for a new truck and the rest can go towards a portion of your rent."

I turned to my dad to see his thoughts. He cracked a half smile, and I knew he was in on this with Swampy. "This is very generous of Swampy," he said. "You have worked hard and put an immense amount of energy into your barefoot water skiing...I think this is fair as long as you stay on track."

"A new truck... wow..." I was stunned. "But you do know that my friend, Dusty, is letting me borrow his truck?"

"I've heard you talk about that truck and it's not what a ski school should have as a vehicle," Swamp chuckled. "You need a reliable vehicle when running a professional business."

Swampy was right. I thought to myself for a few seconds-- there were countless times the little Chevy S-10 left me stalled at red lights when it overheated. I was tired of sweating in the seat while I waited for it to cool down. I knew the truck could not pull a boat. It was great to get me by, but I could not use it forever. Heck, it wasn't even mine!

"I want you to understand this is a unique situation and I don't want you taking advantage of it, I want you to take it seriously," Dad reiterated once again.

I could hardly contain my excitement on the ride over to the dealership. I was in heaven looking at all the brand new Chevrolet extended cab pick-up trucks.

103

I knew I didn't want to let it go to my head--I appreciated everything Swampy and my parents had done for me. They always steered me in the right direction and I trusted them. I was getting ready to turn 21 in a few days and this would be my first vehicle ever. I drove off with a white Chevy extended cab--my dream truck.

Part of the investing process required formally setting up my ski school business. "You need to come up with a name for the bank to use," Swampy explained. For years, I had thought of possible ski school names and everything regarding feet and barefoot water skiing were already taken. The only name that popped into my mind at that time was "Gliding Soles." I wrote it on the forms and signed my name. Just like that, I had a formal name for my business and a source of income for the truck we had just bought. I jumped in the truck, said goodbye to my family and headed back down to Florida on the twenty-four hour drive. Life was beginning to fall into place.

My mom flew in to visit at the end of January to help clean up my rental house. When she walked in, she couldn't contain the disgusted look on her face as she gazed over my living quarters. She got right down to the business of stripping off years and years of dirt on the floors and the cabinets. My mom felt kind of sorry I had to live in such a dump, but with the excitement on my face she knew it did not bother me. My dad had brought us on many adventures when we were young and this was just another adventure and learning experience.

Out of the blue, I heard a bloodcurdling scream. I ran into the hallway with my heart pounding in my chest. Mom was pointing to a drawer hanging open. "What is it?" I walked cautiously toward the wooden dresser.

"It's a spider! And it's huge!" She made a circle with her hands the size of a pancake. I tried to contain my laughter. It was the first time mom had encountered the Florida super-bugs. The tropical climate was home to what I called "bugs on steroids." After a few months of discovering bugs at every turn, I had gotten used to them. Florida is famous for the Palmetto bug, which is simply a flying cockroach. Those things are huge by bug standards and some are two-inches long. They're also very fast--when you turn on a light they hightail out of sight in the blink of an eye. Another comforting tidbit: the Palmetto cockroach is the cleanest bug in the world!

Mom was so shaken by the bugs in the house that she ended up having several nightmares throughout the week. I felt terrible for her. By the second day, she was running a fever, but she continued to polish up the place. The weather had turned cold outside, and the heat could not keep up with the leaking windows and the thin walls. I don't know how--but she kept on cleaning. I guess it was a motherly thing to do plus, she did not want her son living in a dump.

When I look back on this, I can picture her on her hands and knees scrubbing the floor with determination. She was battling a fever and feeling terrible, stuck in an old house filled with spiders and cobwebs; yet, doing everything she could to make the place livable. I didn't realize it at the time, but now I can see how much love she had for me. The memory brings a lump in my throat just thinking of it. I did not fully appreciate it at that time, nor did I truly notice it at the time, but I appreciate it now. That was pure love! Every time the memory pops into my mind, I mentally send a thank you to my mom.

I had a place of my own and new wheels, and the next thing I needed was a boat. When I was living in Montana, I tried my hand at negotiating a deal. I contacted a boat company and tried to arrange for a sponsored deal on a boat. Five minutes into the call, I knew it wasn't going to happen.

I connected with Richard Grant, an older man in his 50's, from New Orleans. Richard participated in clinics I did on the river where his cabin was located. He was a venture capitalist who lent money to companies that bought offshore oilrigs. Richard presented me with a deal: he would supply me with a brand-new boat and in return, I would train him and pull him for free for a year. At the end of the year, we would sell the boat at a profit and obtain a new model to sell. It was a win-win situation for both of us and we shook on the deal.

A couple of months later, Richard decided to bring another boat to Florida. This particular boat was a V-drive and was typically used for wake boarding and cruising--it wasn't designed for barefooting. I had two boats sitting on my property--our goal was to sell the boats, make a profit and start an actual dealership with a show room. In the meantime, I could use the boats for my ski school. Richard's generosity and trust was like no other and I could not have started my ski school without him. I was 21 years old with two brand new boats sitting in my yard. I was being trusted with these boats and given a great opportunity. A trickle of students began to sign up for lessons. *This is it! I'm finally following my dream and doing exactly what I love to do. I'm going to fill my boats with students. I'm going to spend all day in the boat and teach everyone!*

Journey to South Africa

After the tournaments were over, the ski school hit a slow patch until one day, the phone rang. It was Rob Ransom, a skier from South Africa. "Keith, how would you like to come to South Africa in January for a month and do a couple of clinics?" Four whole weeks in South Africa--this was something I definitely couldn't turn down. I would be staying with various families and teaching barefooting clinics on different waterways. This was an opportunity of a lifetime for me to see this part of the world. I would be able to stay an extra week and explore more of the country after the clinics were completed. The last week of touring would be part of my payment as well. It involved visiting Sun City and going on a few safaris and I was good with that!

I arrived at the airport with my itinerary in hand and approached the ticketing counter with excitement. I was grinning from ear-to-ear when I handed over my passport and driver's license. I just couldn't believe I would soon be on a plane to the Southern hemisphere of the world! As the young woman looked over my information, she had a confused look on her face. I watched as she looked at my itinerary and then back at the computer.

"Is there a problem?" I asked.

"Mr. St. Onge, your reservation is booked, but the ticket was never paid for."

You've got to be joking--this was booked a month ago! "The people that hired me told me they would buy my ticket and confirmed everything with me," I explained. "What can I do now?"

"Well, if you want to go on this trip, you'll have to buy the ticket. I can get it for you at the same price that it was booked for."

"And how much is that?"

"That will come to..." She rattled the keyboard and squinted at the screen. "That comes to $2,100."

"Oh, man!" I exhaled. Mentally I calculated what I had in my checking account. There was no way to cover that amount. I pulled out a credit card. The trip had been planned for a month now--I didn't want to back out. I just had to pray that the people who set up the trip would cover the cost of the flight once I arrived.

In the days before 9-11, the atmosphere on international flights was a relaxed one. I was seated on the second level of the 747, which was a new experience for me. The flight attendant asked if I would like to come up to the cockpit and chat with the pilots. For thirty minutes I had a beautiful view of the sky ahead and nothing but ocean below. I'm thankful for that memory, for an opportunity like that would never be available today.

When I arrived in South Africa, the clinic organizers reassured me that they would reimburse me for my flight. I spent two weeks working with one barefoot club, and the next week with the Ransoms and another family, the De Villiers.

Andre De Villiers Sr. picked me up in his boat with a private driver and his 15-year old daughter, Nadine. He hired me to work with Nadine and her two brothers, Andre and Zane. Andre Sr. reminded me of a tougher version of Swampy, rough around the edges and all business. His skin was dark from the sun; stretched tight and rough like a boar's hide. He greeted me with a cigarette dangling from his mouth.

The two brothers had some definite skills on the water. Zane was twelve years younger than I and he quickly became my little shadow, following me everywhere. I could see he wasn't really into barefooting at the time, but loved being around it. He put his wetsuit on with great reluctance, often at his father's insistence. Andre was tough on the water and he had sheer, raw talent. I quickly saw he was going to be a force to be reckoned with if he stayed dedicated to the sport. His feet were huge and flat--a barefooter's dream. The kid could barefoot for miles and miles with nary a complaint. I soon learned people in South Africa often walked everywhere without shoes--to the store, to the car, and around the yard. Andre Jr. was a unique individual and I could see his dad made him tough--just as tough as the bottom of his feet! He was quiet around me, and this reminded me of my early teen years. I could tell Andre wanted to excel on the water--and his father would make that happen. Junior was above the learning curve and I was impressed with his talents.

However, the real star on the water that week was Nadine. She too, was tough as nails and her skills were phenomenal. The first time I saw her doing turns on her feet, I froze in amazement. She could complete five times the amount of turns than I could!

I trained hard as a youngster, but Swampy and I looked like amateurs compared to what I witnessed with Andre Sr. and Nadine. Andre, Sr. was a drill sergeant, barking orders at Nadine during every run. I was taken back by Nadine's work ethic. She was a machine on the water-- practicing her drills over and over. Only a few females have the potential to rise through the ranks of barefooting with skills like the men. South Africa had something special in Nadine--a rare female with the talent and the gumption to handle the falls that would make some grown men cry.

I looked over at Andre, Sr. and tried to hide my stunned amazement. He winked at me. He spun the top of his round cooler off, grabbing an icy cold beer. It was only 10 a.m. and the tenth cigarette of the morning dangled from his mouth. He grinned. He was a father who had the sport running through his veins and he loved every minute of it. It was easy to see the pride on his face as he watched his kids on the water.

The boat idled to a stop.

"So, what do you think, Keith? How can she improve?" Nadine was resting in the water, trying to catch her breath. I didn't know what to say. I stumbled for words. "Umm, that was great. Incredible, actually."

"No, Keith, I'm not looking for compliments here. Technique!"

"Oh...uh... yeah. Um, on a couple of turns, she could stand a little taller to make the turn smoother." I was worried that he might toss me out of the boat if he didn't like what I said.

He grinned. "That's more like it." He spoke to Nadine in Afrikaans and I had no idea what he said, but what I did gather was the sternness that came from his voice. I was scared for her. But I could see the respect Nadine gave her father and the winning attitude she had. Apparently he did repeat the instructions I mentioned, because I could immediately see the results in her skiing.

Relieved, I settled back in the seat. I realized I just had to stick to my familiar teaching style and not allow myself to be intimidated. We quickly developed a mutual respect and I began to enjoy my time with this unique and talented family. The three of them showed a lot of improvement with their skills and by the end of the week we had really bonded.

"Keith, come to the cabin for dinner and we'll go over some techniques," Andre Sr. said. That evening his wife, Ina, greeted me at the door and I could smell dinner cooking on the stove. Andre, Sr. led me into a room that I quickly dubbed "The De Villiers Shrine." The room was plastered with pictures from his heyday, with medals and trophies scattered in the perimeter around the pool table. I spied a picture of Mike Seipel on the wall. "He's one of my idols," I told him. I explained how I had gotten my start on the water with Seipel instructing me. I could see many other well-known, "old-time" barefooters posted on the wall. It was like taking a trip back in time, and realizing how far back the passion for the sport existed. I could see in his eyes that he marveled both in the past and present of barefoot water skiing.

We sat down to a delicious dinner, an abundance of meat; sausages I had never tasted before. The sausages were small, gritty and kind of dense, packed with all different kinds of meat-- none I could recognize. The only type of sausage I could identify was Canadian bacon which was served every morning for breakfast. I must admit, after many days of sausages, I did not want to look at them again. By the end of the week, my stomach had enough-- I cringed at the smell of sausage wafting out from the grill.

"Come on, Keith, let's go outside and go over some techniques," Andre Sr. said. I pushed back my chair and followed him outside. A rope was tied to a post, the handle dangling near the ground. One of the kids stood nearby with a video camera ready to go. "Ok, let's start talking about surface turns. Can you explain step-by-step how to do this turn? I want to get this on video so I can remember what you taught this week." Andre Sr. had me explain my teaching technique on nearly every trick in the rulebook.

I broke a sweat and worked off those sausages as I went over every barefooting trick in extreme detail. Nadine and Andre, Jr. had yet to learn line turns or feet-to-feet toe turns, which are the highest level of tricks to do in barefoot skiing. Andre, Sr. wanted to know everything there was to know about all tricks I could do. I had no problem going over everything because I wanted to help all barefoot skiers improve and that's why I was there in the first place. He understood the sport better than most people I worked with. We enjoyed conversing about technique and the history of the sport for hours while the kids videotaped everything I showed them. I figured if Junior stuck with it, his father now had the perfect training aid to help him along: my homemade instructional video. A few years later I coached the U.S. Junior Barefoot team at the New Zealand World Tournament, and I noticed fourteen-year-old Andre Jr. tricking up a storm. He was using the tricks I painstakingly revealed in the instructional video.

When I arrived back home life settled into a routine. I was scrambling to find students to fill up the schedule and bring in a steady income. Money was tight and I never knew if I would have enough to pay the bills. Whenever I made extra money, I tried to set it aside. There were times I just wanted to pull the plug on the whole Florida gig and move back home. Surely life would be a lot easier back in New Hampshire. I missed my family and I was lonely.

Kendra flew in to visit me for a week. It was the first time the two of us had hung out together without any other family around us. We hit Sea World and Islands of Adventure theme park. We arrived just as the gates were opening so we could be the first in line for the rides. We rode the first ride five times in a row because nobody was there yet. We ran to the next one and rode it several times too. By the end of the third day we could hardly walk and our sides hurt from laughing. After one day of rest, we hit the water and went skiing together. We had a great time truly being brother and sister. It was long overdue.

Although she was still in high school, I could relate to her as a young woman for the first time. She was not a little girl anymore and I treasured the time we spent with one another. It was a week of adventure and fun that allowed us to get closer than we had ever been before. When I dropped her off at the airport my heart sank and I instantly remembered all my family back home that I dearly missed. I always knew there would be sacrifices in chasing my dream, but being away from my family hurt deeply.

Kendra saved me in a way. After she left, I came to realize I loved Florida, it was my new home. Chasing that dream was a choice I made and I could not wimp out and give in. I would have to continue proving to others and myself I could do it--and I would do it!

Letting My Feet do the Talking

At the Nationals in Houston, I noticed an "older" petite lady with a shock of blond hair. Judy Myers was competing in the Senior Division at 56-years of

110

age. She learned to barefoot water ski at the age of 53 on a dare. I couldn't help but notice her beaming smile and friendly personality. I was instantly drawn to her.

Judy was full of spunk on the water and a spitfire on land. For an older lady she had a spicy vocabulary. Every time she let out a couple of choice words, I would do a double take; it was as if my own grandma was swearing. "Watch your mouth," I jokingly reminded Judy every now and then. She would laugh and say, "Okay, Keith, I'll be good-- but if someone comes in with an attitude, I'm not holding back!" Even though she was old enough to be my grandma, I loved hanging out with her.

Judy was carrying some extra pounds, but she didn't let a little weight or her age stop her from learning new things. The more I chatted with her at tournaments, the more I liked her. Judy was planning to retire from her job as a college administrator and she jokingly suggested she should come and work for me. "I'll help you run the ski school if you let me barefoot for free," she said. We continued to toss that idea around from tournament to tournament for several years. Little did we know, it would end up being the beginning of an amazing partnership.

During the second round of the jumping at the Nationals, trouble started to brew. I was skiing head-to-head with a skier from Italy. During a head-to-head format, skiers take turns doing three jumps. The skier fell on his first jump and requested a three-minute injury break. I was sitting in the boat with my crew when the chief judge ordered me to go ahead with my second jump. The guy was still on shore with another skier tending to him. Nearly ten minutes had passed which was well beyond the allowed three-minute break. "I'm not going next, that wouldn't be fair," I protested. "This is a head-to-head competition and I want to see his jump so I know how far I have to land my next jump."

"You have to take the next jump or I'll disqualify you," the judge warned. Inside, I was burning mad but I didn't see any other choice but to go ahead. The change in procedure defeated the purpose of a head-to-head tournament.

I didn't go all out on the jump because I wanted to make sure I could land it and ski away. My goal was to jump a little further than my first jump to put a little pressure on the other guy. When I climbed into the boat after the jump, I could still see him sitting on the shore. The boat crew informed me I would have to go ahead with my third and final jump. I glanced at the shore and he was still sitting there. It certainly didn't look like he was getting ready to jump anytime soon. By now, I was really steaming. A skier who takes an injury break only has three minutes before they have to get on the water again. This guy was taking up far more than the allotted three minutes.

The chief judge got on the microphone. "Keith, you must take your third jump now or you'll be disqualified." I asked the boat crew to push the button on the radio so I could talk to the judge personally and explain the situation. As I did, he barked out orders to jump, reminding me I would be disqualified if I didn't go ahead. I apparently had no option at this point.

I didn't gain much distance with the third jump. Now I felt like a sitting duck. The anger inside was ready to spill over. I watched as the skier took his second jump with no sign of an injury holding him back. He knew how far he had to jump and he walked away with the win. I returned to the dock in a foul mood and met up with my wetsuit sponsor. "Did you see what happened?" I seethed. He admitted he wasn't happy with the turn of events. I turned to my dad and Swampy. "I want to protest this! What he did wasn't right," I grumbled. There was no time to protest because ESPN was getting ready to film the next event, a combined trick and jump tournament on the same site.

I was standing on the starting dock, gearing up for my ESPN run, when the chief judge sauntered over. "Hey buddy, I'm sorry about what went on earlier," he said. "It was the wrong thing to do."

"What the hell!" I spat out. "I'm in the middle of a competition. I think you're trying to screw me and mess with my head!" I turned and jumped in the water. It took every ounce of energy to hold down the anger inside and focus on the competition ahead. I gripped the handle and readied myself for a mandatory flying dock start which required a jump off a 15-foot tower. I was fueled by a hungry desire to win. I had nothing to lose and everything to gain at this point! In a matter of seconds, I quickly put a crazy trick run together in my head and added a different trick than what I originally planned. I knew I would win if I had a great jump. I just had to execute it and land it. It was a risky thing to do, but I was so pissed off inside I didn't care.

> ## Let Your Ability Do the Talking
>
> "Let your skiing do the talking!" Swampy was famous for saying. Rather than telling the world what you can do or hope to do, show them through your actions. Actions speak louder than words. Instead of bragging, let your ability do the talking.
>
> This quote constantly kept me grounded.

As soon as my feet hit the water, I was "in the zone." One trick meshed beautifully into another and when I landed the jump I knew I had it. The run was so sweet that I skied right up to the shore. I pumped my fist in the air as I walked up the shoreline. I looked like I owned the joint and I knew at that point no one could beat what I just did! I sat back and watched the last few jumpers struggle to catch up with me. The anger finally subsided. I ended up walking away with the first place trophy and a cash prize. This was another one of Swampy's lessons in action: let your feet do the talking.

My First Endurance Tournament

Toward the end of the summer, I was riding high. I was slowly gaining experience and building up confidence in tournament after tournament. There was one tournament I was curious about: Footstock, a figure-eight tournament held in Crandon, Wisconsin. Footstock is a special kind of tournament; a laid-back, yet fiercely competitive endurance barefoot tournament. The concept was simple: the boat would pull two barefoot skiers in a figure-eight pattern around the lake until one of them fell. The skiers were required to step off of a water ski before the start buoys. To complete a figure eight, the skier would have to barefoot 1.5 miles and cross over two sets of rollers (boat waves created by the boat wake). Each "eight" took one minute and twenty seconds to complete. The winner of that round would advance to the next round. The tournament winner was the last skier standing. I had never skied a figure-eight tournament before and I wanted to give it a try.

I recruited two buddies to join me in a rental car and we drove from Florida to Wisconsin. We were dead tired when we arrived 21 hours later but headed straight for the bar in town and tossed back a few. Footstock was legendary for the partying that went on before, during and after the tournament.

The next morning, I was nursing a massive hangover when I arrived at Lake Peshtigo. The lake was really a drainage pit and the water was as brown as leftover coffee. I shuddered to think what was in it. I was signing a few autographs when a young boy walked up. "Who are you?" he asked. I explained I was a three-event competitor and had just won the National tournament. The kid shrugged and walked off. I was definitely out of my element and very much an unknown among the grassroots barefooters.

The whole Figure-Eight tournament was new to me and I could feel the nerves coming on. I grabbed a ski off the pile and headed down to the dock. I had so little experience with putting one foot in the water and kicking off a ski. I mentally wished I had practiced it more before the tournament. All too soon it was my turn. I sank into the water, high-fived my opponent, and braced myself for the start. As the boat took off I wobbled a bit as I got up but quickly balanced myself. I let out a huge sigh of relief as I kicked off the ski and found myself barefooting. *Hmmm, maybe this wasn't so bad.* My opponent quickly went down. I advanced to the next opponent and won again. On the next run, I caught a toe on a roller and went down face first. Since the tournament was double-elimination, I had one more chance.

The nerves were still rattling inside of me as I readied myself for the next run. I kicked off the ski and instantly knew I was in trouble. I pitched forward and hit the water on my side, but I quickly tumbled back up on my feet. I didn't make it past the buoy in time. The boat stopped and the judges in the boat determined I was disqualified. Just like that, my first experience with Footstock was over and the tournament had just started!

Chapter 12: Don't Give Up

Being challenged in life is inevitable, being defeated is optional.

~Roger Crawford

Fergus Falls, Minnesota was the site of the 2000 World Championship. My Australian friend, Matty, and I flew from the Nationals to spend two weeks in Montana with Swampy. It was like old times hanging out with Swampy on the water and being coached again. I put together a challenging new trick run. My skiing wasn't consistent though. One day I could complete a run, the next day I would fall or mess up. I just wanted to kick Ron Scarpa off his throne as he was the king of three World Championships in a row. I had confidence on the water when it came to competing against him in the Nationals, but in my head the World Championship was a whole different ballgame. Ron had a lot of experience and it showed in his performance.

I hadn't seen Swampy in two years. He owned a lake home on Dicky Lake, just fifteen minutes outside of Whitefish. Spray and Swampy ran several businesses and their investments in the market and overseas were quite successful. They accomplished many things since my last visit and were doing exceptionally well.

Swampy picked us up from the airport and we drove towards the lake. As we began to get closer he pointed out the lake from the road and it glowed like the ocean in the Caribbean. I was amazed to see such beauty in a lake surrounded by mountains. "Hey, Swampy." I said, "That lake tells me two things. Color like that usually means the water is super clean and super cold!"

Swampy grinned. He knew I was right. We drove around the lake and came to the driveway of his lake house. The house was encased in knotted pine and sat on gorgeous piece of property. As the garage door opened, I was stunned by all the toys packed inside of it. Four-wheelers and snowmobiles! "Things seem to be going pretty well Swampy," I laughed.

"I love it up here, Keith!" he said. "This is where I always dreamed of being and I don't ever want to leave." I was so happy to see Swampy in his realm.

We brought our bags inside the lake house and the glowing lake captivated me. I put my bags down and peered out through the large sliding glass doors. The deck was massive-- a great place to host a crowd. A rock pathway curved down the hill to a set of stairs. At the base of the stairs sat a hot tub. *I'll be putting that to good use!* Two jet-skis and a barefoot boat were parked at the dock. "The landscapers did a good job on those rock walls, didn't they?" Swampy came up and stood beside me. I nodded.

Swampy was very successful and he shared his success with his family. He bought his father a new truck, his brother a new snowmobile and many other things for people just because he loved to give. I thought back to everything he had given me throughout the years. He had given me something I could never repay--the gift of his time. For countless hours he trained me on the water as a youngster and now I was thrilled to see how far he had gone with his own success. I was so proud of him and I could see the happiness painted on his face.

After two weeks of intense training on the water, Swampy, Matty, and I drove to Fergus Falls. I had a decent chance of winning the World Championship but my confidence level was at a 50-50 point. Half of the time I felt positive and the other half of the time doubts filled my head. Throughout the year and the weeks leading up to the tournament, many people expressed their confidence I would win the Worlds. Instead of the comments putting me in a positive place, each one felt like a load of bricks on my shoulders. Just before heading to the Worlds I told a reporter, "I will give the competition a run for their money, for sure. Hopefully, they'll be chasing me. I have everything I need to win. I just have to put it together."

I had a really good shot at winning the slalom event as I skied hard on all of my passes. I was going all out in the final run, cutting hard across the wake. The shape of the wake was sharp with a steep drop off. On the very last cross I went airborne and slammed my foot through the water. As soon as I tumbled to a stop I knew I was going to have to try and play catch up to win the Overall.

I sat on the dock trying to mentally prepare myself for my trick run. I dangled my feet in the water and closed my eyes trying to visualize the runs I was about to do. In the background I heard laughter and people talking loudly. It was hard for me to block them out and focus. My legs felt like Jell-O because the nerves were really overtaking my body. I was afraid if I stood up my legs would collapse. I started to wonder how I was going to get through my trick runs.

Halfway through my run, the doubts did me in. I fell on my first run. During my second run, it was the same scenario: another fall and another incomplete run. I was upset but I had to push it out of my mind and concentrate on jumping and slalom. Matty grabbed a video camera and filmed my jumping. "Keith, I noticed something when you approach the ramp," he said. "Just before you go over the jump ramp you are pushing your heels out in front of you. No wonder you've been complaining of bruised heels!" It was too late to change anything at that point. Matty's observation made sense. Every time I connected with the jump, my heels would slam into the fiberglass and every time I approached a jump I would brace myself for pain. I could jump high and far, but I couldn't land the jumps consistently. As a result, I was playing mind games with myself before every jump and only managing to land a few.

Jumping was not Ron's strong event, but he trained with Jon for two weeks at the Worlds site to prepare himself. Every once in a while Ron would pull out all the stops and rocket off the jump, and he did that at this tournament. Once again the Overall trophy was added to his collection. I had to settle for second place.

Is the Dream Worth It?

Back home, Gliding Soles still wasn't taking off in the way I hoped it would. Lake Minneola was drying up from the severe drought. There was no way for me to get through the channels to the other lakes. To make matters worse, I shared the lake with a wakeboarding school. Wakeboarding requires the opposite wake conditions behind the boat than barefooting; the bigger the wake, the more air a boarder reaps. This meant the lake was constantly in motion with rollers everywhere. My ski school students began to complain and the word began to spread to other customers.

I went over to talk to the wakeboard crew to try and come up with an agreeable schedule for both schools, but they merely shrugged their shoulders and refused to come up with a compromise. "We are running a business here too, buddy," was their response. The fact I was there first did not seem to matter.

After the Worlds, Matty and I headed down to my place to hang for two weeks. Matty did some skiing, but I just wanted to decompress. I didn't want anything to do with barefooting at that point. All we did was drink beer and chew tobacco as we sat on the back of my boat trying to figure out what we wanted to do in life.

At the end of the week the phone rang. "I've got some bad news," said Swampy. "You know the money we invested? Well... it is gone." The news was indeed bad: Swampy lost everything he invested. The account with the money was laundered and all of the money had vanished. Swampy was barely hanging on and he was worried he would lose everything. The years of success had taken a sudden downturn. Losing the investments meant I no longer had the monthly income that covered my truck payment and part of the rent. Between the drought, the wakeboarders tearing up the lake, the lack of ski school students, and the loss of monthly income, I was in a tough spot. I was running on empty at that point. I sank into a depression. With all of the challenges facing me, it was just too much. Was the dream worth it?

I lay in bed going over my options. *Should I go down the educational route and get a degree in physical fitness exercise physiology?* I could not see myself sitting in the classroom week after week. I was not an enthusiastic student in high school. The tests I took to enter college showed I would have to retake some high school classes. The last thing I wanted was to be confined to a classroom again.

Another option I considered was moving back home to get a job as a prison guard. Several of my friends were working at the local prison and the job included benefits, health insurance, and a steady paycheck. A regular paycheck was something I was striving for at that point. I was tired of not knowing when my next student was going to sign up at the ski school. I didn't know what to do or which way to turn. It seemed like the dream of a career in barefoot water skiing was drying up. I picked up the phone and called my mom. All at once it came pouring out. "I don't know what to do," I confessed. "It's so hard right now. I'm not sure I can do this much longer, Mom. I can't run the ski school on this lake with all the wakeboarders roughing up the water--and I'm not bringing in enough money to support moving somewhere else."

"You always have a place to come home to, Keith," she said. "You can come home to Berlin and get a job in the prison as a guard. With that kind of job you can retire in twenty years!"

I looked up at the ceiling and thought about home. I missed my family and my friends. It would be so easy to just walk away from it all and go back home. Yet, going back home would mean feeling like a failure. Deep down, I wanted to accomplish my dream. I wasn't ready to give it up. I wanted to be a World Champion. I wanted to run a popular ski school. I felt a lump forming in my throat and I closed my eyes to keep from crying. "I know I can do that, Mom, but I've put a lot of time into barefoot skiing and I can't give up just yet. This is my dream. I just need a little more time and a good location to run this ski school. If I can find a great location, I know I can build the school. I have to keep on trying."

"Whatever you decide to do, you know your Dad and I will give you support," she said. "And you can always come home. You'll always have a place here." We went back and forth discussing all of my options. Mom never wavered in her encouragement and this spurred me to continue.

"Good night, happy dreams, I love you, God bless you, and sweet dreams," we ended our call. This little saying started with dad and me when I was nine years old. We started saying "Good night" then we added, "happy dreams" and so on. Even today, my family and I still say it to each other.

I hung up the phone an continued to peruse my options while lying in bed. *A steady paycheck… or an uncertain future?* I wasn't sure what to do. I couldn't see myself giving up without achieving what I set out to do. I couldn't leave the sport knowing how much time I had put into it over the years. I had a dream to fulfill. Instinctively, I knew I wasn't ready to give up and go home. I felt like something better was just around the corner. I was halfway right.

A New Job, A New Path

A few weeks later I received a call from a lady named Becky. Becky's daughter, Melanie, was one of my ski school students. They drove in once or twice a month from Tampa. "Keith, I've got a job proposition for you," she said. "I'd like to interview you for a marketing position at VDO Sports. This is a new company I've set up." I did the interview with Becky and we discussed what the position would entail. I would work to build VDOsports.com and handle the marketing and promotion. VDOsports was an early version of the modern day YouTube. Individuals would submit videos showcasing their best trick or maneuvers in their sport and upload them to our website. A panel of judges would rate each video and record the number of hits that each video received. The first-place video received a sponsored prize.

I figured I had stumbled into an incredible opportunity. I said yes to the job, and suddenly, I went from not knowing what to do or where to go, to making fifty thousand dollars a year. I had to move to Tampa quickly, so I signed a lease with an apartment complex next to I-75 just outside of Tampa.

The other side of my job required me to continue to train Melanie. She was an extremely talented and motivated barefooter. She was only thirteen at the time and she took her training seriously. She trained on the water as if it was her job. Melanie had a huge heart for the sport and an amazing work ethic! She was by far the best female Junior skier in the country, and coaching her was a great way to get my name exposed in the sport.

My job at VDOsports required me to work both in and out of the office. A colleague and I drove around Tampa for hours, visiting sports retail stores and speaking with the managers. We gave presentations about VDOsports and asked them to donate products for the prizes. In return for the sponsored prizes, we would feature their logo on the website and promote their company. Ideally we wanted as many videos as possible from a large variety of sports. This would diversify the website and get more athletes to watch the craziest videos caught on cameras.

This was my first typical Monday through Friday job and I truly loved it. It was nice having a secure job with a steady paycheck. I liked knowing what I was going to make on a weekly basis. I did not have to sit and wait for the phone to ring, hoping it was going to be a new student. I drove to work, did my job and collected a check. It was a nice change from sitting in the boat all day, churning out the same training tips day after day. At three p.m., I would take off to go train Melanie after she finished school. I had no problem skipping out of work early. I could deal with that!

When the lease was up on the rental house, I went to pick up my boat and parked it on the far side of the apartment complex. I could see the boat from the window of my apartment and I just hoped the management wouldn't complain. For several weeks, it was quiet and the boat remained in the same place. Then management came knocking at my door. "You can't park your boat here."

"We've got a problem then," I said. "If I can't keep my boat here, then I can't run my ski school, and the ski school helps pay my rent."

I had one thing going for me--the apartment complex was somewhat vacant and they needed my rent payments. To my relief, the management agreed to let me keep the boat parked in back for the rest of the lease. I continued running the ski school, giving lessons on the weekends. I missed my old house on the lake and had a difficult time adjusting to living in an apartment. Three months into the job, I began overhearing some office employees speak in an uncomfortable tone. I listened closer and discovered a few people were looking for other jobs. Every time I inquired about the stability of the company, Becky told me things were fine and I completely trusted her.

One month later which was four months into the job, things were beginning to unravel. Becky, a strong woman who usually kept her composure, was showing stress throughout the week. Everyone was working hard to launch the parent company and get it to take off, but rumors were flying among the staff that the investors from the parent company were not coming through with the finances. Becky reassured us everything would work out and that the company would take off.

Two weeks later my paycheck bounced. I knew this was a bad sign, but I continued to trust Becky and figured it was just a temporary thing. She continued to reassure me the funds would come through. "The investors are working on it," she said. I continued training Melanie and collected a small amount of cash, but it was not enough to pay the bills. Two weeks later the second paycheck bounced. The office was shut down shortly after and I suddenly found myself unemployed. At first I wasn't too worried because I had a little money saved up. The reality was a whole other ballgame: I was in a state of denial. I held out, hoping my job would come back. Becky kept telling me I would get my job back and I wanted to believe her, but month after month there was no paycheck. Meanwhile, I had my truck payment, rent, food and utilities to pay for. In the midst of it all, I stubbornly held on to my habit of going out to the bar and spending money on beer. As the months went on, my savings began to dwindle and I became extremely nervous. *What am I going to do when the money runs out?* I stayed in my apartment most of the days watching TV like nothing ever happened. I was experiencing depression and didn't even realize it. 9-11 happened right in front of my eyes since I was glued to the television morning and night.

Luckily, my roommate, Matz, kept me somewhat sane. He paid my rent for two months. "Keith, aren't you worried about not having a job?" he asked. There was a concerned look on his face. "I don't think it's good for you to stay inside all day hoping your old job will come back. Maybe you need to focus on your barefoot skiing again since you're so good at it." I shrugged him off. I felt like a housewife cooped up all day, but in reality I was hiding from the outside world. I didn't want anyone to know what I was going through. I would look like a failure. I was scared and didn't have a clue which way to turn. Matz kept telling me how good I was at barefoot skiing and he wished he could do the things I did on the water. He tried barefoot skiing a few times and wasn't overly successful. He reminded me of how much time and effort I put into my skiing. Just thinking of my efforts in the past tangled my head up even worse. I brushed off his attempts at cheering me up. I wallowed in self-pity. *How did I end up here? Why me? How am I going to be successful when I'm hiding here in an apartment?*

I continued to feel like I had no options and I kept looking for a break of some sort. I trained Melanie for another month and Becky continued to dangle hope the company would be up and running again. Becky made it sound so promising but I felt my fate was in her hands. I didn't like that feeling. Then one day Becky informed me that she would have to stop Melanie's training sessions. The family was going through their own crisis from lack of funds.

For two long months, I operated in a state of denial. In the late mornings, I stumbled to the fridge and ate whatever unhealthy thing was parked on the shelves. I sat around day after day numbing my mind with TV programs. As soon as evening rolled around, I parked myself at Barnacles, the local sports bar. I was scared to go out into the job market and work a real job. I barefoot skied my whole life and fell into what I thought would be a dream job with Beck--and now that was gone. After two months, I knew I had to kick the ski school back into gear again. I was burning through my savings at a rapid rate, paying $580 per month on a truck I couldn't afford. I loved that truck, but couldn't afford it. Without a steady income, I was rapidly spiraling downward.

Tampa was no place to build a ski school with the lack of skiable water. When I moved to Tampa the ski school basically disappeared from the barefoot scene as many of my old clients had no idea where I was. I was fortunate to have one customer, Christian, who kept me afloat during this time. I knew I had to develop my own website and start marketing the ski school, but I didn't know much about website design. After a couple of nights of piecing together graphics and writing the content I developed <u>glidingsoles.com</u> and it came to life. It was a corny looking website with a black background and orange font but it got the message out: I was open for business.

During that spring, Chris Atinella from the Eastern Region came to my ski school. He was skilled in building websites and he offered to help me out. We bartered equipment and ski sets for his work on my website. He redesigned the site and gave it a professional look which brought it to a whole new level. He was heaven-sent and I thank him for helping me during such a tough period of my life. It goes back to the lesson I learned as a kid: there's always someone around to help you when you need it if you keep your eyes and ears open. No one knew how close I was to going broke and I was too embarrassed to tell anyone.

My Most Important Tips for Buying a Car/Truck:

This is what your goal should be for a vehicle:

Never have a car payment!

Make a budget and start with what you can afford, paying 100% cash to avoid a payment. If you're a young adult, saving up for your first car will allow you to have more opportunity in the future. Many first time buyers forget that they will have insurance payments, gas and maintenance to pay. This all adds up fast.

I recommend never going to a dealership. This is the way they make their living and you end up paying for it. A brand new vehicle depreciates fifteen percent as soon as you drive it off the lot.

Always buy used, which is easy to do nowadays because people drive their cars for a year or two and trade them in. Obviously you need a vehicle that is dependable, so look for something with low mileage--a vehicle that has been taken care of inside and out. Check NADA.com or KBB.com to find the market value of a used car.

If you absolutely cannot afford a vehicle by paying 100% cash, then aim to put down at least 25% of the total. Strive for a payment under $200.00 or less per month-- and even that is on the high side.

You will most likely need to get a loan for a newer vehicle and this is what you want to avoid and/or eliminate--so consider an older vehicle or compromise on the size or type.

A paid-off car is money saved and a less stressful life. Take it from me. My payment controlled my lifestyle!

Off to Australia

I booked a one-month clinic tour in Australia during January of 2001 and I was really looking forward to heading down under. I was finally going to be able to hang with Matty in his hometown and see his part of the world. Matty was a skilled, talented surfer and he wanted to introduce me to his sport. I had never surfed before so I was intrigued to try something new. "I'm going to take you to a great place to surf," Matty said. We piled into his boat and drove down the river to a channel that connected with the ocean. We parked the boat and headed to the beach with the surf and boogie boards. "You're going to start off on the boogie board," Matty explained. We started to paddle out and a thought hit me. "Hey Matty, what about sharks? Do you have those around here?"

Matty threw his head back and laughed. "Keith, this shore line is shark-infested! There are probably several hundred sharks under us right now." I tried not to show it, but I was scared. I didn't relish the idea of being eaten by a shark on my first surfing attempt but being a typical guy, I had to squelch my fears or I'd never hear the end of it from Matty. Then another thought hit me. "Hey Matty, aren't those waves a little big for a beginner?" The waves were pounding the shoreline and the whole ocean was roaring. It was intimidating the hell out of me. "Oh, come on you little wimp! Get on the board and I'll show you what to do."

As talented as I was at the sport of walking on water, I had a heck of a time trying to master the art of boogie boarding. I was having trouble getting back out after catching a wave. The boogie board was too buoyant to push down under the waves. I tackled the massive waves by paddling as hard as I could but I kept getting pummeled back toward shore. Exhausted, I headed back to sit on the beach and catch my breath. After Matty caught several waves, he came in. "Here, Keith, try the surf board," Matty suggested. "Maybe you'll have better luck and it will be easier to push the board under the waves as you paddle out."

I tried over and over to catch a wave, but nothing was happening. I was pretty determined to make a go of it because I couldn't stand the thought of going through the day without accomplishing a new skill. I watched and waited carefully for the next wave and I caught it. Slowly, I stood up and tried to balance on the bucking board. I lost my balance and tumbled. The wave engulfed me and pushed me down toward the bottom. I scraped the sand and tried to twist to reach the surface. Another wave pounded me and pushed me back down. I didn't have much air left in my lungs and I struggled to figure out how to swim upwards. The waves continued to barrel over me. My lungs were at the bursting point. For an instant I was transported back to Lake Umbagog and I remembered what it felt like to be trapped under that kneeboard. *Oh my gosh, I can't breathe! I'm going to die here!* I thought I was going to pass out. I popped to the surface and gulped a mouthful of water and air at the same time. Another wave pounded me back down again. It was like tumbling inside a washing machine--around and around again. I was disoriented and running out of oxygen. Just when I wanted to give up the ocean spat me out once again. I sucked in some air and another wall of salt water forced me down to the bottom again. Finally, I felt the sand beneath my feet and crawled toward the beach. I coughed and sputtered, sucking in the much-needed air. The salt water settled in my lungs and stung my eyes. Matty paddled up. "What's the matter, Mate? You look a little beat there!"

I squinted at him. "I can't do this. I almost drowned out there! No way in hell am I going to do this again!" I started to swim back. I was afraid to go back, I was afraid of the sharks, and I was afraid of not having enough energy to make it back to the boat. *Surfing was not for me.* I was done.

World Games Japan

The highlight of that year was the invitation to compete in the World Games in Japan. The World Games are introduction sports for the Olympics. Two skiers from each country are selected for the Games, one male and one female. Rachel George was the other American. Rachel was a talented ballerina with long, blond hair and blue eyes. She was slim and slender with the perfect ballerina body and she had a tough side just as most female barefooters do. You can't take up an extreme sport without persistent determination or you'd never last on the water. Rachel grew up on a private lake in Ohio where she learned to barefoot with her father and two brothers.

Oscar "Foot" Mann who was working as the tournament homologator joined us on the plane. His job was to calculate measurements to ensure accurate scoring. Foot and I had butted heads in several past tournaments and became friends. When people say, "Oh, you Americans are so loud," you can blame Foot for this. He has a great sense of humor. Whatever is on his mind, he's sure to share it. The three of us were sitting on the plane contemplating whether or not we should sleep on the long flight or stay awake. Rachel dozed off. Foot decided we should stay awake for the entire flight and then crash as soon as we arrived in Japan. With that plan our sleep cycle would line up with the Japan time zone.

"Let's have a couple of beers to get us through this flight," Foot suggested. We kicked back with a few beers, a few jokes and some good laughs. By the time the seventh beer arrived, the server put it down in front of us with a stern look. "All right boys, you've had enough. There will be no more beer for you two after this one!" Foot and I were undeterred. We wanted to keep drinking to stay awake and get through the long flight. Foot stood up. "I'm going to get us some more beer," he said. I laughed as I watched him make his way toward the galley. He waited until the coast was clear and snatched several beers out of the refrigerated drawer. He came waltzing back with a grin and handed me a beer. Every time the server came down the aisle we hid the cans. Foot made another beer run during the last leg of the flight and scored some more cans. By the time the plane touched down on Japanese soil we were two very happy Americans.

After the flight, we had a three-hour bus ride, and then dinner. We sat down in the dining room in front of six wooden boxes piled up at each place setting. Each box contained a different food. There was rice, fish, sushi, salad, and some vegetables that I didn't recognize. Some of the skiers wouldn't eat anything as they weren't comfortable with the flavors and textures of Japanese food. I loved it and ate everything! The next morning I woke up gingerly and looked around. I lifted my head and squinted in the sunlight. No headache. No hangover. No jet lag. In fact, I felt like a million bucks! Foot's plan worked like a charm!

At the World Games barefooting takes second stage to water skiing. This fact was evident when we arrived at the dock and learned that there was no boat for us to use. We each took a few passes behind a wakeboard boat. We switched to a 95-foot rope so we could cross the steep wake, but the farther back from the boat you go, the wider the wake becomes. I tried to decide whether to attempt to cross the wake on one foot for the slalom event or play it safe with both feet and a lower score. I went through my practice runs and I felt confident I could get through on one foot. We had another unusual challenge too: there were bamboo shoots floating in the water and we occasionally skied right over them. Luckily, most of the bamboo had been floating for days and they simply felt like a wet sponge upon impact.

At the dock, I took off my wetsuit and laid it on the floor. I stood and watched the other skiers. Stepping back, I felt a sharp pain. My heel landed square on the upright zipper sticking out of my wetsuit, puncturing a hole in my heel! I let out a stream of profanity. I pulled my foot away and blood began spurting out. I didn't want anyone to know. I slipped on my flip-flops and went off in search of Super Glue. Grabbing a bike from the hotel, I took off for the nearest department store. I went up and down the aisle hoping to find the glue. "Super glue?" I asked. No one seemed to understand me. "Glue?" There was none to be found. I settled for a box of Band-Aids and headed back to the site.

It was my turn to compete and there wasn't much I could do but remove the Band-Aid and jump in the water with my gaping heel. The lake water wasn't exactly clean but I couldn't worry about it. I had to focus on the task at hand and block the pain out of my mind. I readied myself for the start of the slalom run and made the decision to ski on one foot. It was a fateful decision that brought me a score of 16.4 and allowed me to take the lead for the Overall title. David Small, a rising competitor from Britain, was not far behind me. I didn't take much notice of him, but he was a barefooter with a lot of raw talent. Despite the heel wound, I managed to trick well and land my jumps. The moment I landed my first jump I cinched the Overall title and won the World Games.

Chapter 13: The Power of a Quote

Too often we underestimate the power of a touch, a smile, a kind word, a listening ear, an honest compliment, or the smallest act of caring, all of which have the potential to turn a life around.

~Leo Buscaglia

When I arrived home from the World Games, I received a call from my cousin, Nathan. He decided to discontinue college and wanted to experience life in Florida. I immediately offered him a place at my apartment and he agreed to move in. I was thrilled because he was a cousin who was more like a brother to me. As soon as I hung up the phone memories flooded my mind. Nathan grew up just down the road from me. Every single weekend during the winter we rode the chairlifts on the mountains in New Hampshire spending hours skiing and snowboarding. I couldn't wait to hang out with him again.

Nathan drove down with his dad in February and settled right in. My friends quickly warmed up to Nathan because he was a natural social butterfly. He was a skilled barefooter and I was hoping he would eventually end up partnering with me at the ski school. The first time I taught him to jump he immediately accomplished an inverted jump, something that most skiers took years to accomplish. Nathan landed a job as a bartender at Barnacles Bar and Grill. This became one of our skier hangouts and Nathan would always slip me some free drinks.

One night I was looking over my website and scouring through the web when I came across an article published by another barefooter. He published several untruthful things about me and indicated that my ski school was closed. *Closed? What the heck is this all about?* The ski school was very much open and I was trying to bring in new business and clients. I couldn't figure out why a guy who basically knew nothing about me was taking the time to discredit me and my business. I sat down and quickly fired off an email to him and requested he remove the erroneous article immediately. In his response he told me he would not remove the article. I called him and I tried to plead with him and explain that my ski school business was very much alive and well. My concerns did not faze him one bit.

As soon as I hung up, I called Paul Stokes and explained the situation. Paul was working for him. "What is his problem? Why is he trashing me on the Internet?" I wanted to know. Paul defended him but he didn't give me a reason why I was being targeted. Instead, he invited me to work with the guy. "There's an e-commerce business starting up and I'm going to write articles for the website," Paul explained. "It's going to be an online magazine all about barefoot water skiing." Stokes was extremely excited and he tried talking me into joining this business. "He's a good guy, he's not that bad-- you can trust him," he continued. "If you join us we can grow and become really big. We need a person like you on the team and this is a great opportunity!" I was unconvinced and took a pass on the opportunity.

I turned my focus on looking for a new location for Gliding Soles. I came across a house rental by a river that I thought would work perfectly. Nathan and I packed up the apartment. I hooked the boat to the truck and took off for Temple Terrace. We settled into a Pepto-Bismol pink rental house that was just a half-mile from the Hillsborough River. I was only 25 minutes from the Tampa airport, one hour from Clearwater Beach, an hour away from Disney World, and ten minutes from down town Tampa, an area that was famous for nightly entertainment. The house was just four miles from Busch Gardens and I figured it would be a good location to draw some of the tourists over to the ski school.

I was so excited about finding this location that I basically overlooked the neighborhood and the surrounding areas. Once we settled in we drove around more and saw just how run-down the subdivision was. My own rental should have been an indication. It was much too nasty to run a ski school and there was no place to set up a pro shop. I had a beautiful Chevy Silverado extended cab towing a sweet Mastercraft boat, but I was living in a run-down house reminiscent of a trailer. The front of the house looked like a garage. The inside consisted of paneled walls in nearly every room. Because Nathan worked at the bar at night, he slept all day. We took on college students to help pay rent and fill up the four bedrooms. All of this meant I had to meet my ski school students at the boat ramp each day, as the house was no place to conduct business. Every day I had to tow the boat to the ski location and haul it back home at the end of the day.

One of our roommates was a member of a local ski team and he wanted to host a fundraiser at the house one weekend. "Let's have a big party and charge everyone admission," he suggested. "This will help us raise money for our water ski club." *A party for a good cause?* I was game. We created flyers and passed them around at the University of Southern Florida. We hired two bouncers and a DJ. Kegs of beer were lined up outside with stacks of cups next to them. One of the two living rooms was designated as a "VIP" room, stocked with fancy foods and hard liquor. In the other living room we set up an inflatable pool filled with water, ready for the wet t-shirt contests. At seven p.m. we opened the doors and waited for the crowd to arrive. Ten dollars for all the beer you could drink. A few people began showing up and then it turned into a crowd arriving at the front door. We had over 350 people milling around inside and out. The noise was deafening and the energy was unbelievable. More kegs were added to the bunch. The women were jumping into the pool and slopping water all over the floor but no one had a care in the world that night.

Halfway through the party, I suddenly had what I thought was a brilliant idea. I grabbed the battery out of the boat and picked up a pump that was lying nearby. I connected the battery to the pump and dropped the pump into my beer mug. The beer flowed through the hose and I sucked it down in gulps. I was the center of attention! It didn't even occur to me that the pump had previously sucked up who-knows-what from the river water and the hose was filled with mold. Everyone was laughing at my impromptu beer fountain but I paid a heavy price: I was sick for days afterwards.

The drinking didn't stop there. Nathan and I would gather with the college students at Bar Tampa in Ybor City. The bar served free beer for an hour. We often didn't have enough money for beer, so it was a cheap way to drink our tails off. Bar Tampa was "Eye Candy City." Most of the girls were dressed in outfits which left little to the imagination. "I can get any girl's phone number here," Nathan bragged. Girls were naturally drawn to Nathan. Tall with blue eyes, striking blond hair, and a smooth personality—he was a real ladies man. I didn't stand a chance next to him in a roomful of girls. I decided to challenge him. "All right, Nathan, let's make a bet then. I get to pick out the girl and you have to come back with her number."

"You're on, buddy!" he laughed. I looked around the bar. I wanted to find the hottest girl there, the most impossible one to hit on. I spotted her dancing on the bar. She was a petite gal with long black hair and a very shapely rear-end

131

packed into a tight, short skirt. She was prancing around in tall boots and a shirt that lifted up to reveal a lean stomach. Half of the eyes around the bar were fixated on her. I nudged Nathan. "That's the one. Let's see what you've got."

Nathan sauntered up to the bar and it wasn't long before the girl bent over to talk with him as she danced. A few minutes later Nathan returned with a slip of paper in his hand with her phone number scrawled on it. "And you thought I couldn't get her number?" he grinned. My mouth fell open. "How did you do that?"

"I made it look like I wasn't interested in her." Nathan explained. "She wanted to get my attention so she made herself really noticeable and we began to talk." I rolled my eyes and dug into my wallet. He ended up dating her for a while.

A New Sponsor?

The phone rang. It was the same guy who wrote the article indicating the closure of my ski school. He called to request a ski school review for his website. I debated whether or not to decline. The ski school had never been reviewed before. After giving it some thought I agreed to do a review. I was also hoping to convince him to remove the damaging information on his website that was hurting my business.

As much as I loved my sponsored boat, it was a boat made for all water sports except barefooting. I was a bit worried to see how the boat would reflect on the ski school review. The wake behind the boat was a rough one to cross and the stern roller was quite a ride for barefooters with less experience. I knew I had to make the best of my situation and hope for a good review.

I met the guy at the dock and from the very first moment he was all business. The morning runs went smoothly and I started to relax. By lunchtime, he loosened up as well and began to share his business plans. "I've got a website that I'm putting together that's going to be a hub for all things barefooting," he said. By the end of the lunch hour, he offered me a contract to work with him. "This is the deal--the website will sell barefoot water ski gear," he explained. He named three other competitors he planned to include. "Whoever signs the contract will receive twenty-five percent of the profit on all merchandise sold. I will send a 1099 at the end of the year because it's a subcontractor position. Basically, I'm sponsoring skiers to endorse my business and push the clients to buy from me. In return, I will pay out a portion of the profit and skiers won't have to worry about having any overhead."

He produced a contract, outlined the details and left a copy of it for me to look over. "I'll think it over and let you know," I said.

We headed back out on the water to finish up the afternoon set. As we approached shore and put the boat on the trailer, he asked to see my house. "It's part of the ski school review," he explained. "I want to see where the school is hosted."

I didn't want him to see the house. The gaudy pink rental looked like a trailer with a roof that was ready to cave in. A crappy house in an old neighborhood-- that image certainly wouldn't go over well in a ski school review. What's more, it was a mess inside and I had put off cleaning it for weeks. I had never had a student at the house before, so this was a bit of a surprise. "I run the ski school from here, this public boat launch," I explained. *I wonder if he's just looking for dirt to write about?* I wasn't sure what to do. If I refused, I risked getting a bad review. If he saw what a trash heap I lived in, and wrote about it on his review, it could affect my business. Either way, I was screwed.

"Ok, I'll show you were I live, but I do not sell equipment out of my home or ever take students there" I explained. I wanted to make it clear that it was my home, and the ski school was not a part of it. *Just don't take any pictures*, I prayed. We walked quickly through the dwelling. I tried to get the tour over with quickly. "I think it's best to wrap up the day and settle the bill," I said.

"Oh, I don't pay for ski school reviews," he explained. "I shouldn't have to pay because I'm doing a report on your school." I was stunned and speechless for a moment. *My time is worth something*, I thought. I weighed my words carefully. "You see, this is my livelihood, this is how I keep the business running and I spent all day in the boat. You're going to have to pay for the skiing and instruction that you received today. It's only fair." We wrangled back and forth on the issue until I agreed to give him a deal and charge him half of my fees.

After he left, I toyed with the idea of working for him. After a week of debating the issue over and over in my head, I made some calls to get input from others. I called my dad and talked it over with him. I mulled it over with Swampy. I contacted several others I trusted and went over the pros and cons with them. The conclusion was simple: I had nothing to lose and a lot to gain if it all panned out. If it did not work out we would go our separate ways. I figured the opportunity would result in more exposure for me and hopefully more money. I was in a situation where I had few options. The ski school business was slow and I was barely making ends meet. His article on the web was keeping students away.

I like to see the good in all the people I meet so I chose to see the advantages to this deal. I could see the win-win of the situation. By being sponsored, it would help me grow Gliding Soles and my three-event background with National titles would give his barefooting website a big push. I decided to sign the contract and become a sponsored athlete.

The Pressure Builds Up

If there ever was a time in my life that I felt intense pressure at a tournament it was at the 2002 Worlds. In the weeks before the Worlds, the expectations began to build up. "You're going to win this one, Keith!" Everywhere I turned, friends and family members said the same thing. A month before the Worlds I flew to Vienna, Austria to begin training and become familiar with the site. I decided to skip the Nationals, a decision that I would later come to regret. I stayed with Christian and we trained hard together. Two weeks before the Worlds I drove to France to ski in the Europeans tournament as an international skier. I won that tournament, set a World trick record and came close to breaking the slalom record. When I left, I was flying high. As long as I repeated my performance, in two short weeks, I would achieve my career goal of being a World Champion.

I was favored to win the 2002 Worlds quite easily. My fans and my friends fed me a steady diet of encouragement. I figured if they felt that confident, then I should be as well--and I was. I held two World Records under my name-- jump and tricks, and slalom was my strong event. I figured I had the Worlds in the bag. Ron Scarpa was there, but by now I had racked up confidence after winning so many National titles. Patrick Werner from France was also there. We had met at the 1996 Worlds. He was close in age and also a bit on the shy side. The two of us bonded over the years. He was extremely strong in the tricks event and our jumping was similar. I was sure I could blow him away in slalom.

There was one competitor that I should have kept my eye on but I didn't think twice about him. David "Pitbull" Small was from the United Kingdom. I had met him briefly at the 2000 World Championship, the World Games, and at the recent Europeans tournament, but I didn't pay much attention to him. I figured he would not be too much of a threat because of his age and inexperience. Besides, I had just beaten him at the Europeans. I had myself completely pumped up for this tournament.

I wasn't in the greatest shape at this point in my life. In fact, I was downright chubby. The endless drinking and partying had packed several extra pounds on my 5' 9 1/2" frame. The drinking was like a cancer to me. Day by day I didn't notice the effect, but over time it was catching up to me. The other footers came up to me and gave me a poke in the stomach. "A little beer belly there, eh, Keith?" I laughed and sucked my stomach in. I thought back to my teen years when I was a bit on the chubby side. Spray would take every opportunity to tease me. "Hey, you've got 'torpedo tits!' he would say as he grabbed them and gave them a twist. Here I was in 2002 sporting the extra weight fueled by endless Mountain Dews. I kept the weight hidden under XL t-shirts as much as I could.

My rope and handle sponsor supplied six ropes and handles for the World tournament per my recommendation. The ropes were made from a new, non-stretchable material called Spectra. The material was ultra-lightweight and as thin as a straw. I used the ropes and handles at my ski school so I was confident in the product.

The competition was intense and I was keeping my eye on Ron and another top skier. I blazed through slalom and was in first place so I was feeling confident. I did well in tricks but I fell during one run so I was not in first place. Patrick was leading the way. I knew I had to place well in jumping to win the Overall so I spent a few minutes mentally pumping myself up before heading over to the starting dock. I took my first jump and landed it well. I watched Ron and another competitor but not much was happening with them. David fell on his first jump. Another competitor came off the ramp and as he landed with a hard pull on the handle the rope snapped. I didn't think too much of it. Every now and then a rope snapped at a tournament. A few jumps later, another rope snapped. *Geez, what are the chances of two ropes snapping in a single tournament?* I was concerned, especially since it was my sponsor who supplied all the ropes for the Worlds. I was completely puzzled as to why the ropes were snapping. I used the Spectra ropes many times at my own ski school and I had not experienced any problems with them. By this point, the other skiers were talking about the ropes and speculating about why they were breaking. The word started going around: *hang on to a bad landing long enough so you can break the rope and you will get another chance to jump again.*

I took my second jump and landed it. David went up again and I held my breath as he landed on his butt. He was not able to ski away. I exhaled. I was becoming more and more confident that the Overall title was going my way. I was deep into conversation with another barefooter when Christian came running up. "Keith! We need to find more ropes. Another one just snapped."

"What do you mean, another one? You gotta be kidding me!" I said.

"We better look for some more ropes. If these last three break we won't have any left." We scrambled up to a shed and sifted through the equipment trying to find a tournament-quality rope. Finally, we resorted to asking other barefooters if they could lend us some ropes. We located a rope from one skier and headed back to the dock.

David went up for his third and final jump. I watched from shore as he approached the ramp. David went big on the jump and I held my breath to see if he would land it. He landed on his butt, feet in the air. It wasn't a jump that he could ski away from. I figured the Overall title was finally going to be mine. I mentally started celebrating.

I couldn't believe what happened next: the rope snapped. I shook my head in utter disbelief. David was given another chance to jump due to tournament equipment failure. He rocketed off the jump. The moment I saw him launch off the jump I had a knot in my stomach. I may not have paid attention to David when I arrived at the Worlds but now all of my attention was on him. His feet hit the water and he cleanly skied away. With that last jump he had a chance of securing the Overall title. This qualified him for the next round with three more jumps to possibly improve on.

I got ready for my next jump. All I needed to do was slightly improve and land my final jump and the Overall trophy would be mine. The moment I flew off the jump I wasn't sure if I could make the landing. I knew I had to fight for it. I came down hard. My butt hit the water and as I bounced back onto my feet something didn't feel right. In slow motion, I watched as the handle pulled out of my hands. The jump was not going to count and it was the one that could have secured me with the World Championship Overall title. It wasn't completely over. David still had to improve his jump score the next day to beat me out of the Overall title.

I went out to dinner that night with a few teammates and the Australian team. As usual the talk turned to barefooting. We were all tossing back a few beers. We had just finished dinner when one of the U.S. skiers started giving me a verbal whipping. "My teaching style can be taught to anyone around the world with great results," he began. "Keith, on the other hand, has no style that can be applied to his instruction. Until you can teach someone your style, you haven't really learned how to teach it."

I sat there in stunned silence. I didn't understand why he decided to single me out in front of everyone.

"Every student must be handled differently," I responded slowly. "The same technique does not work for everyone. I try to adapt to the skier's style and teach what I think is best for that individual." My teammate wasn't finished, in fact, he was just getting started. I sat there and took it all in while trying to keep my game face on. This was a guy I looked up to for many years and here he was putting me down in front of my teammates and the Australians.

At twenty-three years of age, I knew I didn't have much experience with coaching and instructing students but to hear it from a legend in my field-- well-- it hurt. I sat there in silence as I listened to him cut me down. I felt two inches tall. I looked over at the Australian guys and rolled my eyes and shook my head. The Aussie's and I were outwardly laughing at the situation, but deep down inside I was hurting. I had a crappy performance on the water as well up to this point. So rather than having a debate, I just turned my head and shrugged it off. Confrontation was not one of my strengths. I hadn't yet learned to stand on my own two feet off the water. I hadn't learned to see the gift in the lesson my teammate was trying to teach me. The gift and the lesson would come two years later.

In the next rounds I won the slalom event. Patrick took first in tricks and I came in second. Everything came down to the finals in jumping. The jump that David landed in the first round got him into the final round and I knew if he landed a bigger jump he would be crowned the Overall Champion. The pressure was on.

As the next round started and David came off the jump I could tell he jumped differently than anyone else. He had his own jumping style and he was clearly full of confidence in the air and on his landings. I tried to reassure myself his jumping was just a fluke. *He is so young and doesn't have enough experience on the jump ramp for me to worry about. It is hard to land larger jumps and if he does go big, well, he'll just land on his butt and not be able to ski it away...just like the previous round.* I watched as David went for the jump with gusto and he didn't hold back. He hung in the air for a long time and landed the jump with ease.

I knew right at that moment I was not going to be the new World Champion. I was crushed. I had my chance and I blew it. I watched as others swarmed around David and issued congratulations. Another fellow footer came up to me and said, "Keith, you'll be thinking of that jump for a long time." His words just twisted the knife much deeper in my chest.

Right then and there I decided I didn't like David. I wanted revenge against the guy. Here's the funny thing: it wasn't his fault he beat me. I didn't reach the goal that I set out to reach. I did not ski to my full potential and I certainly didn't put enough effort into my jump training. How could I hold a grudge against a young, rising star like David when it was me who was not prepared? I was the one with a big head. What a heavy lesson for me to learn and it was a lesson which would still take a few years for me to learn fully.

The jumping continued and as the last of the footers went off the ramp, the impossible continued to happen: every single rope snapped. All six of them were torn in half. We finished the tournament with the borrowed rope. As I sat and analyzed the tournament results, I realized a small irony: if I had not recommended the ropes, David would have never gotten the second chance to jump again. I would have won the Overall trophy. That was a hard pill to swallow!

Two weeks after the Worlds, I headed out to London for a jump tournament, "Splash of the Titans". I didn't train myself at all before this tournament. I was still feeling down from the Worlds and I wasn't even looking forward to competing in a jump contest. The tournament was invitation-only, and all of the accommodations were paid for. I figured it would be fun to see London and the tournament was also a chance to win some money. I skied horribly in this tournament. I skied so poorly the organizers did not issue an invitation for me to return to the tournament the following year. The moment the tournament was done I was done too. The disappointment from the Worlds combined with my poor performance in the jump contest did me in. I just wanted to drink it all away.

I met up with Patrick after the tournament and we headed out to the tournament party. The two of us proceeded to down one beer after another. Drinking was the only way I could drown the feelings stuffed inside of me. The disappointment I felt after the Worlds was some of the heaviest I had ever experienced. I didn't know how to deal with it. By the time Patrick and I headed back to our Bed and Breakfast I had put away quite a few beers. The room everyone was partying in was on the third floor suite. Patrick and I ended up in the bathroom because we could not hear each other speak over all the commotion and partying going on in the room. We talked about barefooting--the grueling training we had taken up, the time we put into the sport, and the goals we had set along the way. Our feelings about the sport were similar and it was nice to talk to someone else who came away with the same understanding. As we got deeper into our discussion, I began to pour out my disappointment. Once I started, I couldn't stop.

"I was supposed to win the Worlds--I should have won--I can't believe I didn't win!" I said. "This really sucks. All this pressure to win really messed me up. So many people were telling me I was going to win--that's why I feel like crap right now. How could I screw it up?" The tears started to flow. I knew part of it was triggered by alcohol, and part of it was just the relief of being able to talk to someone and express my feelings.

"I should have won a few World Overall titles myself," Patrick explained. "There are tournaments that I look back on, which I could have won if I did things differently. But it doesn't do any good to look back and second-guess." Patrick reached in his wallet and pulled out a laminated card. He handed it to me. "This card was given to me by John Penney, a past World Champion. He gave it to me at a low time in my life and told me to hold on to it until I achieved my dreams; and then to pass it on to someone who needed it more than I did. I've achieved a lot of things. I won my first gold medal at this Worlds and that has been a long-time goal. I know it's time for me to pass it on and I want to give this to you."

Blinking back the tears, I looked at the card. It read: "If you can imagine it, you can achieve it. If you can dream it, you can become it." The quote was by William Arthur Ward. "Keith, when you've achieved your goal and your dreams, that's the time you'll look for someone to pass this card to," he continued. "Hold on to it and remember the words on this card. Someday you'll achieve your dreams and someone else will benefit from these words."

"But, Patrick, don't you want to keep it?" He was close to winning an Overall, but had yet to achieve it.

> If you can imagine it, you can achieve it. If you can dream it, you can become it.
>
> ~William Arthur Ward

"I have fulfilled all of my dreams and I am totally comfortable with who I am and what I have achieved," he explained. "You need this more than I do right now, and I know you will take it with pride."

By this time the tears had stopped flowing and the beer was wearing off. I put the card in my wallet. Patrick was someone I had always respected and trusted and the card meant a lot to me. In the years to come I felt a positive energy every time I pulled out the card to read the quote. I read the card a lot and brought it everywhere with me. The card gave me a reason to continue to pursue my hopes and dreams of becoming a World Champion. Little did I know that the card was going to make its way through several hands and change some lives as well.

A Lesson About Achieving Your Personal Best

If there was one thing Swampy taught me well it was to compete against myself. "If you worry about your competition, they will simply play mind games with you," he explained. At every tournament I tried to remember to simply improve my personal best with each event. Without a doubt, I wanted to win at every tournament. I wanted to be the best, to be number one. The competitive person inside of me always itched to beat my rivals, but I long ago learned to set my own personal goals and work toward them. One of the goals was to win the Worlds--to become a World Champion. I couldn't and wouldn't rest until I achieved that goal.

At the beginning of every year, Swampy taught me to set up barefooting goals for the year and aim for them. We would sit down together and write the trick run out on paper and make our plan. "This year our trick run comes up to 6000 points, which should be doable." Swampy would say. "Do you have confidence in that, Keith?"

"I know I can do all the tricks in the run. With a little work I'll be able to memorize them and get them to flow smoothly so yes, I can do this," I replied.

Swampy would get me to commit to the goals and we began our journey on achieving them. When I achieve personal goals I gain a deep sense of satisfaction as a result. This is true of any goal in my life-- there's a sense of accomplishment when I achieve goals under my own strength and power. I encourage others to approach life this way. There's no pressure about being better than someone else—only a personal best to achieve. Over the years I learned to focus on the personal goal and when I reached the goal I would be number one in my own eyes.

When I was interviewed by ESPN in 1997 at the National tournament, the reporter asked me, "Do you worry about your competitors before you ski?" I had a simple answer: "I ski to the best of my ability and when I do that, I 'place' where I deserve to be."

Chapter 14: Hitting Rock Bottom

A dead end street is a good place to turn around.

~Naomi Judd

With the Worlds coming up, I was scrambling to find someone to drive the boat so I could get some training in. I was on the Hillsborough River coaching a student when an old school barefoot skier, Jimmy Taylor, pulled up on shore in his truck. Jimmy was a pure, "rough around the edges" redneck, complete with a southern drawl and profanity-laced speech. His body was as thick as his Southern drawl and he was intimidating at first. "How's the skiing going?" he hollered out the window.

"It's tough," I said. "I don't have anyone to drive me or coach me these days. I'm doing the best I can at this point pulling students during the day and getting some water time in whenever I can."

"If you want to commit to some serious training, I'll coach you," he offered. "I will drive and pull you every day after work."

"That would be awesome," I said. "I'd love that."

Jimmy was a serious barefooter in his younger days-- a big guy with the misfortune of having small feet. Despite the disadvantage he was a strong skier and he coached the previous world slalom record holder, Don Mixon, Jr., years ago. For the first time in seven years I had a coach again. Every day after work, Jimmy came out to the river and tirelessly worked with me. I felt like I had Swampy with me all over again. Jimmy gave me a kick in the butt when I needed it most; he tweaked my routine and kept me going. We skied in the rain and through endless cold evenings. I was able to focus strictly on my skiing that way.

I came to a sinking conclusion about the sport: I hated jumping. I was sick of being sore. I was sick of the mind games. I was sick of the struggle to get it right. I didn't want to jump anymore. I came up with every excuse under the sun to avoid the18-inch ramp. Every single time I zipped up my wetsuit and slapped on a helmet, the heavy blanket of dread would wash over me. The negative mind games kept playing in my head like a broken record. *Maybe I don't have what it takes to be a champion?*

Now that I had harnessed Jimmy as a coach, there was no getting out of it. I had to face the jump and figure out what was holding me back. It was good to have a coach again, to have someone do all the analyzing for me. I was slightly intimidated by Jimmy at first but he soon had me laughing. Jimmy pierced the air with his Southern accent with F-bombs every other word. The cussing took the edge off and as funny as it may sound, it relaxed me and made me laugh. There were times I couldn't believe the string of profanity he managed to sling together. "Come on, hold those arms in, you #$%&!" Jimmy hollered as he idled back toward me. "An, ya know what, I don't give a #$%& what those other #$%& think. You're going to kick their #$%&! Now get back out there and give me another #$%& jump but this time, hold on to the #$%& handle when you land."

Jimmy fired off instructions with the speed of a machine gun. *Do this. Do that. Keep your arms in before the ramp. Squeeze your shoulder blades together. Feet wide on the landings.* Jimmy got me pumped up while staying focused. On some days it worked and I rocketed off the ramp. Other days I climbed into the boat sore, tired and no better off than before.

I wanted to focus on my jumping and try to make some changes in the way I approached the ramp and flew through the air. If it weren't for Jimmy, I would not have done any jump training. I absolutely hated jumping and wanted nothing to do with the event. I feared the unknown. I did not know how to jump properly and instead of figuring it out I pushed it under the rug every time. Jimmy helped me tweak a few things here and there. I was coming off the ramp better. "Your feet are still coming together too close on the landings," he pointed out. That habit was giving me inconsistent landings. Sometimes I would go big and land them but other times I would simply crash. Most days I ended up frustrated but I held out hope I would land a big jump or two at the World Championships.

Jimmy and I headed out to the river one day and worked on fine-tuning my trick run. We were three months into the training and I was struggling with a particular trick. Climbing into the boat, I sat on the engine cover and tried to figure out what was wrong. "I need to change something," I told Jimmy. "That trick doesn't feel good to me. I'm struggling with it out there. I think I need to take it out of the run."

"No, don't do that," he said. "You've been working on it for three months and you haven't fallen on it once. Don't change it now." My gut instinct was telling me to take the trick out or take the time to figure out what was going wrong. Jimmy was right, I had not fallen on it once in three months of training, but it simply felt awkward to me. I just couldn't put my finger on the problem. My confidence level was low every time I executed the trick. Yeah, I could do the trick, but I was not comfortable with it. I ignored my gut feeling and headed out to the Worlds hoping for the best.

Gut Instincts

Over the years I learned to trust my intuition or gut feeling as most people call it. When intuition nudges me, I work on understanding why something may not feel comfortable. I always try to go with my first intuition. I have now gotten to a point where I use my intuition in my work. If I feel a skier should take a break I tell them to stop and get in the boat. I have had many skiers say, "Come on, Keith, let me take one more run!" and sure enough... they get hurt. I used to let my students ski as much as possible but now I take control and put a stop to it because I don't just sense it, I simply know!

A Heavy Lesson

I arrived in Australia a week early to compete in an Xtreme Weekend event and work in some practice time. Competing in the Xtreme event turned out to be a bad decision, the format screwed up my jumping and tricks. I didn't even place in the event. When I arrived at the Worlds, I was rattled by my poor performance in this event and wished that I hadn't competed in it.

Dad wanted to join me at the 2004 Worlds in Mulwala, Australia, but the $1,500 for the ticket was steep for him. He wasn't sure if he would be able to go, but he decided to put his intentions out to the universe and see if there was something that would come up. Sure enough, he was put in touch with Andrea Eggert, a footer who donated her frequent flier miles to him.

I was getting ready to start slaloming, but Dad hadn't arrived. I was worried, and wondered if something had happened to him. I sat in the back of a van with another barefooter, trying to get some relief from the heat and the sun beating down. Just as I got up to head to the dock, Dad came running up. "Am I too late? Did I miss the slalom event?" We hugged. It felt great to have my dad there for support. "You're not late-- I'm just about to head down to the dock for my slalom run."

As it turned out, Dad had a bit of an adventure getting to the Worlds. At the airport he was stopped and thoroughly searched, all because he had an apple in his bag. International travel strictly forbids the transport of fruit, but Dad wasn't aware of that. Once he picked up the rental car, he spent hours on the road completely lost. A patrolman pulled him over for speeding, but Dad caught a huge break and some guidance on the road. After all, he had to drive on the other side of the road, which was confusing.

During my practice runs before the start of the Worlds, the gut instinct about my trick routine reared its ugly head. I was feeling good after the first round, but during the second round of tricks things began to go downhill. I fumbled on the very trick that Jimmy and I battled over. Rattled, I struggled through the rest of the routine. Suddenly, I took a hard fall but I hung on to the handle. I was hanging on by three fingers, sliding along the water on my back and frantically trying to recover so I could finish up the run and score one more trick in time. I could feel the muscles in my forearm stretch beyond capacity as I pulled the handle in and got back up.

There was a problem after that run--I had trouble closing my fist and my grip was weak on the handle. I wasn't sure how I was going to be able to finish up my runs. I did something I had never done before in a tournament: I donned a glove on my injured hand. It was the only way to keep a grip on the handle for the rest of my runs.

The injury wasn't serious enough to hold me back but I wrote an article and sent it to my sponsor to post on his website. I included a picture of a masseuse working on me. I hoped it would throw my competition off and make them think I was not able able to ski. It turned out to be a dumb move on my part. Showing the picture only drove my competitors to ski harder.

In the middle of the tournament, I had some unfinished business to deal with and this meant finally facing a teammate. I wanted the opportunity to address my feelings about his confrontation with me at the 2002 Worlds. Even though I outwardly blew off the conversation that night, I let it fester inside of me for two years. Every now and then I would reflect back on the harsh words he hurled at me. I tried not to let it bother me, but it did. I couldn't face another World Championship without letting him know about the hurt I had been carrying inside for two years.

The U.S. team was lounging outside the hotel room one evening and my teammate happened to be sitting right across from me. I was a few beers deep and had a little liquid courage in me. It wasn't the right place, nor was it the right time, but I decided to bring it up. "Hey, do you remember what you said to me at the 2002 Worlds?" He turned to look at me. "Yes, I do." *This might be easier than I thought!* Being under the influence of alcohol was not a good thing for this kind of situation but I plunged ahead. "Did you know that you have been one of my idols for many years?" I continued.

"I guess so." He looked a bit uncomfortable and shifted in his seat. He wasn't sure where I was going with this. Fueled by the alcohol, I continued. "Didn't you find it disrespectful saying what you said to me back in 2002 at the World championship?"

"Well, Keith, I was trying to explain the difference in how I teach compared to how you teach," he explained.

"It's not about teaching styles, it's about you putting me down," I shot back. I had been holding a grudge for too long and I let loose on him. The two of us continued our exchange and it became pretty heated. The team members sat around in silence watching the two of us verbally duke it out. One of the team members walked off to find Jon, the team coach. We were still slinging sharp words when Jon stepped between us. "Zip it, you two! Come with me, I want to talk to both of you," he ordered.

We walked back to the hotel room in silence. Jon motioned us into the back of the room and slammed the door. "How can you two be arguing in front of the whole team during the World Championships--you two are supposed to be leaders!" He lit into us. The stern look on his face was almost painful to watch. "The conversation you two were having will not continue. I want the two of you to apologize to each other and get over it."

I sat there in silence as I waited for him to go first. I was ashamed to admit it, but I needed that apology even if it was a forced one. My teammate apologized and I did the same. "It was not right of me to bring it up in front of the team--it was wrong of me to do that," I admitted. "I guess two wrongs

147

do not equal a right." The two of us repaired our relationship that night and went back to being teammates again. As for me, looking back, I came to realize I had overreacted and read far more into the situation than necessary. I had missed the lesson my teammate shared with me and it took me two long years to learn it.

The situation taught me several lessons at once:

Being under the influence of alcohol will skew your judgment and thinking.

Conflicts should always be dealt with in private.

It's not healthy to let something fester over a long period of time without addressing or learning from it.

And finally...I developed and refined my own style of teaching by taking everything I learned over the years and shaping it into something that worked best for my students.

When the final round approached, I found myself in second place for the Overall. I knew I had to go all out in tricks and land a decent jump to beat David. I was pushing myself hard through the final slalom round. During my final wake crossing I felt a sense of déjà vu coming on. I caught air and slammed into the water--just as I had done at the 2002 Worlds.

At this point, I really had to scramble to catch up from being behind on the tricks. I talked with Jon and we decided to do something bold: change my entire trick routine. It was a crazy gamble, but one I had no choice to make. If I stayed with my current trick routine I wouldn't score enough to secure the Overall. I had to make a full, all-out attempt at racking up enough points to put David down a notch. I spent the rest of the night doing dry land practice and going over my new trick routine. My first pass was pretty good; I was satisfied with my results. It all came down to my final pass: if I could complete the entire run with the new trick routine, the Overall title would be mine.

I was three-fourths of the way through my tricks when I caught a foot and went tumbling down. Just like that, another Overall title went down the drain. Another World Championship completed with an unrealized dream.

I have always prided myself in being a good sport, so as soon as I was dropped off at the dock I headed straight over to David who was getting ready to ski his run. "Looks like you won. Congratulations!" I shook his hand. "Job well done."

I returned home in a depressed state. For the third time in six years, I came in second place at the World Championship. I began to question my skills, my commitment, and my passion for the sport. David was six years younger than me and he was blazing his way through the ranks. He was ranked number one and I was ranked third. At the Nationals that summer, he jumped his way to another World record with a jump of 89.9 feet.

I dreaded seeing Jimmy. I knew he would be disappointed after all the time he put into my training. Sure enough, he let me have it. "Damn it, Keith, all that time we put into this and you let the others mess with your head! You never should have put that picture of you getting injured on the Internet. That just showed your competitors you were hurt. If I were out there with you, I wouldn't let anyone get close to you or talk to you. They only get into your head and get in the way!"

I thought of Patrick's card: *If you can imagine it, you can achieve it. If you can dream it, you can become it.* I had come all this way in my career--just to go down in my own sinking ship. The feelings I had made me feel lost in what I was doing, lost in Florida, lost in my tiny ski school, and lost in completing the only dream I had. Shoot, I was favored to win four years prior to this. I knew it would only get harder with many younger skiers coming up the ranks. It was beginning to look like I might never achieve the World Champion status I dreamed of.

Ditching a Bad Habit

Looking back, there was one bright accomplishment that year: I finally gave up chewing tobacco. For a year and half I tried willing myself into giving it up, but I never felt ready or strong enough to stick with the idea. I couldn't push myself to stay away from it. In the middle of a clinic in Texas, I scraped the last bits of tobacco from a tin. I didn't want to ask anyone to bring me to town just to buy more because that would be embarrassing. Once I thought of that scenario, I realized chewing tobacco was pretty stupid.

149

Well, I wanted to quit for a while now--might as well be today.

It was grueling trying to fight the urge to put tobacco in my mouth. I was stuck in the boat for hours and there was nothing I could do to battle the cravings. I was so used to the habit of having something in my mouth. I brought along mints and sunflower seeds to keep my mouth active and to keep my mind off the gnawing desire for chewing tobacco. I thought about tobacco for every second of every minute that went by that week. It was a constant battle dealing with the temptation to take up the habit again.

Quitting the tobacco habit was one of the hardest challenges for me to overcome. The craving was so intense and I fought the urge to "pick up one more can" on a daily basis. I knew if I gave in just once, I would never conquer the habit. When I arrived home, I stocked up on bags and bags of sunflower seeds and brought them with me everywhere. Cracking open the shells and spitting them out kept me occupied. I littered quite a few lakes with empty shells that summer.

Habits

When I look back, I realize how much of my life revolved around this bad habit. I allowed others to influence me because I wanted to fit in and be accepted. I should have done what I knew was right. My Pastor said it best, "Do what your heart knows is right."

Influence can be a good thing, especially when you choose to surround yourself with those who influence you in the direction of success toward your dreams. Be yourself--be the better person you know you can be. Challenge yourself!

When something feels wrong deep down inside of you, it's time to sit back and rethink your situation before going forward. Often, we have options and the more options you place in front of you, the easier the decision-making can be.

The Low Point

I moved into yet another crappy rental house in yet another area I wasn't happy with. I had few options at that point in my life so I settled for it. Swampy moved in with me and he began working as a courier for a car parts company. The ski school slowed down for the fall and I found myself with time on my hands. Swampy and I didn't talk much about barefooting at that point. We were two depressed guys just going through the motions each day. "I need to train you and get your butt going," Swampy said. I just shrugged. "I'm not gonna work my butt off trying to be the best," I retorted. "This sport doesn't pay. I'm not making much money from the sport and the ski school barely pays the bills."

Swampy tried to snap me out of it. "You are a professional athlete and you must give it your all and act the part if you are going to keep on barefoot skiing!" he said with a loud voice. "You're throwing your career away with all the partying. The window of opportunity is closing. When the window is shut—that's it--you're done. You will never get that again! You will have lost your potential. You have the opportunity to be the greatest skier ever. Don't throw that away."

It was hard taking advice from him. He had lost everything and was in no position to lecture me with optimism. I took advice from Swampy for years, but why should I listen now? He was depressed and miserable, so how could I take advice from a man in his position. We were simply not the same team we had once been.

> Never be afraid to ask someone's opinion...you do not have to do what they say but take in the knowledge. Use what you think will benefit you and leave what you do not need.
>
> ~Keith St. Onge

"Who is going to train me?" I grumbled. "You work full time and I can't slalom behind the boat I have, so there is no point! I'm not going anywhere with this!" I was slinging out excuses but I didn't care. Swampy put his head down and for a second I realized I was tearing his heart out. All the years of work we had put in—and here I was tossing it away by whining. Swampy had steered me in the right direction for so many years but at that point I just wasn't ready to listen.

151

"I don't get paid the millions like other pro athletes so why should I put all my energy into it!" I continued to rant. Deep down, I knew I didn't want to give up the sport but I was at a point where I felt I either had to give 100 percent of my energy toward it...or nothing. I had no energy left. For six years, I aimed for the goal of winning the one thing I wanted: a World Championship title. I couldn't achieve it. How much more did I have inside of me to keep working at it? Was the price too heavy? Was the reward too little?

Maybe my competitor was right after all... Maybe I should have gone to college and earned a degree as a backup plan.

It was a tough time for both of us. Swampy wasn't comfortable living in Florida. I wasn't happy living in Tampa. We were two individuals just barely making it through life. The only reason we both had a roof over our heads was from all the hard work we did training together for years before. I was a National Champion and the title carried enough clout to keep a few students coming to the ski school and just barely enough money to pay rent. Swampy wasn't earning enough money to pay me his portion of rent so I let it slide. After all, he had given so much of his own time and money when I was younger and it was time to do the same for him. I felt good being able to help Swamp when he needed it most, but it was a difficult time for both of us.

Swampy and I were often open with one another but during this time together there were some things we left unsaid. In the past, we used to talk openly about our feelings but I sensed something had shifted this time around. Living the normal, everyday life with each other was fine, but there was an unspoken tension around our unhappiness. We were both foul at the world and the situation we were in. Our position in life was not where we expected it to be and this was not the outcome we planned years ago. Money was tight for both of us and this created some unease. Towards the end of the one-year contract on my rental I knew I needed to move on without him. I did not have to tell Swampy my plans because we both came to an understanding: it was time to part ways.

I was at the point in my life where I was ready to buy a house. It would be a great investment for me and also for the future of the ski school. I made up my mind--I was going to find a fixer-upper on the water and move the ski school there. I did not invite Swampy to come live with me and I assumed he was fine with it. He was also ready for a change and moved near his sister in Alaska.

One evening, I was lamenting to a friend about the extra pounds I was carrying and I mentioned I needed to become more serious about a fitness regimen. "Why don't you come to a kickboxing class with me?" my friend suggested. Kickboxing sounded masculine enough and I needed a regular workout that didn't involve water sports. As soon as we walked into the class I discovered it was 90 percent female. That was more than all right by me! Kickboxing proved to be the perfect workout for me. My shoulders loosened up and I enjoyed the quick movements. After sitting in the boat all day, sometimes with challenging customers, I looked forward to working out and punching the bags. It took me two months to be able to complete the one-hour class without stopping to catch my breath--and that was a reality check.

There was one floor exercise that was tough for me to complete at the end of every class: it was an exercise I dubbed "Fire Hydrants." Picture a dog decorating a fire hydrant. Now picture yourself on your hands and knees, raising your bent leg at a 90-degree angle. That exercise was a killer for me. The females in the class loved this exercise--it supposedly produced shapely butt--but I didn't have much use for a butt-shaping exercise! I would do a few reps and quit right away. It was a little embarrassing to watch the gals complete the exercise with ease. Obviously my back and leg muscles were screaming because they were weak from under use. After a few months I began to take the exercise seriously. I found the more I pushed through the pain and increased the movement the easier it became to lift my legs over time. This exercise truly helped my lower back and hip flexors. I have used the same muscles for so many years that working the opposite muscles was the key to balancing my body. Kickboxing was the best thing for me.

As for the females in my life, I dated a few girls here and there but the relationships were never serious enough to consider a lifelong partnership.

The Alligator Encounter

During my daily lessons with students, I noticed a guy swimming near shore. *That's crazy, there are alligators in the lake!* I idled near him. "You ok out there?" I hollered.

"I'm fine! Just going for a swim!" he said. I was flabbergasted and a bit puzzled at his bravado. The alligators in the lake didn't daunt him. As for me, I couldn't imagine swimming among them. Every day, I watched the guy as he casually swam outside the swamp areas. I couldn't figure it out-- how was he able to swim among the gators without being attacked?

One day, I walked over just before he was about to enter the water. "Hey buddy, I've been watching you swim--are you crazy? How it is that the alligators don't get to you?" He laughed. "I've got a trick I use," he explained. "Before I walk in, I look around for alligators. If I see one, I walk toward it. Then I walk into waist-deep water and go underwater for about ten seconds. The alligator views me as a predator and takes off."

I shook my head. "That's really wild!"

"I had a close encounter once, though, years ago," he continued. "I wasn't looking carefully enough that day and missed an alligator nearby. It must have gone under the water before I could notice him. As I waded in the water I brushed the side of the gator and it turned on me. It hit me with his mouth open. It didn't full-out attack me. The gator was probably just scared, but it left me with a few broken ribs and some puncture wounds."

A few months later I was floating in the water after a practice run and I noticed an alligator near shore. The six-foot beast eyed me lazily. I figured I'd have some fun and test out that little trick. Letting go of the rope, I slid underwater and counted to ten. Everyone in the boat had heard about my neighbor's little trick, so they knew why I disappeared under the water, but from their vantage point they couldn't see the alligator. I popped to the surface and scoured the shore.

At first, I couldn't see the gator. The thing had disappeared. Then, I froze. I locked eyes with a very angry reptile. Instead of scurrying away from me, the alligator was slithering right toward me.

"Go, go, GO!" I screamed. I grabbed the rope. The handle was still a few feet behind me. I heard the boat crew laughing. The alligator was moving faster. "It's a gator! Damn it, go!!" A helpless feeling washed over me. As soon as I felt the handle, I held on tight. The crew finally noticed the gator swimming toward me and the boat took off. I wasn't going to let go of the handle because my life depended on it!

I later learned why that trick didn't work. First, it was mating season and the gator may have been a female protecting her eggs. Secondly, I had blocked the alligator from accessing the open water. His natural response was to see me as a threat and it had nowhere to go. Needless to say, I never taunted another alligator again.

Career Growth

My business relationship with my barefoot sponsor started to grow that summer. We began getting to know each other and sharing ideas about how to expand the sport. One of our best ideas was to create barefooting videos that we could upload to the website. My sponsor filmed and edited the videos. He had a very creative side to him and it showed in our videos. For the first time in my career, all of my tricks were captured on video and the ability to show them on the web exposed me to a larger audience around the world. Skiers from everywhere were using the videos to teach themselves tricks. There were very few barefooting videos on the Internet so my videos quickly became popular. I was helping my sponsor's business and he was helping me gain exposure. It was a win-win situation for both of us.

One of the most popular videos circulating among the barefooting community was titled, "All My Life," set to the same song by Foo Fighters. At one of my clinics, the wife of a barefooter came up to me. "Are you that Keith guy in the video?" she asked. I laughed. "Yeah."

"I'm so sick of hearing that same damn song while my husband plays your video over and over," she said. I laughed again. "Sorry!"

One day I stopped in at a competitor's ski school for a photo shoot and I heard the familiar beginning chords of the "All My Life" song. I walked over toward the office and craned my neck to see who was viewing the video. One of the workers was parked in front of the computer watching my turns, toe holds, and jumps--and he was nodding along to the music. I couldn't help it--I threw my head back and laughed as I walked into the office. "Hey, buddy, I see you're watching my video!"

"I watch this thing ten times every day!" He looked at me with a sheepish grin. "I love it!"

Chapter 15: The Turn Around

Keep working hard and you can get anything you want. If God gave you the talent, you should go for it. But don't think it's going to be easy. It's hard!

~Aaliyah quotes

It was getting to the point in my career where many barefoot water skiers knew my name, but I wanted to find a way to gain more media exposure. I was doing more photo shoots with WaterSki and Water Skier magazines and my goal was to get on the cover of one of the magazines. I had six National titles but continually took runner up at the last three World Championships—I wasn't sure if it was enough to deserve a cover shot. I networked with Todd Ristorcelli from WaterSki magazine and he invited me out to his lake house for a photo shoot.

"What will it take to get a cover shot?" I asked. He told me what he was looking for and I spent three hours doing all sorts of poses and tricks. During the last hour, he wanted me to jump off the water and do some sort of snow skiing move. I was so worn out I could hardly get into the boat when we finally called it quits. "I think we may have a cover shot," said Todd.

I was so excited and when I left, I wanted to tell everyone but I kept quiet. During the fall, I got the call from Todd. "You'll be on the cover of Waterski magazine next month," he said. I just about fell off my chair and thanked him a million times.

A month later, I opened the mailbox and there was a shot of me suspended above the water, *on the cover!* I could hardly believe it. Another dream fulfilled! I ripped the cover off and put it into a frame. I didn't care what was in the rest of the magazine--I just wanted the cover! I ordered several more copies and told everyone I knew. Friends and relatives were calling to tell me they saw the magazine on newsstands at the airport and in bookstores. Business at the ski school was still slow and the cover shot kept the trickle of students coming. I was barely staying afloat financially, but I continued reaching my goals on the water.

A Place Called Home

I met up with some friends one day and we went skiing on a lake in Winter Haven that I had never seen before. I was amazed at this lake--there was a strong wind blowing out of the north yet the water was smooth. There were no other boats on the lake which meant no rollers or waves to deal with. "What's the name of this lake?" I asked the guys.

"This is Lake Rochelle. There's another ski school which comes here once in a great while but only when running three boats in the spring," they explained. "This lake is connected to several other lakes via a series of channels. You can always find calm water here."

We went through a canal to Lake Haines and found more of the same calm water. For the last several months, I entertained the idea of buying a house in hopes of opening a pro shop. I had to get serious about the ski school business and take it to the next level if I was going to be able to continue in the sport. I was planning to look for a house in Tampa but after skiing on the lake in Winter Haven I wanted to rethink my plan. I had been back and forth on purchasing the house I rented on the river in Tampa but that looked like a dead end road. Other houses in the Tampa area were too expensive on the river and in some areas, the neighborhood was not desirable.

I bought a map of Winter Haven and studied the lakes. During the next several months, I explored the lakes with my boat observing the wind and the water conditions on each lake. I looked at the shorelines of each lake and the houses that surrounded them. On the days I didn't have students, I explored the neighborhoods. With 554 lakes in the county, I put a lot of miles on the truck!

There was one neighborhood I continually drove through and the more I saw it, the more my intuition kicked in. The neighborhood had two lakes on either side. The subdivision only had one street that entered it from the main road, which looped back around. There was very little traffic and the homes were older. Large oak trees lined the road with Spanish moss hanging from the limbs. It's what they called "Old Florida" and it was beautiful and spooky-looking at the same time. I was pretty confident I could afford to purchase a house if one came up for sale.

Every time I drove through the community, I'd pray to see a "For Sale" sign being displayed on someone's lawn. At the dead end street, I often pulled into one driveway to turn around. The yard was overgrown and unkempt. Several orange trees lining the driveway were overflowing with unpicked fruit.

"I bet there's an old guy who can't handle the upkeep anymore," I said to a friend one day. "I should knock on his door and ask him if he'll sell the house to me." I couldn't quite summon the courage to do it though.

For the next three months, I kept driving by the same neighborhood, turning into the same driveway, and hoping for a "For Sale" sign. A cousin came to visit for a long weekend and I showed him around the area and the house as well. My dad took a tour with me one day when he was visiting. "This house would be perfect," I told him. "It's on three-fourths of an acre, sits between two lakes, and it's next to a canal that connects the two lakes. Plus, it's water-front property!"

It was mid-day when a friend and I were driving yet again through the same neighborhood. As we drove by the house, I said it again, "One of these days, I'm going to knock on the door..." We drove off and were a few miles away when my friend looked at me in exasperation. "I'm sick of hearing you talk about that house. Turn around and let's go back. I'll knock on the door for you."

"Really? Are you serious?" I swung the truck around and we headed back. I drove down the driveway further than I ever had before and put the truck in park. "Ok, go do it!"

My friend hesitated. "I was only kidding. I didn't think you'd actually drive back here!"

"Oh come on! I've been driving around here for three months and I've turned around in this driveway so many times--I'll do it!" I got out, walked up to the front door and knocked. Just as I expected, an old man appeared at the door.

"Hi there!" I smiled. "I've been looking for a house on this lake. Are you interested in selling your house?"

He looked me over. "I was actually going to put it on the market next week but I don't want to deal with a realtor."

I was floored. "Really? I don't want to deal with a realtor either! How much do you want for your house?" I asked. I knew the market was hot in the area--lakefront homes were going quickly and often ended up in bidding wars. I could only afford a certain amount and there was no way I could do a bidding war with my limited budget. He named his price and it was within my budget. My heart was skipping several beats. I tried to remain cool. "I'll buy it," I said. I accepted his price and I hadn't even stepped inside the house. I knew this was the right house to buy and the price he gave me was low enough--there was no need for negotiating.

"We've got company right now and the house isn't cleaned up," he said. "We're going out of town. Come back in two weeks..." He paused a minute to calculate dates. "Which makes that Labor Day...and bring a down payment. We can sign a contract then." We shook hands. The whole discussion took just a few minutes. I hopped back in the truck with a huge smile on my face. "I bought the house!" I tried not to scream until I was well away from the house and I let it out. "Whoohoooo! I got it for a great price! I can't believe how quickly the whole thing fell into place. He could have gotten thousands more for this!"

The two weeks crawled by as I impatiently waited for the day I could take a look at the inside of the house. The day before I was scheduled to see the house, the phone rang. It was the guy's wife. "How interested are you in the house?" she asked.

"I'm one-hundred percent interested," I replied. "I'll be stopping by tomorrow to look at it and write up the contract."

"Are you really sure you want it?"

"Yes, I do. Is there a problem?" I gripped the phone tighter. I could feel the hair rise up on my neck. I wasn't sure what was going on.

"There's a guy in my front yard and he is holding a check for a deposit," she explained.

"What--what are you talking about--your husband agreed to sell it to me!" I tried not to yell. "I'll come over right now and give you a deposit. How much do you need?"

When she told me the amount I nearly fell over. I wasn't sure I could scrape together that amount. *I want this house so badly.* I mentally calculated the cash I had on hand and what I had in savings. "Hold a minute, please." I turned to a friend sitting nearby. "How much cash can I borrow from you?" The amount was enough to proceed.

I got back on the phone. "I can bring you cash and the remainder will be a check, but it won't be the amount you're asking. I can only do half of that right now and I can be there in thirty minutes." It was nearly an hour's drive. I thought my heart was going to pound right out of my chest. I wanted the house. I didn't care what it looked like on the inside. I knew it needed work, but it was a great location for the ski school and my intuition told me it was the right thing to do.

The woman continued to hassle me a bit about the deposit but she finally agreed on the amount. I grabbed the checkbook and made a beeline for the truck. I barreled down the highway well over the speed limit, praying there were no cops on the road. Ten minutes into the drive, the phone rang again. It was the same lady.

"This man is still here and he really wants the house. He has a nice family, they really need a place to live, and they seem like such nice people." This unknown guy with a family was taking the house away from me! I wasn't sure what I was going to do if he was actually standing in the yard when I arrived. For all I knew, she could have been stringing me along. The housing market had almost been at an all time high and many people had bidding wars against each other. I knew I was getting a once-in-a-lifetime deal on this property! The old man let it go for thousands less than what he could have gotten in this market.

I stepped on the gas and the speedometer hit 90. "I will be there in a few minutes and I want to buy the house. I promise you, I will be right there. Please...hang tight?"

I screeched into the driveway and I looked around. There was no one standing outside. The blinds were closed. I walked through the tunnel of overhanging oaks that led up to the door. Elmore, the owner, met me at the door. "Come on inside," he motioned. I stepped in and was engulfed in the odor of carpet that had seen too many days and too many pets. The interior was dark and it took a few moments for my eyes to adjust. I had a disturbing thought: *This would be a perfect place for someone to be tied up and held hostage--no one would know!*

Elmore drew up a contract and asked me how much money I had brought with me. "I don't have as much as you wanted, but I'm only a few thousand off. Thanks for not selling it to the other guy." Elmore looked at me with a bit of a perplexed look. "Why do you think we would have sold it to him?"

"Well, your wife called and asked if I was still interested in the house and..." I cut myself off as I glanced at his wife. I had the feeling that Elmore was not aware of his wife's dealings. Perhaps the other guy hadn't really shown up after all. Elmore stepped in closer to me. I caught a hint of breath sorely in need of a mint, but I didn't care. His deep blue eyes met mine. "You and I made a deal," he said. His voice was humble and confident. "Of course I would not have sold the house to anyone else...we shook on it."

For the first time since the whole deal began, I let out a sigh of relief. "Thank you! I wish everyone was as trusting--like it used to be." My small town, New Hampshire roots were showing. He laughed. "When I shake someone's hand, I keep my word."

As I walked back to the truck I was on an incredible high. The house needed a lot of work, but I wasn't afraid of the work ahead. *This is my future*, I thought. *This is where the ski school will be located for years to come! How perfect this is!*

Little did I know that buying the house was the easy part--getting a mortgage was a whole other ballgame. I was extremely naive about the house buying process and just assumed I would be able to go to the bank and borrow the money. The very next day, I had to leave to teach a clinic and I was going to be on the road the rest of the summer. I underestimated the vast amount of paperwork that was needed to obtain a mortgage, especially while being away from my files. I flew home from the clinic the day before Nationals and finally signed the mortgage contract. It was then I noticed Elmore's real name: Claude. It was my dad's name and my middle name as well. I also noticed the address, 3915. My parent's home address was 39. I took it as a sign: the house was definitely meant to be mine.

The Turnaround

I was out of sorts when I arrived in Austin for the Nationals because my mind was on the many things I would have to do in the house. A mortgage was a new responsibility for me so I wasn't as focused on the tournament as I should have been. This was the final tournament for Ron Scarpa. He made it clear he was retiring from the sport and wasn't going to compete anymore. He hadn't skied in the previous Nationals so he planned to go out with a bang in the Austin tournament.

I skied at my normal slalom pace behind the boat but I found the wake difficult to feel. The tournament boat was one I had not trained on and it had a horrible wake. The judges did not credit a number of my wake crossings and I ended up with a very low score. I was not happy about skiing behind that boat. I grumbled inwardly, but there was nothing I could do about it. Ron and I faced off on the tricks and the competition was close--he took the lead.

Another competitor and I faced off on the jumping and I took the lead. On his third jump, he landed and skied away but the distance wasn't enough to beat me. I started to celebrate my win.

My celebration was cut short as I watched my competitor request a re-ride. He told the boat crew the driving was not correct. He went up for another jump but didn't land it. The skier continued to ask and was granted re-rides after every jump, for a total of four re-rides. I sat on the bank watching the whole thing unfold. "I can't believe he's getting all of those re-rides," I fumed to another barefooter. "Are they really going to let him jump until he beats me or what?" It is one thing for judges to grant a re-ride without a skier asking for it but to grant four re-rides due to a skier's request--that's a whole other ballgame. On the fourth and final jump the skier gained enough distance to take the lead away from me. I ended the tournament in a foul mood.

The Nationals was a nice parting gift for Ron as he walked away with the Overall trophy and ended his career with a bang. I went and got nicely drunk at the banquet. It was the last time I would drink for a year. When I left Austin, Texas, I knew I was going to make some major life changes. After losing three Worlds in a row as runner up and now losing a National championship, it was time for some serious soul searching. I did not want to end my career without achieving my dream. All the hard work, all the years of training, all the time spent on the water--I wanted something to show for it. From the time I was thirteen, I wanted to be the best; I wanted to be the World Champion. "I'm going to be *the* best," I told my mom as a teen. As a naive thirteen-year-old I set goals for myself whether I knew they were realistic or not. The goals gave me something to strive for.

I had been floundering for so many years, coming close each time but always walking away with second place. Second place Overall at the last three World Championships was a record--and not the one I wanted! I was tired of second place. It was time to make some changes to get to first.

There's a tradition in the National Hockey League where players grow a "playoff beard" for good luck when their team enters the playoffs. I was from a hockey town; my dad and all his brothers played hockey. My dad was captain of his team during his last two years in high school. His twin brother, Andy, and his younger brother, Ray, played on the same line and they went on to win the state championship one year. I played hockey when I was very young and I told my dad I didn't enjoy it. He pulled me out of the league but I continued to skate for fun. I enjoyed skating and was pretty agile on the ice. I went ice-skating every Friday night with my friends and played pond hockey once in a while. I was often asked, "Why didn't you play hockey seriously? Your dad was amazing at it!" All I could come up with was, "I'm just like my dad, I play a sport on the ice...it's just melted!" I think skating gave me great balance and prepared me for barefoot water skiing. After all, the two sports are very similar: you can't lean forward onto your toes and you can't lean back. In both sports you must stay centered directly over the center of your feet.

So it was at that point in my life the turnaround began. It was playoff time. For one year I was going to let my facial hair grow out. For one year I was going to make changes in my life and go "all out."

My sponsor sent me an email which changed my life and taught me an important skill. "Here's something I want you to think about," he wrote. "Sit down some day and write what your goals are from a business, competitive, and personal standpoint." He gave me an example:

My #1 goal is to win a 2006 World Overall Title. In order to assure that, I will spend at least three hours per day on the water, focusing on my personal performance. I will stick to a very rigid diet and training program. Business growth will not be a focus in 2006, but I feel securing a World Title will result in a 30-40% growth in 2007.

If you're going to focus on business growth you should prepare a mission statement that shows what Gliding Soles stands for and your goals for the business. He encouraged me to explore myself more. Write down the answer to these questions: When people are asked to describe

164

Keith St. Onge, I want them to say _____. When my close friends and family are asked to describe Keith St. Onge, I want them to say _____. Are they two different answers?

There was more:

Write down the things you must do personally and professionally to make it happen the way you envision it. Do all of this and you'll have a quick snapshot of what Keith St. Onge is all about. By sticking to your principles, goals and beliefs; the decisions you make and the opinions you give verbally or in writing, will reflect those values and carry more weight.

> To achieve any goal in life, dream about it, think about it, picture it, and write it down.
>
> ~Keith St. Onge

For the first time in my life, I sat down and put my goals in writing. For years, Swampy was the one who wrote down our goals and now it was my turn.

I knew the drinking had to stop. For the next twelve months, I vowed not to touch a drop of alcohol. It was going to be a tough commitment because I spent so much of my life partying with the guys and now I would have to resist chugging down a beer. I also committed to changing my diet and eating healthier foods. This meant saying goodbye to Mountain Dew--and I lived on that for years. I set a goal to work out on the water at least four to five times a week, one to two hours per day. I kicked the jumping up a notch, adding practice jumps three to five times a week. After being in the boat all day with students, it took some effort to make myself get out on the water with intensity and get the practice time in.

Another goal was to become comfortable and confident with every trick run and jump. No more going into a competition wondering if I could make it through an entire run--I wanted to go into the next Worlds knowing exactly what I was capable of doing on the water. I knew if I could ramp up my effort and concentration I could take my skiing to the next level. I wanted to shift my mindset and approach the sport like a true job with rules and guidelines in place for me to follow.

I wrote out my goals in explicit detail, filling an entire page with my plan for the upcoming months. *I will win the World Overall Title following this vision*, I wrote. I signed my name with a flourish on the bottom of the page. It was November 25, 2005.

I flew home for Christmas and my parents met us at the airport. I hugged them tightly--our visits were few and far between. I missed spending time with them. It was late at night so I hopped in the driver's seat of the Ford Explorer. I wanted to give them a break from driving. My parents settled in the back. Unbeknownst to me, both of them left their seat belts off. We were deep in conversation and about twenty miles into our trip when I glanced in the rear view mirror. A pair of headlights came around the corner behind me quickly, barreling straight for us. There was no way to avoid the speeding lights coming directly at us.

"We're gonna get hit!" As soon as the words were out of my mouth, the car slammed into the back fender. I was pushed deep into my seat with no control over the vehicle. We spun around almost in slow motion as I yelled "NOOOOO!" I feared we were going to go over an embankment that dropped off into the darkness. We slammed into the right guardrail and spun toward the opposite guardrail. We bounced off and continued spinning into the other guardrail once again. Six hundred feet later, we spun a final time and came to rest in the opposite lane of the highway. I could hear my dad in the back. "Stay calm, Stay calm." He had his hand on my mom's arm.

"Is everyone ok?" I asked. For the most part, upon initial inspection, we seemed to be all right. My back ached, but I was otherwise fine. I took worse barefoot skiing falls than what we just experienced. My dad was sporting a bruise on his head and my mom had whiplash.

A cold chill came over us as the temperature outside was nearly twenty-eight degrees. We got out and I walked over to the other car. The nineteen-year-old driver was obviously drunk. "I'm so sorry," he slurred. "I'm so, so sorry!" Several state troopers pulled up and an ambulance arrived. We declined the offer to take us to the hospital after the initial examination. Our injuries seemed minor at the time and I think we were in a state of shock. The tow truck driver dropped us off at a nearby hotel. The next morning, Dad and I walked a mile to the nearest rental car company. As he bent to sign the papers, Dad realized his reading glasses were missing. "They must have flown off during the accident," he said.

I signed the papers for him and we left to pick up my mom. "Let's go back to the accident scene," Dad suggested as we left the hotel. "I want to see it in the daylight." We drove back to the highway and pulled over to the shoulder. The skid marks were obvious and showed the path of the accident. "I'm thankful it

166

wasn't much worse," said Dad. "It's a blessing nothing happened to us and no one was killed. We've got spirits above looking out for us." We walked along the shoulder back to the car when Dad spied his glasses up ahead. He jogged over to pick them up. "I can't believe it, my glasses are intact!" He held them up. "They've got a few scratches on them but I can still use them!"

The other driver didn't have insurance and my parents were called to court when the state decided to press charges. The young man received a dishonorable discharge from the military as a result of his actions and he was required to pay restitution for the accident. My dad wanted an opportunity to sit down with the driver and encourage him to learn from it but the attorneys would not allow it.

Eventually we received a copy of the accident report showing the driver was going approximately one hundred and twenty miles per hour on impact. Angels were indeed looking over us.

A Tough, New Coach

Eugene Sam had a reputation for being a tough, disciplined coach with a new style of teaching and I wanted a piece of it. I met Eugene and his son, Heinrich, at their first Jr. World Championship when I coached the U.S. Junior Team in New Zealand back in 2003. Heinrich was a young, enthusiastic skier. I gave him my rope and handle at the end of the tournament since I knew they could not afford a new one. The South African Rand currency was at an all time low. One U.S. dollar equaled sixteen Rand. Heinrich and his dad were extremely grateful and we remained good friends.

I decided to fly down to South Africa to train with him and Heinrich for three and a half weeks. Heinrich was poised to become the next World champion and Eugene's teaching style was reputed to produce results on the water. I was serious about training in preparation for the World championships and flying to the other side of the world proved it. "I'm open to what you have to teach me," I told him when I arrived. "I just want results. I want to learn as much as possible on the water." I was the oldest "kid" there and Eugene ran me as if I were a teenager.

Picture two parents: if one says yes to everything the kid never learns to respect the parent or to respect himself. The other parent is the strict one, the one who explains the rules, the reasons why, and dishes out punishment. Most kids are responsive to the parent that clearly outlines the expectations and discipline. Eugene was like that second parent--the kids in the boat couldn't get away with anything. His monstrous size had something to do with that: six feet tall with massive arms, a broad chest, and a low, deep voice that commanded attention. He was tough on the water but the kids loved him and respected him. Once a kid realized he could accomplish a trick under Eugene's instruction they learned to look up to him and follow his teachings. Eugene pulled the best out of young skiers.

Eugene was hard on me just like Swampy used to be and I liked that. I needed it at that point. He motivated me, he kicked my butt, and he pushed me to the edge of what I could do. I had struggled with one trick for so many years: the one-foot 180. I had no consistency with that trick. I fell so many times over the years and I dreaded doing this turn.

"All right, Keith, for this trick, I want you to move your ankle up near your knee when you start your turn," Eugene commanded. I hesitated. The technique was a much different position than what I was used to doing. "I'm not sure about that, Eugene. That position feels much too awkward. I'm not sure I want to do it like that."

"Shut up, get in the water and try it," he barked.

Jeez. I jumped in the water. Just as I anticipated, the whole thing was very foreign at first and the position didn't feel right. Eugene kept yelling, "Pull the ankle up higher and bring the knee back!" I worked at it with discomfort. But the more I worked at it, the better it began to feel. The result I was looking for finally materialized: I was able to complete the turns smoothly with amazing consistency. I was thankful that Eugene pushed me when he did. I was absolutely reluctant at first, but I did not buck the system. I was willing to give it a go. I actually teach my students that trick the same way he taught me and it produces clean results on the water.

> ## Stay Open to New Ideas
>
> The new style was extremely uncomfortable to me, but because I remained open to trying it, I found consistency in that trick for the first time in my life.
>
> Keep your mind wide open to new ideas even if they seem uncomfortable at first. New ideas can lead to new experiences that will open doors to you in life. Put people on your life team who will push you in new directions.

During practice runs I was slaloming past the world record. When we took off for a local tournament, I was determined to set a new record in wake slalom. I accomplished it! My slalom record of 20.6 still stands today.

The jump training was another story. My back was sore from the accident and the constant jumping made it much worse. My 28-year-old body was screaming in my attempts to keep up with the teenagers training with me. I was aiming for distance and consistent landings but nothing was working. After each jump, I kept plugging away but there were no "aha" moments, nor a sense of "Hey, that worked." There were some sets where we would do fifteen jumps in a row instead of the normal three or four jumps. During the last several days of training I was reaching the breaking point with my back. At one point, I lay in the water waiting for the boat to idle back to me and I was writhing in pain. "My back hurts like hell," I moaned.

"You wuss! Get back out there, you little baby," Eugene shot back. "A little pain won't kill you."

I wanted to win the Worlds, and I didn't want to give up, so I got back out there and grimly completed jump after jump. I was willing to do whatever it took. With every jump, I had David Small on my mind. I wanted to take him down and move him out of my way. He was the only thing keeping me from my dream of becoming the World Champion. Two days later, I had enough. I could not keep going. I grimaced in pain as I hauled myself in the boat and sat down with a heavy sigh. "This isn't working, Eugene. I can't take any more jumps. I need a day off. I've accomplished nothing with my jumping. I'm just done."

For the next three days, we explored South Africa and went on a safari ride. I looked at my back pain as a blessing for I was able to stop and enjoy the country. I had no idea the pain would turn out to be even more of a blessing and later lead me to a woman who would change my life.

When I returned from South Africa I was still looking for the magic "key" that would correct my jumping. I turned to another competitor who was one of the best jumpers at that time. He had a style all his own and I hoped by adopting a different style I could rack up more distance and consistency. He came to my lake and pulled me through two jump sets and quietly observed my mangled landings.

"Keith, you've got to work on landing on your feet and not your rear end," he said. "You need to land more upright." For years, I would lean back during the landing, bounce on my butt, and if I was lucky, I could get up and ski away. He worked with me on the training boom off the side of the boat, churning out advice after each jump. To my surprise, I was landing the jumps much better by the end of our session. Unfortunately, I couldn't transfer his advice behind the boat where I continued to struggle. I understood his advice and I tried to follow it, but I continually allowed the bad habits I built over several years to take over.

By spring, business was starting to boom. I turned an old boat storage building into a pro shop and stocked it with wetsuits and my sponsor's apparel. Judy and her husband, Casey came to work for me. For years, we joked about her working for me and we got along so well. When I finally needed help, I went straight to Judy for advice and asked her to come and work for me. From the beginning she was committed to seeing me grow. The two of them were an incredible blessing to my business because teaming up with them meant I could focus on the students. Judy handled the business calls, paperwork, and the student schedules. Casey took care of things around the house. For once, the business began to run on a smooth and professional course.

Close Calls

Whenever I teach a clinic, my students often want to see me ski on the water. If there's time and the conditions are good, I will usually jump into a wetsuit and get a little workout on the water. It's good for business and it's good for me. At least it's good *most* of the time.

170

During one clinic, I decided to do some barefooting to show the students a backward technique for crossing the wake. "I'm going to be skiing backwards so be sure to go to the far left side of the bridge ahead," I warned the driver. We skied between the pillars of the massive bridge as they were wide on the left and narrow any other direction. I was powering across the wakes aiming for perfect technique so the students could see my position at each cut across the wake. Like Braille, I was feeling my way back and forth across the wakes skiing backwards. I'd lift one foot up, cross over, shift to the other foot, and then repeat in the other direction. Just as I shifted my weight to cut in the other direction I came within a few feet of the concrete pillar of the bridge.

I nearly crapped in my wetsuit. Seeing a massive concrete pillar fly by me was frightening! Just a few more feet or a nano-second later, I would have either landed in the hospital...or wound up dead.

I climbed in the boat and let the driver have it with a few choice words thrown in. "You don't ever drive that close to anything! I told you to go on the left side, you didn't!" I felt bad for piping up, but my heart was pounding and my emotions were running wild.

During a clinic in Georgia, I wanted to grab some wake slalom practice for the Worlds during a break from instructing students. So when I noticed a metal raft from a dredging barge nearby I pointed it out to the driver and warned him to stay away from it. He confirmed he understood what I said.

Behind the boat, I dug in with each foot and zipped back and forth across the wake pushing for speed. Suddenly out of the corner of my eye I saw the metal raft. Except this time, the raft was literally *two feet* from me when I whipped by. But this time, I didn't yell. "Do you realize what you just did? I could have died," I said quietly. There would be no more practice for me that day.

Risk/Benefit Ratios

The last incident was a turnaround for me. I had to start weighing the pros and cons of every situation before putting myself in positions of trust with drivers I didn't know. My customers want to see me ski and they often request it. It's part of my job, to keep my customers happy and entertained as they learn. But as I've gotten older I've learned to take fewer risks. Ten years ago I would have jumped at any stunt in any situation. As I've matured, I've learned to look at the pros and cons, weigh the ratios, and make decisions based on that.

Even in my best pro/con situations, unexpected things happen. In one instance, I was skiing on the side of the boat on the boom, I let go to glide away on my padded suit and the driver, without thinking clearly, turned the boat right toward me and nearly ran me over. I went straight and the boat cut directly behind me. In other words, the boat crossed my path, which means if I hadn't slid far enough I would have been run over. In the last several years there have been situations where I've opted not to ski, especially with drivers I don't know. Sometimes customers are upset about my decisions to play it more on the safe side, but my intuition guides me more often than not.

Chapter 16: Life Changes

To exist is to change, to change is to mature, to mature is to go on creating oneself endlessly.

~Henri Bergson

One day, I received a call from a lady in New Hampshire who wanted to set up a clinic. Her husband used to barefoot and she and her daughter wanted to learn. "What do you need for equipment?" she asked. "You'll need wetsuits, handles, shoe skis and a boom for the boat," I explained. Without a pause she ordered everything. I had never handled such a large order before. We settled on the clinic dates and I agreed to pay half of the airfare for the trip because I wanted to spend some time at home with my family. Dad picked me up at the airport and we headed to the clinic site. "I've been in this area before," Dad said as we drove near. "I've done some line work out here. Just down this road there are multi-million dollar homes." He paused and looked at me. "What's the name of the family again?"

"The last name is Marriott," I said. All of a sudden, we looked at each other and realized it was *the* Marriott family from the famed Marriott hotel empire. The name simply didn't register with me at the time of the booking. Our suspicions were confirmed when we arrived at the gated entrance. The lake house was set on expansive grounds with immaculate shrubbery. The family met us at the entrance and we learned that the grandson and his brothers owned miles of property down the shoreline. The grandfather had purchased land around the lake years ago and several family members owned homes there. The lake was the site of the movie, "What About Bob." I spent a pleasant week with the family and Dad came to pick me up on the last day. We spent the afternoon riding on Jet-Skis and exploring the lake. After dinner my dad and I were asked to hang a large sheet from the balcony. They brought out chairs, blankets, a small table for the projector and four bowls of popcorn. We sat down to watch "What About Bob."

The Woman Who Changed My Life

Back home, my back continued to give me problems and the pain was unpredictable. Most of the time I could deal with the pain, but I was more frustrated because my back would not hold up. There were some days where I would bend forward and catch myself by bracing my hands on my thighs--it felt as if the muscles in my lower back were completely beat up. The pain was searing and I often felt as if I had no support in my back. I never knew when it was going to give out. I went to several doctors and had X-rays taken. "The discs between your lower vertebrae are inflamed," said one doctor. "They have a little more wear and tear than the average person but it's not bad. Your muscles are just tight. You need to stretch them more." I left the doctors' offices without a solution for the pain.

Sitting in the boat instructing students day after day was taking a toll. Out of all things, sitting in the boat for six hours a day was the worst thing I could do for my back. I didn't have a choice--this was my livelihood.

I took off for a clinic in Helena, Montana and met up with my friend, Adin Daneker. If there were anyone who has seen more sides to me than anyone else, it would be Adin. He is a paramedic and a firefighter; a blond hair, blue-eyed pin-up guy in suspenders who girls drool over in a calendar. He's six years older than me and has been one of my loyal students for years and we've evolved into brothers.

"You remember the crap we used to pull years ago?" I asked him on the way to his lake. "Hell, yeah! I still haven't forgiven you for the wild ride in the back of the truck," he said. I laughed at the memory. Adin was drunk as a skunk one night and I was the designated driver. The extended cab was full of people, so we tossed Adin in the truck bed and headed home. He passed out cold. I swerved from side to side on the road as we all watched Adin roll from one side of the pick-up bed back to the other side. I touched the brake, and we felt a thump as his head hit the wall of the truck bed. I'm ashamed to say that I did this a couple more times until we arrived home. The poor guy woke up the next morning with bruises all over and two small cuts on his head. Adin was a little confused as to how he got all banged up but he didn't complain too much.

Adin and I were helping each other on our jumping during the week of the Montana clinic and our jump landings were extremely inconsistent. Adin happened to be watching tons of old footage on CDs the night before and figured out a technical issue with our landings. He noticed eighty to ninety percent of the jumpers landed with their feet shoulder width apart or further.

"Hey Keith, take a look at some of our landings," he said. "Every time we miss a landing, our feet are glued together. *That's* our problem!"

The next day we both focused on keeping our feet wide and we started landing more jumps than usual. Since we had the bad habit of keeping our feet close together, it took a lot of effort to keep our stance wide on the landings. After flying through the air at 45 mph off a jump, it's only natural for a guy to try and protect the family jewels upon landing. I still couldn't shake the bad habit of landing with my feet together. Every time I landed with my feet together, it created a hole in the water and my rear end would land in the hole. This caused a sudden stop and my back would absorb all the impact. After one rough jump landing, I curled up on the water writhing in pain. The next day I could hardly roll out of bed. *How in the hell am I going to go to the Worlds? I can't ski. I can't get out of this bed! All this time, money, and effort put forth and I feel like I'm eighty years old!*

I stumbled over to the computer and started searching for someone I thought could help. I remembered my mother bringing me to a doctor who had a practice based on muscle testing. I Googled "touch for health" and reviewed the list that came up. One small business looked intriguing so I decided to call. I was ultimately searching for a massage therapist. Maybe I could move if someone just worked out the knots in my muscles. I dialed a woman named Mary Jo Morgan. She was listed as a Touch for Health practitioner under the massage therapy category.

"Hi, this is Keith St. Onge, and I'm in need of some massage therapy. I've injured my back and I'm experiencing some intense pain. Can I set up an appointment?"

"I don't do massage," she answered. "There are other things that I can do to help. I can do an analysis of your muscles and make recommendations on food choices to help you heal. Different foods affect different muscles and I can teach you how to eat properly so you can benefit from that."

"I appreciate that," I said. "But I already eat healthy and I'm very active. As far as health is concerned, I'm fine. It's my back that is giving me problems and I need a massage therapist to work out the tight muscles."

"You need to come into my office because I know I can help you," she replied.

"Thank you for your time, but this is serious, and I need a masseuse."

"I can help you," she insisted. I could hear the confidence in her voice.

"All right, I'll give it a try." We set up an appointment for later that day. Shoot--I was willing to do anything at this point to cure my back. I walked up to the front door of her office and knocked lightly, still wondering why I was here. A petite woman with short, dark hair opened the door and invited me in. I settled into a chair, staring at the rows and rows of herbal supplements lined up on her walls *Maybe she is a witch doctor and I will be healed in a few short minutes.*

Mary Jo was in her late 60's but she looked like a woman ten years younger. The first thing I noticed was her skin: it glowed like vanilla ice cream and looked so vibrant for her age. "I'm Mary Jo and it's nice to meet you Keith." She extended her hand in a firm shake. Her voice was crisp and had a unique sound--she exuded so much energy that her voice vibrated as she spoke. The sound caught my attention and I leaned in with complete focus.

"Take everything out of your pockets--your cell phone especially--and place them here." She motioned to her desk. She stepped back and looked me over from head to toe. "Stand with your feet together, turn this way a bit, and relax." She smiled. I felt like a little boy being told what to do, but I felt complete trust in her. Maybe it was because I was in such pain and vulnerable for any antidote she would prescribe. Either way, I followed every order and took in as much information as I could.

"I'm going to do a muscle test," she announced. She asked me to keep my arms straight out as I held an herb in my hand, a procedure that is part of traditional Chinese medicine. "Your muscles will tell me if this herb or food is good or bad for you. All human bodies are different and not all of us can consume the same foods. I want you to try and resist as I push down on your hand...hold it out straight, like this." Mary Jo was quite small and looked a bit frail, so I figured it would be easy to hold up to any pressure she could give. This would be a piece of cake. She pushed down. My arm went down instantly, I couldn't hold it up. I looked at her puzzled. She gave a calming look with a sureness which pierced right through me. She knew exactly what she was doing. She switched to another herb. "Hold tight," she commanded. "Ok, you need a little of this," she said half to herself and half to me. We continued on--one herb or supplement replacing another. "Now this--push...

okay...this will eliminate the other two things I said you should take..."

The whole process was exhausting. "I need a break, Mary Jo!" I was getting my butt kicked by this petite gal. By the end of the session I couldn't hold my arm up any longer. "Give me a few minutes to go over this," she said. She put together a list of herbal supplements and sat down to explain her findings.

"This eating plan is designed to balance you," she said. "Food affects your organs in many ways. Your liver needs help, and these are foods I want you to eat to help support your liver and get it strong again." I glanced at the eating plan. There was a specific outline of foods, and during specific times of the day I would have to consume a particular food. Mary Jo explained that my liver had to work overtime with the amount of alcohol I had consumed over the years. "No more alcohol, no chocolate, no peanuts, no tobacco and no caffeine," she insisted.

She continued to rattle off a list of forbidden foods. "No yeast, no white flour, no pasta, no cookies, no refined sugar, no milk, no cakes--none of that! You will eat millet bread and almond butter instead of white bread and peanut butter." Instantly, I knew my days of eating peanut butter and Fluff sandwiches were over.

"You will drink hazelnut milk instead of cow milk," she continued. "You will eat an organic Gopal's Pineapple Nut Rawma Bar at three in the afternoon--instead of a power bar. Before you go to bed you must eat seven rings of fresh pineapple and this will act as a natural anti-inflammatory for your back." *Wow, I won't have a problem going to the bathroom after this*!

She continued down the extensive list. "Every time you get in the boat you need to chew on some whole cloves." Not only was my liver working overtime to process the alcohol I had consumed over the years, she explained, but it was also working hard to process the engine fumes I was exposed to daily in the boat. "Cloves block out the absorption of fumes. Chew it--and swallow it when it becomes soft. The clove will then cleanse the liver and help restore it."

I was dubious to say the least when I left her office. It was a huge leap of faith to follow her plan, but I was out of alternatives and I wanted the pain to go away. I wanted to get well again. Mary Jo was diagnosed with seven different types of cancer at the age of 21 and she healed herself naturally with the assistance of holistic doctors. If she could accomplish that with natural remedies, then certainly I could give this a try. It was a challenge to follow her eating regime but I forced myself to comply with every step of it.

I began to research information about food and health and what I learned was an eye opener for me. For instance, I now consider white flour to be just as bad as tobacco. White flour turns to glucose in the body and it doesn't allow insulin to do its job. It is stored as fat instead of being digested properly. Europeans eat a lot of bread, but they aren't piling on the pounds like Americans. Yet, when they come to America and adopt our eating habits, they gain weight. In Europe, they make their bread with the whole stock of wheat, which contains oil filled with fiber. In America, we take the wheat germ out of it so it has a longer shelf life which strips the nutritional value.

In less than a week my back was feeling better and I could move it without experiencing the searing pain. I regained nearly all of the range of motion a month later and the pain had almost diminished entirely. Mary Jo was a God-send and for the first time in my life I realized the importance of consuming the right food. She set me on a life-changing path to a healthy lifestyle.

You Are What You Eat

When my dad adopted a healthier lifestyle he told me, "If you cannot pronounce or understand the word you are reading on the ingredients label you should not put it in your body!" I did not agree with him years ago, but I totally get it now. You are what you eat!

You can easily find replacements for everything. Instead of drinking cow's milk, I drink almond, hazelnut or hemp milk. Instead of eating white flour I eat millet or spelt bread. I never realized how clouded my head was until I changed my eating habits. After a month of eating clean foods my head was clear, I slept better, and I had more endurance. I even became more limber.

During the week of the Nationals, the phone rang. It was Ron Scarpa. I tried to hide the surprise in my voice. Ron and I had only spoken on the phone maybe two or three times prior to this. "Do you remember that conversation we had ten years ago?" Ron said getting right to the point.

"Yes, if you're referring to the time I asked if I could work for you," I replied.

"Yeah, I would like to discuss this again sometime this week over dinner."

"Let me see what night I have open and I'll call you back." My sponsor was staying with me so I figured I'd talk this out with him before making any decisions. "Don't talk with Ron because you have a good thing going," he said. He was partially right, I did have a good thing going—I had a steady paycheck from my sponsor. Thinking it over quickly, I took his advice. I called Ron back and said, "Thank you for your offer but I'm happy with how things are going for me right now."

Looking back, that was a stupid move on my part. Both Swampy and my dad taught me to put all options on the table before making a decision. As a businessman, I should have consented to the meeting and discussed the options to see what Ron had to offer. It could have been an opportunity to pursue, but I simply brushed it aside. It's like closing a door without knowing what's behind it. Always put your options on the table before making a decision. The more options you consider, the easier the decision is in the right direction.

The 2006 Nationals were held in Polk City, just fifteen minutes from my house. I announced that I would host a party at the house with several businesses sponsoring the event. My dad flew in to help me coordinate the event. The pro shop was stocked to the hilt with my sponsor's products but sales were slow. I was getting requests for my own line of t-shirts, hats and outerwear, not my sponsor's products.

We erected a large tent in the backyard and set up a massive barbeque grill. I hired a guy to do the cooking and set up an area for the DJ and dancing. Barefoot Wine sponsored the wine and we had a few kegs lined up. We were all set for some fun, but first, I had to do some skiing to snag another National title under my name. Slalom and tricks were easy enough and I placed first, but I feared the jump event. I was worried that I would injure my back and be out of commission for the Worlds. The very thing that I was afraid of happened: I rose too early and felt the familiar pain return on the landing. I held back on every jump, fearing that if I went big, I would injure my back to the point of not being able to move again. Fear had taken over me and I had no clue how to compensate for it. As a result, I didn't place in the top three with jumping, but the distance was enough to score the Overall trophy. I racked up my seventh Overall title and was happy with the results.

Banana George arrived fashionably late at the party that night in his trademark, bright yellow three-piece suit complete with a yellow hat and yellow cowboy boots. The party was in full swing and people clapped as he walked through the crowd, greeting everyone with a wide grin. He grabbed my hand and started to pull me toward him. I decided to fake a sideways flip. He grabbed me in a hug and laughed at my antics. That's one thing about Banana George; the energy around him was always vibrant. Everyone was always fired up around him.

My sponsor supplied the U.S. Worlds team wetsuits that year and he let me design them. I called the team up front and told them that I had two announcements to make. "I've been saving my U.S. Worlds wetsuits year after year," I said. "Every time I save a suit it seems like I have bad luck at the Worlds. This year I watched a movie called 'Walk the Line.' In the movie, Johnny Cash wore black and he strutted around with an attitude. Well, the movie has motivated me--I've developed an attitude with my skiing this year, and we're going to do something different." I paused a bit and looked around at the team. "The old style isn't working. I love my country and I love the red, white and blue but something had to change for this World Championship. Instead of the usual red, white and blue wetsuits--we're going with...black!"

There were cheers and groans from the crowd. The team gathered for a picture with the new wetsuits. While most of them were happy with the all black look, a few grumbled about how small the red, white, and blue emblems were on the front and back. I just shrugged and went on to my second announcement.

"For years, my ski school has been known as 'Gliding Soles' but no one ever calls it that. Most people simply refer to my school as "Skiing with Keith". Well, to reflect my relationship with my sponsor and to have a name that symbolizes a barefoot school, I'm using my sponsor's name for the school."

I wasn't prepared for the negative reaction I received from those around me. "You're nothing but a puppet now," a friend snapped. "Anything your sponsor says, you jump and do it." He walked away in disgust.

I'm not his puppet. I came up with the name myself! I wanted to shout but I kept quiet. The reaction from many people had me pondering things in a new light. I seemed to always be defending my position. My sponsor and I were butting heads on a more frequent basis. Maybe I wasn't seeing the big picture.

My dad approached me with a sad look on his face. "I have to admit, son, my heart dropped when you announced the new name of your ski school. I loved 'Gliding Soles.' That was your original name and it was unique. But on the other hand, this decision is also about growth--you're making your own decisions now."

Judy came up and she didn't hold back. "Keith, I'm a little disappointed in that announcement," she said. "Frankly, I just want to kick him in the balls— because he's got an iron-tight grip on yours!"

The whole name fiasco soon became a moot point and because of insurance reasons we could not name it after my sponsor's business. I had to come up with a name to replace Gliding Soles. For years, people referred to me by my initials and I sported a wetsuit with KSO on it. So just mere weeks after my announcement Keith St.Onge's Barefoot Ski School became the new name of my ski school and we simplified it to KSO's Barefoot School. It was much easier than pronouncing my last name.

Chapter 17: The Pinnacle of a Dream

> **Champions do not become champions when they win the event, but in the hours, weeks, months and years they spend preparing for it. The victorious performance itself is merely the demonstration of their championship character.**
>
> ~T. Alan Armstrong

This was it: the 2006 Worlds. I had a year of major preparation under my belt and I had made some serious lifestyle changes. Now it was time to find out if I was finally going to achieve my dream. I flew to Washington two weeks before the Worlds and stayed with my good friend, Adin Daneker. He was a paramedic and a firefighter; the kind of blond hair, blue-eyed pin-up guy in suspenders who girls drool over in a calendar. He was one of my loyal students for years and we evolved into brothers. "You remember the crap we used to pull years ago?" I asked him on the way to his lake.

"Hell, yeah! I still haven't forgiven you for the wild ride in the back of the truck," he said. I laughed at the memory. Adin was drunk as a skunk one night and I was the designated driver. The extended cab was full of people so we tossed Adin in the truck bed as we headed home. He passed out cold. I swerved from side-to-side on the road as we all watched Adin rolling from one side of the pick-up bed back to the other side. I touched the brake and we felt a thump as his head hit the wall of the truck bed. I'm ashamed to say that I did this a couple more times until we arrived home. The poor guy woke up the next morning with bruises all over and two small cuts on his head. Adin was a little confused how he got all banged up but didn't complain too much.

Adin lived on a private, man-made lake in a beautiful house he built. He owned an inboard Malibu, but we decided to borrow a friend's Sanger, the same type of boat that was being used in the World Championship. Ryan Boyd, another talented barefooter and friend joined us. I was filled with confidence every time I went out on the water. The trick routine I put together was new to the barefoot community; it featured many multiple turns and a new order of tricks no one had ever seen. I worked each trick individually for months to produce perfection. I was at the same ease and comfort I had felt only one time before in my life--at the 1997 Nationals when I took first place.

I took it easy with the jumping and made sure I did not over train--I didn't want to risk injuring my back. It was still sore after several jump sets. I called a friend to get a referral to a chiropractor--I figured some adjustments would help with the pain. He recommended someone two and half hours south in Portland, Oregon. The drive was worth it. After a few adjustments and some stretching exercises, I left the office with the confidence that I would ski well.

It was apparent to the guys I had made some changes over the last year and they weren't quite sure how to deal with the "new" me. Every morning I downed a shot of paprika per Mary Jo's instruction. The paprika was for my adrenal and parathyroid gland. The guys made fun of me every time! "Look, there goes Keith, taking his Pap-Rik-A shot again," they mocked. I didn't care... I trusted Mary Jo as a holistic practitioner. I was willing to do whatever it took to win a World Championship.

One evening, the boys tried to cajole me into joining them for drinks. "Come on Sally, we're going to the bar." Adin clamped his hand on my shoulder.

"Go ahead, I'm going to stay here. After all this training I can't screw off just before the tournament," I said, holding firm.

"Just one beer won't kill ya." Ryan shot back. I felt like an old man who changed directly in front of my friends. It was difficult to say no because I always went out with the boys. But I knew how much time and work I put into this endeavor and I could not fold. I know I seemed moody, but I did not want to regret a thing. If I did not win this tournament, at least I knew I gave it my all and that would be something to be proud of. If I skied my potential and lost--then hats off to the guy who beat me. I spent an entire year making sacrifices and I wasn't about to give in now, especially so close to the tournament.

"There will be time for drinking afterwards," I told them. "Go ahead and have fun. I'm just going to kick back and hang out here."

The morning of the World Championship, we arrived at the entrance of Lake

Silverado in Adna, Washington and I stood in awe of the sight. A wooden archway stretched over the road, supported on both sides by a stacked-stone foundation. Off in the distance I could see Mount Rainer framed in the archway. As we approached the parking lot just before the lake, I began to get those butterfly feelings in my stomach. I used to get similar feelings in my gut years ago as a kid before a tournament, but it was different this time. It wasn't a sense of nervousness but more like a sense of excitement. I was arriving at the big show and I was more prepared than any other time in my career.

The 2,670-foot lake was surrounded by thousands of trees averaging eighty feet in height, forming a perfect hedge when seen from an aerial view. The man-made lake was perfectly designed for barefoot water skiing--the surrounding trees almost always guaranteed glass calm water even on the windiest days.

My parents arrived and I was thrilled to see them. This was the first time my mom had attended a World Championship and I was looking forward to sharing the experience with her. My dad had gone to several tournaments over the years, but having my mom supporting me in person was a real treat. Kendra was working at the time, but she was cheering for me at home. I could always count on her support, even with the miles between us.

Swampy had moved to Alaska so he wasn't able to make the trip. I knew he would be there in his heart because he was following the results on the Internet.

Swampy, on becoming a champion:

If you want to be a champion it takes several things: you have to have talent, you have to have the heart, and you have to have the work ethic. The heart can overcome the talent. There are people who are talented, but they never take off because they get cocky or they don't want to work. You have to have the heart and a deep desire.

Champions are those who are willing to commit and work hard with their talent. If you have the talent and the desire, then the heart--the passion--will pull you to the top. You have to have all three to reach success.

185

The first round of slalom came up and I had my game face on when I arrived at the dock. I was suited up and ready to go--far more ready than I had ever been in my entire life. I had Patrick's card in my wallet. I knew myself better than I had ever known myself before. I knew exactly what I was capable of doing on the water and I was filled with the confidence to execute it. If someone beat me this time, they would truly deserve it.

I skimmed the wakes smoothly, placing each foot down with precision and ease. It was a great run and I scored well. I was more than ready to face the trick round next. I studied the schedule to see when my turn would come up. As I scanned the lineup, my heart stopped. The tournament directors had switched the events--I would have to *jump* next. A wave of anxiety washed over me. I had struggled with my jumping all year long and dealt with the resulting back injuries--what if I hurt my back again? How would I get through my trick runs if I hurt my back? I couldn't shake off the anxiety. My mom tried to soothe me. "You'll land your jumps, I can feel it," she said.

"But Mom, we always trick first and that would allow me to get a good score on the board before I jump and possibly hurt myself." I fretted.

"You'll do great!" She reassured me. "You are going to be the champion. You are going to win." My mom has an uncanny ability to use her intuition so I tried to have faith in what she shared with me. I could feel the tension subside. The soothing words from my mom were all I needed to hear and it took the edge off my anxiety. That is what it meant to have my mom there. I loved it!

I prepared for the jump event with a positive attitude and had my plan. I knew I had to focus on a few things as I raised and when I landed. I swam out to the boat and climbed aboard. I gazed at the crowd on the bank and took a few deep breathes. A voice from the boat judge's radio came on and as the driver listened to it he looked at me and said, "Course is clear, jump in." This round would be my fate and it was time to put a good score on the board. I had to jump far enough to make the second round.

I rocketed off the jump and everything felt great. *This is big enough to make the cut and win the Overall!* I brought my feet forward for the landing and as soon as I hit the water I knew my feet were too close together. My rear end sank into the water instead of sliding smoothly. The rope jerked me forward and I felt a painful wrench in my back. When I tumbled to a stop, I couldn't move. The

186

pain was searing. "Crap! I can't believe this!" I looked on shore at Ryan and asked, "How far apart were my feet on the landing?" He put his hands together just a few inches apart and shook his head. I crawled into the boat. I had two more jumps to complete and I was dreading each one of them. *Come on. Push the pain out of your mind. Just focus on one jump at a time. Just one jump at a time, dammit! It doesn't have to be big either.*

It was a long, painful ride to the jump. I cringed as it came near, bracing myself for the pain that would explode through my back. Coming down on the water from twelve to fifteen feet in the air can hurt even when it's done properly and I was as tight as a banjo string at that moment. A horrible feeling washed over me. The fear had set in and I knew what was coming. I came down hard and missed the landing.

Cursing again, I waited for the boat to pick me up. I started to think about the tricks event and how difficult it would be with my battered back. I could physically deal with the painful misery, but what I could not deal with was a back that would not support my body. What I heard next was music to my ears. "The boat path was too close to the jump, Keith," the judge said. "You have an optional re-ride." I couldn't believe what I had just heard; the judge was offering me another jump for a bad boat path. "I'll take it!" I knew I still had one more jump left after I took this re-ride. This was an added bonus. I figured I'd take the re-ride and push the envelope for a big jump knowing I still had one more left.

I missed the landing yet again, with more torment added to my back. As I let out a stream of silent profanity, another miracle occurred. I received yet another re-ride. This time the speed was too fast. Out of the corner of my eye I could see David on the shore waving his arms in disbelief. He had a scowl on his face and it was clear to see he wasn't happy with the re-rides. I was pretty sure he was swearing at me. I didn't care. It was payback time for the re-ride David chalked up at the 2002 Worlds when the rope broke.

I accepted the second re-ride, but unbelievably, I missed the landing yet again. Everyone on the shore knew what was going on. If I did not land a jump I would not be an Overall contender. My tournament depended on me landing a jump! I took my last jump with the realization I had to land it--or I would be out of the running for the second round. If I missed it, I could kiss the Overall goodbye. I played it extremely safe: I made myself rise off early and purposely jumped short. I landed it and glided to a stop. There was still more cursing going on in my head as I floated in the water. *I can't believe I did such a baby jump. What the hell is wrong with me?*

My mind was battered, my back was throbbing, and I couldn't think straight. The jump was so short I wasn't sure if I was still in the running for the second round. Trudging through the water to shore, I climbed out and I went up to Jon Kretchman, the U.S. Team coach. "What are the numbers, Jon?" I asked. "Did I make the cut?" Jon did the calculations. His face was grim as he looked at me. "I'm sorry, Keith, you didn't make the cut." Every muscle in my body went weak. I couldn't believe it--an entire year of preparation just went down the drain. All of the work I had put in, all of the training I had done on the water all year, and all of the time devoted to this tournament--it was thrown away in an instant. I did not care about winning individual titles at this point. I had just lost the Overall title.

A jumble of emotions swirled in my head as I walked down the shore toward my parents. *I can't believe this! That stupid jump! I lost it all because of that stupid jump! I should have landed my first few jumps. They were so close to being perfect and they would have put me into the second round for another chance to improve. All because of my back--if my back wasn't giving me so much trouble I could have trained harder...*

A wave of shame flushed through my veins. A true athlete hates to use excuses for his mistakes. For the first time in my life, I was filled with uncertainty, doubt, and confusion. Maybe the dream of achieving a World Championship was nothing but a dream. I came to a sinking realization: I might never hold the Overall title to my name. Without that accomplishment, I would feel incomplete for the rest of my career. I was getting older and time was running out on me-- the younger skiers were coming up fast on my heels. My barefoot water skiing "shelf life" was closing in. I thought I had put together a perfect game plan to win the Worlds--and now I was feeling a sense of hopelessness.

"Keith!"

I turned at the sound of Jon's voice. He was running toward me. "Oh my God--" he said. "We have one jumper left. I just figured it out--if this guy doesn't land or jump further than you, you'll be the last one to make it into the second round!"

"In other words, I'm on the 'bubble'!" My heart was pounding. "Who's coming up?"

"Don Baker from Canada." Don was a hit-or-miss skier with his jumping, sort of like me. He constantly went huge, but had difficulty landing consistently. "I hope he doesn't go big and land one, or I'm out for sure," I said. I do not ever wish bad things upon another person but I so wanted to move on to the next round!

Don took off for the ramp and I held my breath as I watched him come up off the jump. It was a large jump. Don flew through the air with a sense of tightness and confidence, but the handle popped out of his grip on the landing. I exhaled. *One down. Two more to go.* The second jump was beautiful through the air. I almost wanted to turn away because I couldn't bear to see him land it. To my relief, he couldn't hang on for the landing. Don hit the water slightly twisted, bounced sideways, and tumbled to a stop.

Don, I love you buddy, but I hope you miss this last jump. I saw my parents walking toward me, but I couldn't take my eyes off of Don as he ricocheted off the jump once again with beautiful form. *Oh damn, he's going to friggin land this one! No, no, dammit, no!* Don's landing looked very similar to mine with his feet much too close together. His butt hit the water and he did a perfect front flip. Another incomplete landing! He should have landed it.

I felt bad for him for a brief second and then I let out a yell. "Yeah, yeah, yeahhhh!" I pumped my fist in the air. My mom ran over screaming with joy and both parents engulfed me in a group hug. We walked back to the car so I could take my soaked wetsuit off and all of a sudden I doubled over in pain.

"Keith! What's wrong?" I could hear the concern in my mom's voice but I couldn't straighten up to look at her. "My back is locked up," I winced. Back at the hotel, I hobbled up to my parents' room. Crawling on the bed, I rolled over and tried to stretch my back. Pain shot up my spine like a thousand alternating needles. "I don't think I can ski--I can hardly move!" I said. "I think my shot at the Overall is gone. I have no idea how I will be able to ski the rest of the tournament."

"Let's go back to the chiropractor," my mom suggested. I dreaded the thought of the five-hour round trip to Portland, Oregon but I was desperate at that point. I picked up the phone, called the chiropractor, and he agreed to meet with me. I lay sideways in the back seat as my dad drove. Every bump of the road jarred me with pain. Thankfully, I fell asleep and escaped the pain.

189

The chiropractor managed to pop my back and make some adjustments. He cranked on me so hard I thought the tight muscles in my back were going to snap. I normally love chiropractors, but on that day I was lying in the torture chamber.

I was sore in spots I should not have been but I was able to move when we left his office. On the way back I called the team massage therapist. "Char, I'm on my way and I need you to do some massage work on me." Char worked on me for two solid hours as I lay there completely exhausted, both mentally and physically. By the time she was done, most of the tight muscles had loosened. My back somewhat worked again but I continued to struggle with the pain. *After this is done I won't be in so much pain anymore so deal with it!* Yes, the pain I could deal with, but the bigger problem was the fact my back just could not hold my body weight up. I could not lean forward without bracing myself on my thighs.

The next day, I woke up to even more intense pain. I winced as I tried to sit up. "How's your back this morning?" My mom asked.

"Not good," I said. "My back is killing me. I don't know how the hell I'm going to ski." I stood up and tried a few stretches. I gave up after a few attempts. "If I can just make it through this round and post a good score maybe that will be enough for the Overall." I mused. I briefly contemplated pulling myself from the competition after the first round of tricks because there was no way I could continue to ski like this. "Let's just get to the ski site and go for a walk. Maybe I can shake this off."

On the way to the site, I mentally prepared myself for one of the hardest tournament rounds I ever faced. I wasn't even sure if I could get up on the water. *I have to ski it perfectly and not have a bobble. If I don't, I'm going to hurt myself out there by pulling my back out of position. If I lose position the whole trick run is shot!* I tried to prepare myself physically by doing some dry land practice when we arrived. I walked down a dried up creek bed behind the large trees that outlined the lake and tied my handle to a tree. I slowly began to go though my trick routine. I was careful not to move fast for fear of pulling my back. The pain was deep and exhausting. How in the hell am I going to do this, I wondered. This was going to be the toughest challenge of my life.

Getting into the wetsuit was torture. I eased off the dock into the water and

190

readied myself for the start. "OK!" I signaled the driver. *Just let me get through my start!* Placing my foot in the water, I leaned forward to stand up, and for a brief second, the pain caused me to pause. I wasn't sure I could trust my back muscles to come through. Gripping my leg, I leaned forward through excruciating pain and I was finally up. *That was close.* I pushed thoughts out of my mind and just let each trick unfold. What happened next is something many athletes describe as "in the zone." I executed each trick perfectly and I felt no pain on both passes. All the fears I had of falling were gone from my mind. When I sat down on the water and released the handle at the end of the run, I was ecstatic. All I had to do now was ski my second pass back to the dock. The same thing happened, one trick melded into another as I completed my run. The runs were perfect because I was so focused and totally in the zone. I simply knew if I got out of position my back would not hold up during the run. I had no other option but to concentrate on executing each position perfectly. Back at the dock, I was greeted with the news that I set a new World Record in tricks. I couldn't believe it! Just moments before I wasn't sure I could even ski.

I had to face another round of jumping, and frankly, I was scared. I calculated the numbers I would need to jump to hold a strong lead for the Overall position. A jump of at least 78 feet would ensure that I would be a contender for the Overall title. *I'm going to aim for 78.8*, I told myself. *This way, no one can beat me.*

"Keith, you landed a 79!" the crew in the pickup boat told me as I climbed in. I pumped my fist through the pain. The distance was exactly what I knew I could do all along. I was baffled why I could not put it together in the first round. I must have had my feet wider this time around because the jump was easy to land.

David would have to jump over ninety feet to swipe the Overall from me and I was eighty percent confident he couldn't do it. But I couldn't be too sure. He had come close to jumping 90 feet in other tournaments, and I knew if anyone could do it, it would be David. I wanted to go a little bit further in my next jump to seal the Overall but I missed the landing, twisting my back painfully again. I debated whether or not to go for the third jump. I wanted to win the Worlds so badly--so I decided to go for it. Any improvement on my jump distance would help. I jumped high and far, but I couldn't hang on for the landing. The pain came screaming back.

I swam to shore in slow strokes and walked over to Jon. "I screwed up my back pretty bad," I said. "I have to head out to the chiropractor and see if he can work on it again." I asked him not to share this with anyone. I didn't want to show my weakness to my competitors and they did not know I was injured in the first place.

I walked to the car with my parents and every breath was painful. "I can't get the wetsuit off, it hurts too much to even bend my shoulders back," I said. "Please help me get this off." Dad slowly peeled the wetsuit off and I changed into a dry swimsuit. The same ritual began: two and half hour drive to Portland, two and half hours back and then another massage session with Char. I dosed off and on during the massage. The pain kept jarring me awake. I didn't fall asleep until 11:30 p.m. which made for an extremely long day.

David did not jump over ninety feet in the final round, so I was able to take the pressure off and celebrate an unofficial win. Before the finals started on Saturday, I decided to shave off the beard I had been sporting for the last year. By the time the final rounds were over, I won gold medals in tricks and slalom and the coveted Overall title. Even more astonishing, I set three new pending World Records in tricks--one record per round, a feat which had never been accomplished at a World Championship before. It had taken me five World tournaments to finally stand on the top of the podium.

As I hugged my parents and thanked them, I was engulfed in a variety of emotions. In the midst of the celebration and excitement, I realized I missed Swampy. He should have been there. He had been with me at the very start and was such a huge part of my life for so many years that I felt empty without him being present. I wanted to share this victory with him. Tears began to run down my face. "Quitters never win, and winners never quit," I could hear his voice in my head. He sacrificed so much of his time, love and money to help me achieve my dreams. The gold medals belonged to him as much as they belonged to me. Right at that moment, I silently thanked him. The tears kept coming.

Lisa Bouchard, steadies me during my first ski show.

Left to right: Nicole Bunnell, Paul Vien Jr., Keith, Grandpa Don and Swampy

The calm before my "drowning moment."

Keith's first time on skis.

Mike Seipel with Keith and cousins, Tim and Ryan

Mike Seipel signs autographs

Barefooting at 9-years-old

First tournament. Left to right: Keith, Paul Throm, Matt Gengren

1989 Regional's Paul Throm, Matt Gengren, Keith

Keith (11 years old) with Coach Swampy. First Regionals, 3rd place.

Keith,
11.5 years old,
Doing a toe hold.

"Look Ma, no hands!"

Spray Danny, my big brother and ski partner.

Keith and Spray performing "Rope in teeth" trick

Swampy and Keith, August 1993

Swampy, best coach in the world! Off to train in the cold water.

U.S. Team, 1996 Worlds. Keith, second from right

Swampy and Keith, 1996 Worlds

First rental – Dusty Vines helped pay the first two months of rent

Keith and Dusty Vines

My first sponsored boat from Richard Grant

Keith, Ron Scarpa, and Patrick Wehner. 1998 Worlds, Sydney, Australia

Keith and Claude, 2000 in Houston, Texas

Lane Bowers, Keith, and Jon Kretchman at Nationals

2002 Worlds
Tricks
Keith, Patrick Wehner and David Small

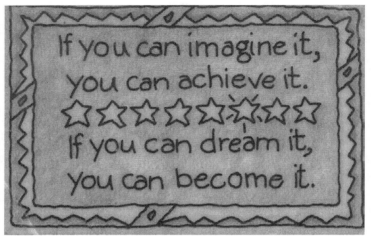

The card Patrick Wehner gave Keith at the 2002 Worlds

Banana George (90th birthday) and Keith

Keith's chubby days as an athlete:

2006 Worlds, Bill Brzoza, Keith, Lane Bowers

2008 Worlds Heinrich Sam, Keith and Andre DeVilliers

2005
Cover of
WaterSki magazine

2006
The Water Skier

2007
Cover of
WaterSki
magazine

2009
Australian
Waterski
Magazine

2009
The Water Skier

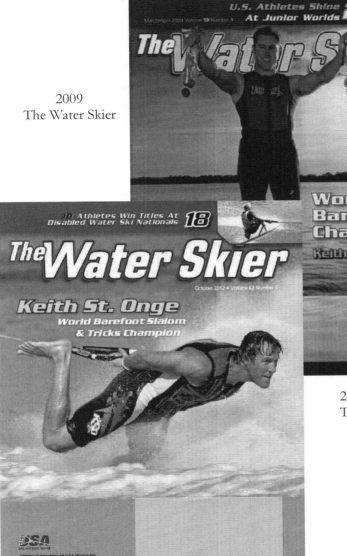

2012
The Water Skier

Judy Meyers, Karen Putz and Keith

Dave Ramsey and Keith

Keith and Lauren, Edmonton, Canada

Glen Plake and Keith

Barefooting Across America Tour

Kendra and Keith

Lauren, Keith, Jackie, Claude and Kendra

Keith and parents

Keith and David, Worlds 2010

WBC Staff: Swampy, Ben, Ashleigh and A. J.

Chapter 18: Passing on Inspiration

> There will come a time when you believe everything is finished. That will be the beginning.
>
> ~Louis L'Amour

The moment I realized I had secured the Overall Champion title, I eagerly prepared a speech to give at the award banquet. "Sit back and get comfortable, because this is going to be a long one," I announced. "It took me many years to have this privilege of standing in from of you tonight and I am going to enjoy every moment." I took my sweet time thanking everyone who played a part in my success. I made a few jokes to lighten the mood and noted how I was blessed to have my parents there supporting me like they had been from day one. I wished Kendra were there to share the moment. Thanks went out to my friends who drove the boat countless hours and the many people that had a part of my career prior to winning my championship title. In my speech, I gave Swampy the credit he deserved, but I also realized it was nice being able to do this tournament on my own. I had finally grown up and proven myself on my own merit.

At the bar, I announced I was buying everyone a round of shots to celebrate. There were over forty-five shots handed out. Thank goodness they ran out of shot glasses or it would have been a much larger bill! I hung out for an hour, but was extremely tired and called it an early night. The "high" that came from winning had taken its toll on my body and I was crashing fast.

Life Transitions

For a few days after the World Championship, I hung out with my parents and explored the area. We drove up to Mt. St. Helens as a caravan of "footers" followed us up. Eugene and his son, world Jr. Champion, Heinrich Sam hung out with us for the afternoon. After saying goodbyes, I flew off to Missouri to do a five-day clinic.

On the Cover of The Water Skier Magazine

The Water Skier magazine called and requested a cover shot of me. I had never been on the cover of this magazine before and I was looking forward to it. We had perfect glass for water and I wanted to do something a little different instead of just barefooting. I decided to wrap my medals around my neck. Four hard-earned gold medals--I wanted to show them off. I put them on, grabbed the handle while the boat was going at full speed and gently hopped out on the water. Immediately, I knew I had a problem. The medals began to swing and clang in the wind. I got back into the boat. "This is not going to work! I don't want to lose the one Overall medal which took me sixteen years to win!" I told the photographer. We found a few rubber bands and hair ties in the boat and wrapped them around the back of the ribbon that held the medals. I was being choked to death, but at least the medals would not flap in the wind. At the end of the shoot, I discovered the Overall medal was barely hanging on. When the November 2006 issue arrived with me on the cover, I was on top of the world again, at least for a little while.

Life became routine again and the "high" from winning the World Championship didn't last long. I should have remained ecstatic from the accomplishment, but instead, I hit bottom. I had worked so long and hard on my dream and now that I had accomplished it, I felt lost. I didn't know what to do. There was nothing for me to work toward at that point and I didn't have a goal to attain. The ski school had slowed down for the fall. My roommate was constantly bugging me to get back on the water but I had no energy or desire to do so. My body was worn down. I was burned out and I didn't want to touch the water for a while.

I started heading to the bars and drinking again. The partying was an escape from everyday life. I even started bumming cigarettes here and there. The tension escalated with my sponsor--we started butting heads over business decisions more often than not. The pro shop was stockpiled with my sponsor's brands but customers were requesting shirts with my name on them. I wanted to produce my own line of Team KSO shirts, hats, and ski school stickers but every single time I brought it up to my sponsor, he shot down my ideas. "You are sponsored by me and represent this business—focus on the business," he reminded me.

I felt like I was stuck. On one hand, my sponsor had rocketed my career to a new level and exposed my name to skiers all over the world through the videos he produced. I received a regular paycheck and security in a seasonal business. On the other hand, I couldn't grow or expand my own ski school or myself professionally. My sponsor threatened to restrict my funds on numerous occasions if I did not do as he commanded. I found myself in turmoil.

Swampy Moves Back

While I was struggling to pick myself back up and get motivated to ski again, Swampy was dealing with his own troubles. He had lost everything when the financial deals fell through and he bounced from place to place. He lived with Spray for a while, and then went up to Alaska and found a job. He was not happy there so Judy found him some work in Arizona. Swampy stayed in Arizona for a few months. He finally decided the best place to settle down again was back home in New Hampshire. "I'll be driving home with my two dogs," he said during a phone call.

"Hey Swampy, why don't you swing by Florida for a visit on your way home?" I suggested. I missed him and I wanted to hang with him a bit before he headed up north. It had been almost two years since we last saw each other. I had plenty of time to relax before training started again. Shoot, I had a year to relax and be lazy before any preparation began for the next World Championships. "I may swing by since I'm heading out East, but I'm not sure yet." Swamp replied.

"Come on, Swampy, we can talk about the old days over a few glasses of wine," I cajoled. "I want to see you." I really wanted to catch up and see how he was doing.

"All right, maybe I'll stop by for a week or two," he said. Swampy rumbled into the driveway five days later. I grabbed him in a bear hug--and there was a lot more of Swampy to grab. We had a great time kicking back and talking about the past and all the barefoot tournaments we attended together. There were several bottles of wine left over from a New Year's Eve party, so each night, we shared a bottle and reminisced.

Before I knew it, the weeks became months and neither of us was pulling the other out of the doldrums. We continued to drag through the motions of "woe is me." Life had dealt Swampy a tough hand and he was wallowing in it. I was feeling a little down as well. I had accomplished everything I wanted to in my career, but I was unsure what my next goals were to be. I was confused and I didn't know what I wanted to do next. The ski school had reached a plateau--I was seeing the same customers and I felt burned out by the process of sitting in the boat day after day. Swampy couldn't bring himself to leave for New Hampshire. We were both in a place where we felt stuck.

After a few glasses of wine one night, Swampy began to open up and he filled me in on his last several years. He had lost everything--his lake house, the ski boat, and several businesses. He was surviving on pasta and processed foods because it was cheap and readily available. His truck was close to getting repossessed and he had nothing but his two dogs by the time he arrived at my house. "Do you remember when I called you two years ago and asked you if you would take my dogs?" Swampy asked. I nodded. "Well, I was living out of my truck at the time. It was probably one of the lowest times in my life and there were moments there...when... I didn't want to go on."

I was stunned. I had no idea how rough life had become for the guy who was a pillar for me for so many years. To think how close I came to losing him brought tears to my eyes and I let them flow. Soon we were both crying. I got up and wrapped my arms around him as we cried together. This was the man who gave so much to me when I needed it--his time, his expertise, his money. He loved me like a son. It was time for me to do the same for him, to give back to him what he gave to me over the years.

"Swampy, I have something I want to give you." I reached into my wallet and pulled out Patrick's card. I looked at the words of William Arthur Ward once again:

If you can imagine it, you can achieve it. If you can dream it, you can become it.

"Patrick gave me this card in 2002 after I lost the Worlds," I explained. I told Swampy the story of the card and how it was passed from barefoot skier to barefoot skier. "Patrick told me to pass this on to someone else when I achieved my goals. I've done everything I wanted to do, especially becoming the World Champion." I handed the card to Swampy. I watched as his eyes took in the words. "When you achieve your goals or find someone that needs this card more than you, you can give it away." Swampy looked up and shot me a wry smile. I was no longer his student--I was now the teacher. We laughed lightly and he slid the card into a small pocket of his wallet.

Swampy never made it home to New Hampshire. Without intending to, he found his calling again at the ski school in the form of a shy teenager. A.J. Porreca, a high school student with incredible talent on the water entered our lives. I first met A.J. at a clinic I did in Wisconsin years ago when he was a young teen. He was heavy-set and quiet, but he possessed a passion in his eyes that made him memorable.

A.J. was skiing at another ski school during his spring break. One of the ski school employees came over to see one of my students and A.J. tagged along. "Who is this little guy?" I asked. I didn't recognize the lean young man in front of me.

"This is A.J. He's from Illinois." My mouth fell open. I could not believe it was him. The baby fat was gone, replaced with lean muscles. "What's new with you, A.J.?" I tried to squelch the surprise I felt.

"Not much," A.J. shrugged. I could see he still hid behind some shyness. I thought back to my own shy teen years.

"So, how's your skiing going? Do you plan on attending tournaments this year?"

"Yeah. I am going to compete at the Nationals for the first time."

"That would be a great experience for you. You'll have fun! I haven't seen you since the clinic last summer in Wisconsin. When are you going to come and ski with me here?" I asked.

"Yeah... um... maybe someday I can come. I'll have my dad contact you," he said. Little did I know, my drinking reputation had preceded me and A.J.'s father refused to let him train with me because of my "wild, partying ways." It was not the first time parents refused to let their teens come to my ski school, but I didn't learn this until much later. I had changed, but there was no way to convey this to my students.

A.J. was persistent with his father, and he came to train with me the following spring. We struck up a rapport and I enjoyed working with him. I began to call him a "Mini Me," in reference to his long face and big chin.

"You gotta see this A.J. kid ski," I told Swampy one night. "He's got a lot of heart for the sport and he kind of reminds me of myself at that age." Swampy

223

met A.J. briefly that week but had yet to see him on the water. "I wanna show you something." I connected the video camera to the television and hit the play button. "Watch this kid." We sat back and watched him jump. "See how he comes off the jump?" I said. A.J. had a gymnastics background and he learned how to jump inverted quite easily. Swampy and I were working on a new technique on the jump to correct the bad habits I had and we talked about looking for someone to experiment on. I knew A.J. could be our little guinea pig. Out of pure instinct, Swampy began to comment on several things A.J. needed to correct and I could see a bit of passion for the sport come out of him. "Maybe you should take him out for a set, Swampy," I suggested.

"Yeah, I think I will." He shot me a suspicious look. He knew what I was up to. Swampy was becoming alive again. I could see the fog lifting. "All right, get him in here," Swampy said. "I'll talk with him and see where he's at." I grinned. It was the first time I saw the spark of the old Swampy I knew. Swampy was about to do what he did best and what he was born to do: work with kids!

Reflecting on Choices

The future of my business was in jeopardy regarding its growth because of the choices I made. My past continued to haunt my future and I knew it. It hurt to look back and know my actions impaired my ski school. I was embarrassed and wanted everyone to know I was not like that anymore. I ate healthy, did not party and took my business seriously, but it would take a lot of time for people to realize that. I would have to swallow my pride and be patient. I knew my choices and behaviors were coming full circle and biting me in the butt.

Looking back, I wish I would have made better decisions, but unfortunately, I was learning the hard way. This is why I'm passionate today about helping others by sharing the poor decisions I made--if just one person has a smoother journey as a result of what I've shared, it's worth it.

The ski school started becoming busy with many more students than previous years. It was becoming more and more difficult for me to juggle the students, the pro shop and my sponsor's business. When the tension piled up with my sponsor, I unloaded on Swampy. Instead of keeping it inside, I let it all out. The frustrations and stress of the previous years all came tumbling out and I shared my escalating discomfort in working with my sponsor. It was great to have a sounding board and to have Swampy's opinion about the business. I felt as if I had released a belt that had been pulled tight around my chest for too long. In the process of sharing my thoughts and expressing myself out loud to Swampy I came to realize I was not happy at all.

In one particular incident, I submitted an article for my sponsor's website describing my views of a controversy that took place at a barefoot tournament. My sponsor wanted to add a different slant to the events. We went back and forth on the article but I was not comfortable making the changes he was asking me to do. "I'm truthfully sharing what I saw with my own two eyes," I told him. "That's what I wrote and I don't want to change it." I submitted it to him for publication.

A few days later, I started receiving angry emails from tournament participants. "Why did you write this...and why did you say that about me?" The tournament director sent me an email as well and he was quite upset with what I wrote. I was puzzled. I knew what I wrote was not controversial and the anger pouring forth from the emails was perplexing. "I don't understand why you're so upset," I wrote back. "What are you talking about, where is this all coming from?" I decided to read over the article again to try and figure out what caused the angry emails. I pulled up the article and sat there dumbfounded; the article expressed a very different view of the events. And there was my name in the byline: Keith St. Onge. The angry emails finally made sense.

The problems continued to escalate when my sponsor purchased the wetsuit company that also sponsored me. I had proudly worn this wetsuit for many years and I was extremely loyal to the brand. I received a steady salary from the company until the ownership changed hands and ironically, my sponsor had negotiated the last contract for me. Three months went by and I didn't receive my usual check. I called to inquire and discovered my original contract with the company would no longer be honored. "Why didn't you tell me about this three months ago?" I was infuriated. "I would like to be paid the same salary as before because this contract carried over when you bought the business!" We went back and forth, but we couldn't reach an agreement to honor the original contract. They offered a new deal based on sales; if the sales increased above their baseline, I would receive a certain percentage. I wasn't happy with the deal because I had no way of tracking the actual sales.

The business relationship was no longer a comfortable one. I had dropped the ball on this and had assumed the contract would stay the same and the payment would be honored. I should have followed up immediately after the lapse in payment. I was loyal to my sponsor and the business but I felt locked in a vise. I was walking on eggshells all the time with my stomach in knots.

My sponsor was flying into town in a few days and we were organizing a big project: to barefoot water ski behind an ultra-light airplane. Mike Seipel had done a similar stunt in the past. I was so excited for this extreme version of barefoot skiing. The pilot, Rhett Radford, was known to be one of the best ultra-light pilots in the world.

The whole idea first came up when a TV show, Stunt Junkies, approached me and asked if I could break the world barefoot water ski jump record behind an airplane. I worked with the company for one month and came up with a plan on how to accomplish this goal. I told them I could break the record but it would not be official as it would have to be performed behind a boat to actually set a new record. Jumping behind the plane would be a whole new record in its own. After some discussion, Stunt Junkies decided to drop the stunt, but I couldn't get the stunt out of my mind. I wanted to go ahead with it. We invited WaterSki magazine to come out and record the stunt.

Mike Salber and I tested the stunt out the day before just to see if it would work. "All right, Keith, here's the plan," Mike said. We've got a ninety-foot rope hooked to the plane. The boat driver is going to chase the rope. As soon as you grab the handle, you can barefoot away." Mike was a paramedic fire fighter so I knew he could attend to me quickly if something went wrong.

The plane came over the treetops and I felt my heart beat quickly. As the plane came near, we took off with the boat. The plane passed over us and left us behind. It couldn't slow down because it needed the speed to hold its elevation. We tried again and again to time the plane's approach with the boat speed but after several attempts we gave up.

We were screwed. WaterSki magazine, along with ten other people would be coming the next day and we didn't have a working plan in place. They were planning to place video cameramen, professional photographers, and more than one boat in the water. From the looks of our attempts, we would have nothing to show them. Mike had an idea later that night. "I've got a friend with a Jet Ski that can go up to 60 mph," he said. "That would be plenty fast to catch the plane and make it easier to maneuver in the water." It would be scary as heck chasing the plane down but it could work. Mike arranged for the Jet Ski to be there the next morning. All we could do was cross our fingers.

We got to the lake early and unloaded the Jet Ski. Mike idled to the end of the lake and circled slowly. In the distance, we could hear the low whine of the plane coming closer. Mike looked over his shoulder at me. He had a stern look on his face and I could hear the same sternness in his voice. "Keith, if you feel like something is wrong or you are not comfortable, don't do it."

I laughed. "If I get that handle in my hands, I am not turning back!" No one had ever done this stunt the way we were going to do it and there were many unanswered questions. Could we do it? How would we do it? I wanted to be the one to answer them.

The plane came ripping over us at fifty miles per hour. The handle was bouncing off the water and Mike made a beeline for it. The handle bobbed ten feet off the water out of reach. It came down within my reach and I missed it. Mike took off faster and caught up to the plane again. I stretched for the handle overhead and got my fingertips on the grip. The Jet Ski went right and the plane went up and the next thing I knew I was being pulled off sideways. I bailed out, landing on my head sideways on the water at 50 mph. I rolled to a stop. "Are you ok?" Mike rushed over. "I'll be sore tomorrow morning, but let's do this again. I almost had the handle!"

After a few more attempts Mike was starting to get the hang of getting me to the hovering handle and I could feel it all coming together. I finally grabbed the handle as it bounced off the water and was able to hold onto it. A slack in the line gave me a chance to steady myself. Mike peeled away at the same time the plane hit turbulence, pulling me off the Jet Ski. For a brief moment I was suspended in the air then I quickly landed on my feet and skied away. *I did it!* I was so pumped that I immediately started looking for cameras to show off. Skiing behind a plane was quite a different experience. The plane accelerated and decelerated, making it difficult at times to stay upright. There wasn't any consistency in the speed and the wind was effecting the elevation, but it was not enough to throw me off. I did a few tricks that had never been done behind a plane just to make sure they were caught on video. I let go after several minutes to rest up and prepare for another try. I only needed a minute of rest as the adrenaline was pumping. I couldn't wait to try it again.

"Ok, Keith, this time let's line you up with the jump and go for it," said Mike. It took a couple more attempts before I finally got off the Jet Ski smoothly. Rhet lined up for the jump ramp. Fear and excitement mixed together all at once inside of me. I was about to do something crazy and I loved it. Truth be told, I *lived* to do things like this! I blasted off the ramp and to my surprise it was a short jump. The plane pulled me off the jump early. It was difficult to ride up the ramp with the rope pulling from such a high position. I was pumped and wanted to attempt it again. The coolest thing about barefoot skiing behind the airplane was that nothing was in front of me--just endless water! I was so used to a boat wake next to me.

I lined myself up for another jump and pulled back as I rode up the ramp. I went much further than I ever had before and it must have been close to one hundred feet! I was pleased with our feat. Now it was Mike's turn to have a shot. He jumped off the Jet Ski after a few tries and had a blast barefooting behind the plane. Even though the stunt never ended up on TV, I was thrilled to experience it. When we released the video online it quickly became one of the highest viewed barefooting videos at that time.

I was flying high after the stunt, but my sponsor and Swampy were not. The displeasure between the two grew. Just before my sponsor left, they got into a heated discussion in the living room. My stomach was in complete knots. "I can cut Keith off anytime," he told Swampy just before he left.

"That guy has a lot of control over you," Swampy fumed. "He just threatened to cut you off. That's no way to do business." On one hand, my sponsor was a steady source of income for me. I had worked hard with him to build up the business and we had made a lot of progress. On the other hand, I wasn't growing my own business the way I wanted to. I felt trapped.

"What would you do if you knew you could not fail?"

~Robert H. Schuller

From the moment we conceived the idea for this stunt I didn't allow any of the negatives to get in my way. Some people are auditory learners, some are physical learners, me--I'm a visual learner. I only saw myself doing what I set out to do. I pictured myself doing the stunt from start to finish. I assessed the situation, knew the risks if things went bad and I accepted them. I kept my focus on the goal and blocked out the fear of the unknown.

I teach my students to keep this same focus when they learn something new, even when it is something that is scary and frightening for them to try. I encourage them to visualize themselves doing what they want to do, from start to finish. This can apply to anything in life.

I had trouble visualizing myself jumping properly. I could not make myself hold the correct body position in my mind. I had done improper jumping for so long my mind couldn't even correct it. My jumping did not improve until my ability to visualize improved. Take the time, close your eyes and see what it is you want to do. Once you can control every movement and body part in your mind, then you can translate that into reality. It's all about mind over matter.

Did you know that the mind cannot distinguish between something you imagine and something you do in real life? If you visualize yourself doing something successfully, you can translate that success into reality.

Swampy slowly began training me again. The hardest part was trying to figure out the coach and student relationship. I had acquired so much knowledge and different training techniques over the years that we couldn't go back to the way things were when I was a teen.

"Swamp, this is going to be really hard for me to admit this, but...my jumping just absolutely sucks."

"I know," Swamp smirked. "You need a ton of work and the first step is admitting it! Now that we have that behind us, we can saddle up."

> Everyone has 24 hours in a day. Adjust your day to devote time to your goal. Structure your time so you calculate a certain percentage of your time to meet your dreams.
>
> ~Keith St. Onge

"I need you to help me rework it," I said. "I've got to completely restructure my technique because it's limiting how far I can jump. It's also injuring my back. We have to figure out how to stop that from happening or I'm dead in the water. If I make a mistake in slalom or tricks, I can't hold my own in the jumping against David."

"That's fine, Keith, and I agree with you--your jumping is awful! I'm happy to work with you but we've got to be on the same page with this," he said. "We've got to go back to basics and strip away twelve years of bad habits. You have to be willing to start all over again." I agreed. Swampy went right to work and pulled up video after video of David jumping. We watched each video over and over, slowing them down, pausing them, and discussing each position frame-by-frame. We found a perfect jump of David's and dissected it position by position. We ended up having to buy a new DVD player because it could no longer pause or go in slow motion.

We both agreed on the basic fundamentals and how to break my bad habits. We also knew it was going to take a lot of time. The goal was to break one bad habit at a time and move onto the next. When we headed out to the boat, it was like old times. I dropped my World Champion status, took out my ego, and stripped it all down. I attached the five-foot handle on the boom. I looked at Swampy and laughed. I hadn't jumped on the five-foot line in years. "I feel like a beginner all over again! It's like the good old days!"

"Get used to it--you'll be there as long as you need to!" Swampy shot back. "Remember the rule we had years ago? When we are in the boat, it is business--no hard feelings and no holding grudges. When we step out of the boat we are best friends. What happens in the boat stays in the boat!"

"Easier said than done," I said dryly. "I know the routine."

After two weeks of jump practice I was still no better off than before we started training. Swampy and I began to battle in the boat. "All you need to do is keep your damn shoulders back! Keep your back straight!" Swampy growled. "You raise forward every time you approach the jump ramp!"

"Cut me a break! It's like trying to learn to write with your left hand after twelve years of writing with your right," I grumbled. It was a never-ending cycle. Swampy would bark out what he wanted me to do and I would go all-out trying to deliver a decent jump. Each time, I would end up more frustrated than ever after slamming into the water. We videotaped every single jump and watched it frame-by-frame. I didn't bother to jump on the days we couldn't capture video because if I couldn't analyze my mistakes it was a waste of time.

> He that lives by the sight of the eye may grow blind.
>
> ~Henry Ward Beecher

Poor Swampy was aggravated but he knew after twelve years of doing it wrong it was going to take a lot of jumps and a lot of driving on his part. (It's funny nowadays, because when he works with a skier with the same difficulties I had he says, "Please no, I can't go through it all again!" I laugh every time he says that!)

Swampy wasn't done with me; he decided to revamp my tricks as well. "I put together a new trick run I want you to try," he said. He outlined the new trick run he wanted me to do. I stared at him, incredulous. "*Eleven* tricks and *twenty-four* turns in fifteen seconds? And you want me to start with a line turn? You gotta be crazy--that's too freaking hard to do! I don't think I can get all those tricks in fifteen seconds!"

Swampy laughed. "Let's go out and time each trick individually to calculate how many seconds it takes for each maneuver."

"I'm going to kill myself with this--and I don't feel good leading with a line turn."

"Keith, I'm telling you...you have to at least try. We have to see what is possible."

"Okay. I'll try it. But I'm telling you, I don't like it."

"If you want to win this world title, you have to push the envelope in tricks." He shot me a pointed look. "You know you have to beat David with tricks, because he out jumps you. This is your only way to stay in the hunt for the Overall."

"I know...but...can't you come up with something a little easier?"

"Easy isn't going to give you points. Look, let's go out there, give it your best, and we can reconfigure from there if we have to."

I felt like Swampy was playing with me. He was having fun experimenting with new runs and I was the guinea pig. It was no different than in the past, but this seemed absurd. Eleven tricks with twenty-four turns? It was an impossible trick run that had to be executed perfectly with every second. When I was younger, he made trick runs of what we already knew was possible. Now, he was asking me to do things that had never been done or ever thought could be done. I had a hard time wrapping my head around this. Swampy was pushing me forward. I hated him for it. He was making me work extremely hard--but he continued to motivate me each day. He was like a professional salesman, stringing me along and coaxing me toward the purchase. The only difference was, not only did I have to buy the car but he was making me build it too.

Time and Effort

With your goals in life you have to be realistic, yet gutsy. You have to be willing to do things you don't want to do. Get out of your comfort zone. It is hard to learn all over again before moving on to the next step but a solid foundation in life will keep you strong. Most people want success right away. They're not willing to put in the time and effort in order to become successful or achieve their goals. That's the difference between those who succeed and those who don't: putting in the time and effort to make it happen.

I promised Swampy I would go "all in" for one week. If the runs looked like they were unachievable we would take a step back and adjust. After a few days, I was convinced it was impossible to achieve the trick run Swampy envisioned. I had taken more falls in a few days than I had all year. I was tired, sore, and fed up. I climbed into the boat and sat on the floor.

232

"I don't think it can be done, Swampy."

"Keith, you are so close!" Swampy gestured with his hands.

"I am sick of being close!" I snapped. "All this time we're putting into it, all the falls, and I'm getting nothing but headaches from it. If I can't fit all the tricks in one run then we have to start all over!"

Swampy was unfazed. "Look, you've got to keep your feet together, stay on your pivot foot when turning and do not track from side-to-side. Focus on those things and you *will* get it. Come on, let's do it again."

"I really need to see the light at the end of the tunnel soon! I'm getting tired, my muscles ache, and the sun is going down. Let's do this tomorrow." I was whining, and I didn't care.

"Four more runs and we will go in," he coaxed. "Just four more and you can have tricks off tomorrow. We'll only focus on jumping." I knew there was no getting around it. Swampy was as stubborn as they come and he wasn't taking no for an answer. I grabbed the handle, flung the rope back out, and jumped in. After a few more passes, I completed every single trick without falling. With a tired, triumphant sigh I hauled myself into the boat.

> Sometimes trusting others to see and dream for you will bring you to the next level.
>
> ~Keith St.Onge

Swampy's eyes were twinkling. We high-fived. "You got the tricks in time!" I knew his mind games and he was most likely lying but I didn't care. It was the first good news I heard all week and it was a sliver of motivation for me.

"Do you really think this trick run is possible in a tournament, Swampy?"

"I know you can do this. *You* just have to believe you can do it! Remember, you always get more tricks in during a tournament than you do in practice."

"Yeah, you've always been quick with that timer!" I cracked a smile. "I'll do it...I just need to rest up."

"Let's go in and watch it on video. You worked hard." Swampy said. We reviewed the video and I slowly began to understand how I could link certain tricks together and save time. I could set myself up for the next trick if I landed my previous trick in preparation for the next. I would have to be precise on every turn and that would be difficult. We went back out on the water the next day. I was supposed to jump but I had to attempt my tricks once again. I would not rest until I knew it was possible to complete the entire run on a consistent basis. The sooner I gained that confidence the less stressed I would be. After several passes the tricks became smoother and I stopped falling.

"So Keith, how do you like that trick run now?" Swampy smiled. We had spent an entire week working intensely on the water.

"Well...everything has to be done precisely. I cannot make a mistake. It's by far the most difficult trick run I have ever done...but...I like it." I could complete my trick run ninety percent of the time with all the tricks in time. I could finally see the light at the end of the tunnel. I was squeezing all eleven tricks into a fifteen second run! I could also do twenty-four multiple turns in fifteen seconds. The barefoot world had never seen tricks this fast in a run before. Swampy and I achieved something nobody thought was possible--and it was a great feeling!

"You know...this will put you over 12,000 points and nobody has ever broken 12,000 before." Swampy grinned. A big smile overcame my face. "This run would be so sweet to nail at the Worlds!" I said.

"Now, how come you gave me so much grief when I asked you to try this run?" He gave me a shove. "You have to believe in yourself! You have to want it deep down. You *know* that. You have to keep your head up and continue plugging away."

"I knew it was going to be difficult and a lot of work. I was looking for the easy way out," I sheepishly admitted.

"You were afraid to fail weren't you?"

"Yeah, I didn't want to put all that hard work into it for nothing."

"If you are afraid to fail Keith, you will never move forward. It's okay to fail, that is how you learn--but you cannot be afraid to fail."

"You're right Swampy, again...I was afraid. But now I'm confident and I want to hit this trick run at worlds!"

"Yes, that's the KSO I know and miss!" He grabbed me in a bear hug and didn't let go.

Pay It Forward

After many months of jump practice and hours and hours of reviewing videos, Swampy and I developed a new technique that helped in the development of barefoot jumping. At first, I was torn. Part of me wanted to keep the secrets to myself but the other part of me wanted to share the knowledge I acquired over the years.

Fortunately, it was an easy decision for me. I like to give back to the sport as much as possible so I give all my experience and expertise to my students! Other people have taught me so much over the years and I feel a strong sense of duty to do the same.

The end of the year rolled around and I was scheduled to do a video shoot for a company in Turks and Caicos, a stretch of islands in the Caribbean. The day before I was scheduled to leave my sponsor informed me that he wanted me to draw up a business proposal to continue my contract with him and the wetsuit company. He wanted me to address six items covering a 5-to-10 year plan and he wanted it presented by the end of the month. I fired off a quick email explaining I was about to leave the country and then head home for the holidays. I would send him the proposal upon my return. I was stressed and frustrated.

When I arrived home, I went to work on the proposal and sent it off to my sponsor addressing every point he requested. "For me to continue my business relationship with you, it must be a win/win scenario where everyone benefits, everyone is treated with respect, and everyone is involved in the process of making the business grow," I wrote. I expressed my disappointment with the two-week deadline for the proposal and the timing, especially with my schedule and the upcoming holidays.

Within hours, I received a reply. "After reading your proposal, I have to say

I'm quite disappointed," he wrote. He expressed his disappointment in point after point. He ended with: "The deal you had is gone." Just like that, our business relationship ended. The years of threatening to cut me off had finally come down to this moment.

On one hand, I was relieved. I was finally free to go out on my own and develop the KSO Barefoot ski school the way I wanted to. On the other hand, I was scared to death. I no longer had the security of a steady paycheck and it looked like I was going to lose my wetsuit sponsorship as well. This meant I would have to start from scratch once again. All the time and effort over all those years-- only to see it all disappear in one email.

I called a meeting with Judy, her husband Casey, Swampy and my parents and filled them in. They were the most trusted people around me and they had experienced a lot more than I ever had in life. I needed their wisdom and input. "I don't know what to do or how to respond to this. I need your opinions." I said. I love getting other people's opinions because that kind of input is priceless. I like to call those meetings "Brainstorming Sessions." My parents told me to talk it over with my sponsor but they did not know him like I did. I knew if I called him I wouldn't be able to speak my mind.

"You don't need him," Judy said. She said it in a much more colorful way—I couldn't help but laugh. It was comforting to have Judy, Casey, and my parents providing support.

"The less said, the better," said Swampy. "If this is what you want, send an email with a simple thank you to your sponsor for the help and the opportunities they gave you. Ask if there will still be a business relationship with your wetsuit sponsor. Focus on the good you gained from it." I thought long and hard about the suggestions from my brainstorming team. Swampy's suggestion made sense. I had learned a lot about business and marketing from my sponsor. I just wanted to walk away from it all with a clean break and a pleasant ending. I was emotionally disturbed by the last minute request on developing a business proposal and the sudden execution of the contract. I knew my sponsor never brought emotion into a business deal and I respected that, but this was over the top. A six-year relationship was done and over with at the drop of a hat. I had hoped to continue to ski in my sponsored wetsuits.

A few more emails flew back and forth and it soon became clear a sponsorship would not continue unless I submitted another business proposal more in line with what they wanted from me. The words in the email from my wetsuit sponsor hurt: "You are on a very limited path. I can guarantee that you will not be the World Champion forever and this may be your last year or it may not, but that day will come." It was obvious I would not be the current World Champion forever, but to say I was on a limited path was another story. He ended with this: "If you can afford to do without our sponsorship then maybe you do have a well-developed plan and we are all just talking nonsense."

I instantly knew I did not want to continue my relationship with my sponsors.

I had reached my breaking point. I sent a final email thanking both sponsors for their support and closed that chapter in my life. It was time to move on. The only thing was, I had *no clue* what I was going to do next. I told Swampy what I had done. "Are you sure you want to cut your ties just like that? Even I have a hard time letting that go. I have seen you ski in those wetsuits since you were fifteen." Swampy said. He had a distraught look on his face. We were both sentimental towards the wetsuits--I had proudly worn the wetsuits in every tournament for fourteen years. Swampy could not believe I made my decision to leave both companies in haste.

"You know me Swamp. I'm as loyal as they come. I would rather make less money and be happy. I've made my final decision and I am done!"

I was starting all over again and I didn't know what to do. I broke down. It was the first time Swampy had ever seen me fall apart, and he gave me my space. He knew I had to figure this out and work through the situation. I called my parents every other night and contemplated what to do. Like always, they supported my decision and said they would be there for me no matter

> Sometimes the greatest risk is not taking one.
>
> --Dan Miller

what. I was fortunate to have had great support from Judy, Casey, Swampy, and my parents. They listened to all my emotional bull crap for over a month dealing with this. With the backing each one of these individuals gave me, they made my future look bright instead of the darkness I kept focusing on.

Throughout the whole thing, I had difficulty sleeping at night. I was stressed out and simply a wreck. There's a saying, that "when one door closes, another one opens." That is exactly what happened when word got out I was no longer with my sponsor. Before long, I had a deal with Vortex Wetsuits, a company that sponsored David Small and Ron Scarpa. They made me a deal I couldn't refuse and it was far more than I had ever received in previous wetsuit deals. I worked with a designer to create a new line of KSO Wetsuits. I was back in business! I quickly went to work ordering KSO apparel and accessories. Sales took off, and the pro shop began bringing in money. The whole experience with my sponsor taught me a lot about myself. I learned that I could truly stand on my own two feet.

> Until one is committed, there is hesitancy, the chance to draw back, always ineffectiveness. Concerning all acts of initiative (or creation) there is one elementary truth, the ignorance of which kills countless ideas and splendid plans: that the moment one definitely commits oneself, then Providence moves too. All sorts of things occur to help one that would otherwise never have occurred. A whole stream of events issues from the decision, raising in one's favor all manner of incidents and meetings and material assistance which no man would have believed would have come his way.
>
> ~W.H. Murray

Team KSO

For a long time, I had the dream of creating my own "Team KSO" and now I could finally make that dream come true. I began to sponsor other skiers at a discount. I was careful who I selected to be on Team KSO-- they were skiers I trusted and they worked hard in representing the KSO Barefoot Ski School. For the first time in my life I was truly making my own decisions about my business. I had people around me I trusted and I knew this was the way I wanted to live. As hard as it was to leave the security of my sponsors behind, it was a blessing in disguise, as I learned I could depend on myself to overcome any adversity that came my way. Swampy and I had many discussions and he had a lot of business experience to share with me. He guided and helped me on my final decisions.

A.J. was among the first skiers we selected for Team KSO. Swampy and I didn't select skiers because of their talent on the water, but we selected people who showed a lot of heart, determination, and a willingness to learn. We wanted skiers who were well rounded and personable. If they were weak at a certain barefoot skill then Swampy and I could help them become stronger. A.J. embodied all of what we wanted on Team KSO. He was not only willing to learn on the water but, he was open to learning off the water as well. Swampy and I wanted to be able to shape young lives the way I had been shaped growing up and we saw incredible potential in A.J. He had a love for the sport that fired up his eyes every time he talked about it.

When he first came to us, A.J. was an absolute wreck on the water. Swampy and I would cringe while watching him attempt maneuver after maneuver-- followed by crash after crash. The learning curve was a long one, but every time we idled the boat back to him we saw a passion that burned deep in his eyes, a passion that poured out of every drop of sweat. He soaked in every word we said and he allowed us to push him without a single complaint.

A.J.'s father definitely warmed up to me after I worked with A.J. and he inquired about the possibility of A.J. training at the ski school full time. Swampy was faced with a decision at that point; he had to decide whether or not he wanted to commit full-time to training A.J. the same way he had trained me. It meant giving his time, expertise, and basically his life--and it meant he would be cemented to Winter Haven--there would be no opportunity for another job. Swampy was hesitant. He wasn't sure if he wanted that kind of commitment once again in his life. He thought back to the years of training me--the hours in the boat, the endless tournaments, the relentless sun—those details were nothing compared to the commitment involved. Once committed, a coach devotes himself to shaping a life. You can't back out of it halfway. "Do you think I'm cut out for this?" Swampy asked. "If I commit to this, it's all or nothing. I have to be in it one hundred percent, but the kid has to be too."

"There's no doubt that A.J. has the drive and the talent to succeed. He looks up to you, Swampy, and he wants nothing more than this," I said.

Swampy made the commitment and dove into full-time coaching. He had found his passion again.

> For eight years, I was drinking beer and partying a great deal of my life away. I regret that time in my life. I felt as though I wasted my time back then and would love to go back and have a second chance. This is a horrible thing to feel and regret. This is why I feel so strongly today about mentoring young kids and teens. I want to help shape their lives so they are guided by the wisdom of what I've learned throughout the years. Some of us must learn the hard way, but if you want to be smart about it, learn from other people's mistakes and not your own!

A few weeks before the 2008 Worlds, I received a call from Eugene Sam. It seemed like a friendly call at first, inquiring about my skiing and life in general. Slowly it began to dawn on me that he was pumping me for information, trying to see what tricks I was working on. Eugene's son, Heinrich, was an up and coming skier, hot on my tail and poised to take over the World Championship. In the years before, Sam looked up to me the same way I looked up to Ron Scarpa as a youngster. I sent him ski handles and in his room, he hung up a worn-out handle and a picture of the two of us together. I sensed a shift in him as he rose up through the ranks; the same shift I experienced with Ron as I progressed: no longer the idol, I was quickly becoming the prey.

"It's impossible to trick over twelve thousand, don't you think, Keith?" Eugene asked me over the phone. I was quick to agree with him. "Yeah, twelve thousand, that does seem impossible," I said. I didn't want him to know Swampy had just put together a run that would score me over twelve thousand points if I completed it perfectly. I planned to trick over twelve thousand at the upcoming Worlds.

The trip to New Zealand was a long one and I was thankful to finally share a World Championship with Swampy again. My teammates were hassling me on the plane. They saw a whole new side of me they had never seen before. I brought healthy food and followed Mary Jo's eating regimen. At appointed times, I snacked on dried apricots, nuts, and wasabi peas--much to the amusement of my teammates. I got up at regular intervals and did stretching exercises in the aisle of the plane. I didn't care that my teammates were razzing me. The health changes I made over the years were working for me and the results were beneficial. "You used to be so much more fun," Ryan Boyd

240

joshed. I shrugged. "I made a lot of mistakes in the past and I'm learning from them," I explained.

When the plane landed in Wellington, we drove out to the site and started training the next morning. I struggled on the water all week and none of my tricks were coming together properly. I couldn't figure out what was wrong. Just two days before the tournament, Swampy and I went out on the water to video my routine. After reviewing the video we figured out what was wrong and fixed the tricks. I was still juggling my nerves when I arrived back at the homestead, a huge, old house the whole team stayed in.

I decided to go for a jog to clear my mind. I headed out to the main road along the countryside. The dirt road was lined with trees I rarely saw in the states. I spotted the occasional sheep grazing on the side of the road. The elevation of the road was hilly which added a little difficulty to my jog. My legs felt the jet lag finally release and I relaxed. Ahead of me, the mountains loomed straight up and I thought about the White Mountains back home in New Hampshire. It was like a scene out of "Lord of the Rings." I stopped to stretch a bit before heading back. The sun started to set behind the mountains, painting the sky a brilliant orange. The clouds took on various hues as the sun's rays reflected off them. I stood there for a moment, just soaking it all in. A calm feeling washed over me and a smile came across my face. *I'm going to win this championship.* It wasn't arrogance, just a quiet "knowing" that came over me. I jogged back to the homestead.

At lunch, I stacked my plate with salad and fish. David eyed my plate in disbelief. "Is that all you're eating?" He pointed to his plate. "Look at me, I've got everything--you gotta fuel up before a competition! What you're eating won't get you far." I glanced at his plate. He had it piled with everything offered in the buffet line.

"Yeah, right! I'm staying light so I can trick up a storm," I laughed as I walked away. I knew I was doing what was right for me. I was leaner than I had ever been before so I fielded comments left and right from other skiers as they remarked at the changes in my physique. I had lost my "chunkiness" and looked like a professional athlete.

On the second day, Swampy nudged me. "Take a look at who's here." I scanned the crowd and I saw my former sponsor. He had told several skiers he wasn't planning to attend the World Championship, but here he was. He was sitting between two of his sponsored skiers. A month before the tournament my former sponsor was promoting both skiers far and wide. He was also picking apart my new wetsuits on his public forum. The old feelings began to surface. I wasn't comfortable--I felt like he wanted to see me fail. It was time for me to face him. "I'm going to ask him about the stuff he wrote about me and the wetsuits." I said.

Swampy looked surprised. I rarely stood up for myself in the past. "All right, go deal with him."

I sauntered over to my former sponsor with a smile. "Hey, how ya doing? I heard you had a comment about the wetsuit featured in the program book." He had trouble looking at me. I could hear him jingling change nervously in his hand. "Um, yeah..." he said. He looked uncomfortable and his voice was strained. "I, uh, saw the wetsuit in there. It looks like you're working on a new design."

"Yeah, I'm working on a couple new designs." There was an awkward moment of silence. He didn't say anything. The roles had finally reversed. The man who used to intimidate me no longer had any power over me. I walked away with my head held high. I knew my future would be what I made of it and I would never let another person dictate my accomplishments.

At the start of the tournament, the best skiers climbed into a small boat as we were shuttled to the start dock. We were mostly quiet on the ride over with a few comments here and there. We were packed like sardines on the dock-- there was literally nowhere to suit up or to mentally prepare in private. It was easy to play mind games with each other because there was no escape. Heinrich was the first one up. He skied beautifully and it was easy to see he scored well. He arrived back at the dock pumping his fist in the air and yelling in victory.

"You have to ski perfectly to beat him," Eugene jeered. The pressure was on. The nerves were jangling inside of me. *Let it happen,* I reassured myself. *You'll be fine.* One by one, the skiers came off the water with complaints about the water conditions. There was a break in the shoreline where the wind was getting through and the water seemed rough. I blocked it out and tried not to focus on it. I told myself to ski through it like it was glass calm water.

It was my turn. It was not the best trick run of my life and definitely not the cleanest, but I knew I scored over 12,000 points. It was just a matter of seeing if the judges would credit me for all my tricks. No one else knew as there was no way for them to tally it up. It was the first time a trick run had surpassed the 12,000 mark.

I was hollering and whooping when I arrived back at the dock, passing the pressure on to David. I saw Eugene and smiled at him. He cracked a smile. "Good job," he said. "How many points?"

"It should be good. It will be high, but it depends on what they pay me for," I said.

"Heinrich just tricked his best. He topped it out at over 11,000 points. You have your work cut out for you," Eugene said. I shot him another smile. I knew to keep my mouth shut. Swampy always told me, "Let your skiing do the talking." That's exactly what I intended to do. The score would speak for itself.

I arrived back on shore to a round of applause. I walked up to Swampy and I could see he was mentally calculating the score. Swampy is a human barefoot calculator. He can add up scores faster than anyone can trick them. "Looks like they paid you for everything," he said. "They got you at 12,450 points!"

"No way! I'm sitting pretty right now!" I wrapped Swampy in a bear hug. This was the first time the 12,000 point barrier had been broken in the history of barefoot skiing--and what better place to do it than at the World Championship in New Zealand.

I breezed through the wakes and racked up a 20.2 for slalom and then headed over to the jump. For all the struggles I had with jumping, I set a high goal for the Worlds: I wanted to land my jumps between 82 and 83 feet. In my mind, I was aiming for a distance of 85. Each time I exploded off the jump, I felt in control. I was chest deep in the water, walking back to shore when the boat crew informed me I could take a re-ride. "The boat speed was off," the driver said.

"Ok, I'll take the re-ride," I grinned. On the shore, David was fuming. "You gotta be kidding me--why is he getting a re-ride?" he hollered.

"It's like 2002, when the ropes broke on you," I retorted. I slapped my helmet back on and headed back out. I landed a solid jump at 82 feet before the re-ride so I didn't need to jump again--but there was no way I was going to decline a chance to improve my score. For the *first* time in my career at a World tournament, I received a medal for jumping. Third place had never felt so good! By that point, I had secured the Overall title once again. Victory was just as sweet the second time around.

During the ride to the banquet hall for the awards, I scribbled out my speech on a piece of paper. I reminded myself to thank the committee, my parents, the team, my friends Ryan and Adin for their support in my training, and the locals for the hospitality they extended to us. All too soon, I found myself on stage going through the round of thanks after the Overall trophy was handed to me. There was a pivotal moment in my speech when I thanked the guy who spurred me to a whole new level with my barefooting. "I'd like to thank my competitor, David Small, because he motivated me to push myself really hard this year," I said.

I wasn't quite done yet--there was one more person to thank. My eyes caught Swampy's and I called him up to the stage. "As most of you know, Swampy has been with me since the first time I put my feet on the water," I began. I took off my medal and placed it around Swampy's neck. "This is half his," I explained. "He worked as hard as I did--he drove me, he coached me, and he encouraged me to achieve my dreams. Thank you, Swampy for all of your support. I could not have done it without you." I grabbed him in a long hug as everyone stood up and applauded. It was the first World Championship where we shared the Overall gold medal together--a payoff of the long hours in the boat and the sweat we endured day after day in the hot sun. Our dream of being the best of the best was fulfilled and we could finally enjoy it together!

Toward the end of the night, I worked up a sweat on the dance floor and headed for the bathroom. I ran smack dab into my former sponsor. We looked at each other in surprise. I was elated about my Overall win and was in good spirits. It was time to pay the guy a compliment. After all, I wouldn't have gotten this far in life without growing from the experience. I had learned a lot from him. "Hey, I just want to say thank you for everything--thanks for your support in the past. We had some good times together." I smiled.

After the banquet, David and I walked to a bar and for the first time, we connected on a whole different level. For years, he was the competitor who spurred me on. He motivated me to take my skiing to the next level so I could achieve my dream; but he also was "the enemy to be conquered" and we kept our distance for years. Now that I had my dream in my hands I no longer had a chip on my shoulder against the guy. I let down my guard with David and we shared a few drinks together. For the first time, we dove into conversation. We discovered we were quite similar in many ways and we understood where we were coming from. After all, we were the two best barefoot water skiers in the world and we both worked hard to get there. We recognized a mutual respect for each other. Something shifted between us after that World Tournament.

"The two of you should go into business together," Swampy said after we retired for the night.

Go into business with my competitor? Are you crazy? I balked at the suggestion. I wasn't willing nor was I ready to take that kind of step. I was enjoying my time as a two-time World Barefoot champion and I didn't want to share that with anyone. I dismissed the idea at the time, but I stored it in the back of my mind to mull it over.

The Coolest Cover Shot

When I returned home, The Water Skier magazine contacted me and asked if I would be interested in doing another photo shoot for the cover. "Of course I would!" I answered. "Where and when?" The photographer, Lynn Novakofski lived just down the street from me. "Let's try for a sunset shot," he said. When Lynn arrived the light was poor and there were too many clouds in the sky. I wanted to try something a little different, because well, I like to be different— or maybe "creative" is a better word. "I'm up for anything," he said. "If it doesn't work we can try again another day." I wanted to barefoot ski directly towards the camera, let go of the rope and have Lynn take the shot of me standing on the water with no handle in my hand. Basically, I was going for a photo that made me appear to be standing on the water. "We don't have the time or enough sunlight for that," Lynn said.

I noticed several cinder blocks piled up next to the dock. "I've got an idea!" I said. I stacked the blocks in the water until they were flush with the surface. I grabbed all four of my gold medals from the Nationals and my five medals from the World Championships and held them up in the air as I stood on top of the blocks. Lynn used the flash because the sun was behind me. I looked as if I was standing on top of the water. Many people thought we superimposed the photo. I loved the fact I was not barefoot skiing, yet Water Skier magazine still used it as a cover.

One Good Deed Each Day

There was another highlight of the World Championship that stands out in my mind. Ross Linton was in charge of keeping the boat gassed up and running every day. Ross constantly fueled the boat up and brought five-gallon gas tanks from the trailer. This is not an easy job nor is it any fun. Since I was walking down to the dock, I decided to grab a gas tank and haul it down for him. Our team was getting ready to ski and I knew we would need more gas. Ross had already taken two tanks down. At the awards banquet, Ross came up to me and we made some small talk about the tournament. I thanked him for his help as part of the local organizing committee. He leaned a little closer to me and said "Thank You!" I wasn't really sure where he was going with it and I wasn't sure what he was thanking me for.

"Keith, I took so many gas cans back and forth all week long at the practice site." Ross said. "Out of all the people that walked back and forth to the boat you are the only person that carried a can down to the dock! For this, I would like to say, 'thank you' as this shows your character and what kind of person you are." I was astounded to learn that I was the only person who helped Ross. I felt good at being able to help. His acknowledgement made me feel pride in the way I was brought up. My parents always taught me to help others.

I've gotten into the habit of being mindful of doing at least one good deed each day. I instill this lesson with my team: do not be the person who sits back and watches while others work. Be the person who contributes. Help others in a time of need and in turn, others will help you.

Chapter 19: Put Your Dreams in Writing

Moving on is simple. It's what you leave behind that makes it so difficult.

~Unknown

When I arrived in Chetek, Wisconsin to conduct a barefoot water ski clinic, I contacted Barry Espeth. He told me he would be "water skipping" with his snowmobile. Riding snowmobiles across the open water was something I did as a teenager in New Hampshire but I only went thirty to forty feet across open water. Barry actually had a snowmobile set up to ride the water for long distances--as long as he kept the proper technique.

We arrived at a small pond with the deepest area being six feet. The shallow depth made it easy to recover the snowmobile if it sank. I watched in amazement as the guys flew around the pond with ease. I hooked up a rope and handle to the snowmobile and sat on a knee board about forty feet back "Ok, let's go!" I hollered. We took off down a grassy knoll leading into the water. I bounced slightly out of control when I hit the water but I put my feet in and stood up off the kneeboard. There I was--barefoot water skiing behind a snowmobile! Everyone on shore was going crazy. We posted the video on YouTube and it quickly became a popular video. That stunt continues to bring in the most questions everywhere I go. People cannot fathom a snowmobile on the water let alone barefoot skiing behind it!

Falling for a Girl

I remember the exact moment I saw her--a petite blonde with a smile that lit up her whole face. It was June 2008, at a party in the backyard of a skier's home in Chetek, Wisconsin. I was giving my fifth annual clinic to the Hydroflites show ski team and a group of us had gathered to kick back and play games before the week started. She arrived with a group of girls and guys. *I wonder if she's with one of the guys?* I couldn't take my eyes off of her. There was a gentle calm about her and I was intrigued. She worked the room with confidence and weaved in and out of conversations with ease. Tossing her head back, she laughed at a joke that someone shared. "Hey, is she with anyone?" I asked a friend. "Not that I know of," he answered. I studied her interaction with the two guys in her group to see if one of them belonged to her; it didn't seem like it.

I finally worked up enough nerve to talk to her. Taking a deep breath, I sauntered up to her. "Hi, I'm Keith," I smiled. "I'm trying to remember if we have ever met? Did you ski in my clinic last year?" It was a lame line, but it was all I could think of to start the conversation.

"No, we haven't met," she responded. "I'm Lauren Lindeman. I'm on the Hydroflites team."

Lindeman. I knew the name. Her two older brothers skied on the team and I had met one of her brothers a few years back when he stopped at the ski school with a friend. She flashed me a smile. I was captivated. There was something about her gorgeous, deep brown eyes that pulled me in. I learned she was not just a show skier but she could barefoot water ski as well. I was definitely impressed. In a sport dominated by men, female barefooters were a rare find.

"My parents have a lake house in town and I've been skiing with the team since I was eight-years-old," she explained.

"How come I've never run into you before?" I asked.

"I've been in Florida going to college for the last three years. I haven't been home much during the summer. I like to travel and I studied abroad for three months in Ireland."

A group began to gather for a washer toss game and by a stroke of luck, or rather, an act of God, we ended up on the same team. I discovered she was fiercely competitive and she was quick to show her determination to win when we fell behind in points. Toss by toss, we came up from behind to win the game. Competitiveness was something I identified with and for the first time in my life, I had met my match. Lauren was a gal who could dish out my kind of fun. I wanted to get to know this girl more. That is, if she would give me the time of day.

The next day was cold and rainy. This was typical Wisconsin weather in the middle of summer—hot one day and cold the next. In the previous years I barefoot skied in the Hydroflites ski show during intermission. I decided not to ski in the show that night. The years of hot Florida weather had spoiled me. I didn't want to take the chance of injuring myself in the extremely rough water and I certainly didn't want to deal with the pelting rain and freezing weather. I settled in the bleachers and watched the show skiers get ready for the show.

At that point in time I had been single for nearly two years. After my last relationship, I made two promises to myself. In the first promise, I would not get involved in a serious relationship until I was fully comfortable with myself. In other words, if I couldn't accept my faults and love myself then I sure wasn't in a position to love someone else. The other promise was simple: I didn't want to put a ton of energy and work into someone if I didn't feel it was right. I wanted to trust my intuition. I didn't want a relationship to feel like I was chasing someone. I wanted a relationship that was mutual and I was willing to wait several more years for the right girl if I had to.

One day earlier in the year, I sat down to list eighteen qualities I wanted to find in my soul mate. I wanted someone who was confident, independent, patient, fun, self-motivated and athletic. I wanted someone who was into healthy eating, travel, and water sports. She had to have a sense of humor, as well as common sense. I wanted a woman who could strike up a conversation with someone that she never met. And because my own sense of spirituality was developing--I was looking for that too. In one short night, Lauren invaded my world and turned it upside-down. I couldn't get her out of my mind the entire day. I looked up and saw her making her way toward me. "So...you're not going to ski in the show tonight? I heard you're a World Champion barefooter. What's the matter--you can only ski in perfect weather?" she razzed me. She was giving me crap and calling me out--but I liked it.

"Ok, I'll make you a deal," I smiled. "I'll ski in the show if *you* come and ski in my clinic tomorrow morning!"

"You've got a deal," she said. I looked up at the cloudy skies as rain dotted my face. A shiver ran down my spine with memories of cold, dampness, and wind while skiing in New Hampshire as a teenager. "I guess I have to go and get my wetsuit," I told her. I was faking reluctance, but deep inside I was trembling with excitement. Little did she know, I would do *anything* to get her to like me even if it meant skiing in the cold rain.

During the show, I was showing off and strutting my stuff on the water. I wasn't showing off for the crowd, I was showing off for *her*. Working hard not to make one mistake on the bumpy water, I cruised to a stop just before the dock, stepped up on stage, and waved to the crowd.

The first impression is so important and I hope it was a good one!

I went up to her after the show. "So... I'll see you at my clinic tomorrow morning, right?" I grinned. "After all, a deal is a deal." She flashed a mega-watt smile and my heart skipped a beat.

"I'm training for a marathon so I've got to do some running tonight, but yeah, I'll be at your clinic tomorrow." We exchanged phone numbers and parted. The next morning I sat in the boat waiting to see if she would show up. I sent her a quick text to make sure she would wake up. *Are you coming to ski this morning?* A text popped up. *I will meet you at 9:30 because it's too cold to ski right now.*

Meet us at the dock on the south end of the lake then, I typed back. I couldn't hold back my excitement and I told the students about the amazing woman I had met. Nine thirty came and went. There was no Lauren. I understood her lack of wanting to ski that morning. It was cold and rain was drizzling. *Maybe she won't show up after all.* The students in the boat poured on the teasing--they could see I was waiting for her. The sun started to peek out but the students were getting cold and wanted to go in. I idled near the dock hoping for more time.

I saw her. She was walking toward the boat. *She actually showed up!* My heart skipped a beat again--it was doing that a lot around her. I tried to remain cool. I didn't want her to know how pumped up I felt inside. I pulled up to the dock. She hopped in the boat and sat right next to me. I couldn't take my eyes off her. It was difficult to concentrate on teaching the students. I found myself trying to impress her with my teaching skills. When it was her turn to get into the water, I knew she had to strip down to her bathing suit to put on a wetsuit. Like I had imagined, she was fit from all the water skiing she did during the summer.

Physically fit with a great body... Another check mark off my list.

"How about we get things going with a start on your butt since you have a padded wetsuit on?" I suggested. Lauren had previously learned to barefoot ski by stepping off of a ski so she had no experience with the deep-water start. I walked her through the steps for the start with a little more of a "hands on" approach than I normally used with my students.

"I don't like all this water in my face," she complained after her first attempt. I laughed. I thought back to my own deep-water starts and the countless times I tossed the handle as soon as the water hit my face. I knew exactly how she felt. "You just have to ride it out and get up, then the water won't be in your face." A few tries later, she had nailed the deep-water start. She was a quick learner and soaked in everything I said. I *really* liked this girl.

Later that night, she picked me up and we joined the ski team for dinner. We talked all night. I didn't want to talk to anyone else, I just wanted to sweep her away somewhere and be alone with her. I knew I wanted to see her again. "I've got an opening for Wednesday afternoon. Do you want to join me in the boat again?"

"Sure!" There was that smile again. Wednesday couldn't come fast enough. There was just one hitch. Lauren had to head back to her hometown in Chicago to pick up a friend at the airport. It was a six-hour trip and she would have to drive through the night to make it back to Chetek for the Wednesday morning clinic. It would be crazy for her to drive to Chicago, turn around and drive straight back to Chetek, Wisconsin. That would be twelve hours of driving! I was skeptical she would make it back.

At seven a.m. I sent her a text and asked if she was planning to join us in the boat. I didn't hear back from her. I sent another one a half hour later but there was still no answer. *She must have decided to stay in Chicago and sleep in.* I didn't blame her. I couldn't help myself I sent yet another text. There was no response. At 9 a.m. my phone buzzed as a text popped through. "I'm 45 minutes away," she wrote. My heart pounded in my chest with excitement. I felt like a kid in high school again. *She was coming back! Gosh, she's giving me a chance.* I picked her up on the dock shortly after. And then it hit me-- If she drove all the way back up here to ski with me, she must really like me...sweet! I was filled with a new sense of confidence.

"Are you interested in learning how to barefoot ski backwards?" I challenged her as she hopped into the boat. To my complete surprise, she said yes. She was one gutsy gal. I walked her through the steps to learn the backward start. As I watched her place her feet in the water I could hardly believe my eyes--

251

she stood up on her very first try! By the end of the set, she was barefoot water skiing backwards for short runs. "I'm really impressed! Nobody learns back deeps that fast!" I told her. I wasn't sucking up either--it was the truth. I was truly impressed. The backward deep start was one of the most challenging starts to learn with a steep learning curve and she had nailed it on her first try. *This girl is something else! She's my kind of girl!*

Later that evening I summoned up the courage to ask her out on a date. We were on our way to the show ski site and I had to gas up the boat first. "Do we have enough time to grab something to eat before the show starts?" I asked. "Sure," she smiled. I silently offered a quick prayer. *Please Lord; allow her to give me the time of day. Please let her give me a chance so she can really see the real me. Don't let me make any stupid moves.* I was nervous. We slid into a booth at Side Winders and ordered burritos. As we dug into the food, I found myself becoming more and more comfortable talking to her and the conversation began to flow freely. I thought back to something my dad often said to me: "A great conversation is like a smooth game of ping pong. Don't slam the ball back at your opponent--keep the rally going. A curve ball or spin will knock out your opponent--or in the case of a conversation will kill it."

"You have beautiful eyes," I blurted out. To me, brown eyes are usually plain and common--but her brown eyes were something unreal. "Thank you," she said. I wasn't trying to flatter her. I wasn't someone who would throw compliments out so early on a date but I could not help it. It was the truth. I was mesmerized with the warmth that shined in her eyes. Lauren was stirring up my insides like no other girl had ever done before. She didn't have an ounce of nervousness in her. She exuded confidence. She also had a quick-witted sense of humor with a sarcastic edge and I liked that.

We finished up our dinner and left for the show. During the show, I watched her every move. "Hey, great run on the trick ski!" I told her. "Not too bad yourself," she said after I completed my run. "But how come you didn't do all those crazy turns like you tell everyone you can do?" There was her typical sarcasm coming out. I liked it and actually thought it was quite funny. "I'm saving it for you." I teased her back with a wink. At the end of the show, I waited for her. As we walked to the parking lot she mentioned she was going for a jog. "You're going to jog after skiing in a show? Aren't you tired?" I was spent, and ready to call it a night. I just wanted to kick back. "I have to," she lamented. "I'm running the Chicago marathon in one month."

252

"I'll go with you," I blurted. "There's only one thing though, I can't run as far as you. How about if I ride a bike while you run?" She agreed, and went off to get her running gear. The rain was pouring by the time she started running. "Are you still going to run?" I asked. "I can't miss my run or it will throw my training routine off,' she explained.

"How far do you plan on running tonight?"

"I'm supposed to run three miles, but I'm not sure how far I can go in the rain. I'll shoot for a mile or two. If it starts storming we can head back." I rode on the bike as she ran. I didn't feel the cold chill in the air or the rain pelting down. I was just happy being next to her. We made it about two miles when we rounded the bend to where I was staying. Lauren opted to call it quits just as the rain began to come down even harder. Streaks of lightning began to snake across the sky. We ran under the eave of the garage and for some odd reason we stood on opposite sides. There was too much space between us, but we bantered back and forth with small talk.

A thought popped in my head: *I want to kiss her. How should I approach this?* I went over several scenarios in my head. *Should I walk over and plant one on her? What if she pushes me away? Maybe I should warm her up with a hug first and then go in for a kiss? No--no, that's dumb. What if she doesn't want me to kiss her?*

I had to try something. I had to take a chance---even if she rejected me. I could not let the evening go on without getting closer to her. I decided to try something I never tried before. "Can I kiss you this evening?" I politely asked. A strange look came over her face. Mentally, I kicked myself. I could tell that no one had ever asked for permission to kiss her before. What the heck--I was being genuine and unique. "Yes," she responded. Feeling awkward, I took a few steps over and kissed her. We had our first kiss while dripping wet from the rain. Our lips were cold and we were both shivering, but the mood of that night was blissfully warm as we touched.

Could she be the one at last? I did not want to put any energy into a relationship but this wasn't a chore at all. I loved being around her at every opportunity. I didn't have to work to connect with her—it was effortless—like nature taking its course. At the end of the week, I was looking for a ride to the airport and made sure to bring this up while Lauren was standing nearby. "I might be able to drive you to the airport--let me look at my schedule," she said. A few hours later she called and said she could. My plan worked perfectly!

The next morning, I was sweating bullets while packing my bags. There was no air conditioning in the house and the weather had warmed up. I didn't want to get my shirt all sweaty before entering the car, so I walked out of the house holding my shirt in one hand and my bag in the other. (However, to this day, Lauren doesn't believe my reasons for coming out of the house shirtless. "You were just trying to impress me," she recalled. Apparently I definitely caught her eye.)

On the way to the airport, we talked non-stop. I was desperately trying to figure out how I could see her again. About an hour into the drive, flashing lights appeared in the mirror. A cop pulled Lauren over and issued her a speeding ticket. I guess we were talking too much and she wasn't paying attention to the speedometer.

I came up with an idea--it was a shot in the dark but what the hell... "I'm teaching a small clinic in Edmonton, Canada in two weeks. Greg Gartner is a good friend of mine and he told me I could bring anyone up to the clinic. Would you like to join me--it's absolutely beautiful up there," I asked. I had never invited someone to a clinic before, but this was a relaxed, private clinic and I knew she would be comfortable there. Besides, I wanted to see her again.

"I'll think about it," she said. She flashed that smile again. "The friend I picked up at the airport this week is from Maine and she's staying with me for one month. I'm not sure I can get away." Of course, I didn't expect her to say yes. I knew she loved to travel, but it was crazy--we had just met. It was a long shot but if it were meant to be, it would be. I gave her a long hug and a kiss before I turned to head into the airport. I really didn't want to leave. On the plane, I felt an emptiness inside which was completely unfamiliar to me. I had never felt this way before. *I hope she comes to Edmonton--please God, let her come with me.* A week later, an email popped in. Lauren asked me what days would work out best for her arrival. I shot back a reply outlining the dates. I informed Greg about my potential visitor. The next day, Lauren emailed me back. *I bought a ticket--I'm going to join you in Edmonton,* she wrote. My jaw dropped. I grabbed the phone and dialed furiously. "You're fooling with me aren't you?" I couldn't contain my excitement.

"No, I'm serious, I'm flying in on Tuesday afternoon," she laughed.

"What did you tell your parents?"

"I just told them I was going to a barefooting clinic so I could learn more."

"Wow, you are crazy...and I love it!" As soon as we hung up, I felt like a little kid waiting for Christmas to arrive. I was going to be spending five days with this girl and I could not wait! *I gotta clean myself up.* I looked in the mirror. The hair was fine/ I had just gotten a haircut. Peering in closer, I decided my eyebrows needed a little trim. I grabbed the electric razor and ran it through an eyebrow.

Oh crap! I stared in horror at the gleaming white skin in the mirror. The skin had never seen the light of the sun my entire life. I had practically shaved my eyebrow off! I looked at the razor. "No!" The guard had slipped from my normal setting on five down to one. I looked back in the mirror. *Oh gosh. Now Lauren is going to think I got drunk one night and someone shaved my eyebrow off!* I had four days to grow as much eyebrow hair as possible. Thankfully, no one said a word when I arrived in Edmonton.

When Lauren arrived, I was nervous as heck. This trip would give us the opportunity to really get to know one another. Thankfully, she didn't say anything about my mismatched eyebrows. This clinic was more like a vacation--the skiers were good friends and there was no pressure to entertain them while on the water.

Lauren and I quickly found that we communicated perfectly. She laughed at my corny jokes and understood me right from the beginning. I laughed at her sarcastic jokes in return. I took this as a sign. In the past, whenever I would crack a dry humor joke on dates it would often fall flat--the other person wouldn't even get it. But Lauren "got me" right away. The humor softened the mood between us, which allowed us to connect. Lauren had common sense and we could relate to one another on many different levels. We discovered we were able to talk about everything--and we had a lot to learn about each other. One thing I quickly loved about Lauren was the way she thought about other people. We were eating dinner on the deck one night and everyone had a chair except for one lady. Lauren got up out of her chair, slid it over for the young woman and walked across the deck to retrieve another chair. Her actions showed she thought about and acknowledged other people's needs and did not just think about herself. That moment I was lured even closer to Lauren.

Late one evening, we walked down to the dock with a bottle of homemade wine. We sat and talked while the sun disappeared beyond the horizon. We were still talking as darkness wrapped around us and one by one, the stars appeared. I was falling in love with this girl and it had only been three weeks since we met. I had never felt this way about anyone else, and it wasn't the wine messing with my head, I felt something special! I thought back to the list I created earlier. I wrote down eighteen things I was looking for in a woman. Mentally, I reviewed the list in my mind and I realized Lauren had every single thing I was looking for in a mate. *Every single thing.* My heart was beating fast. A wave of emotions washed over me--feelings so deep I had no words to explain it. As we walked off the dock, a thought popped in my head: *I can see myself with this girl forever.* That very night, I knew she was "The One."

More to Conquer

I was at a point in my career where I felt I had done it all--I had the elusive World Overall Championship title to my name, I won several National titles, and I held all three world records at one point. I accomplished my ski school business goals and the school continued to grow. But there was one tournament I hadn't conquered: the Footstock National Figure-8 Championship--the granddaddy of endurance tournaments. I had competed in several of the Footstock tournaments but I could never win.

Footstock was sponsored by my former sponsor and this was the first time I was not going to be wearing their wetsuit or be associated with them. For the first time in my career, I was able to market my own name without anyone controlling me. Breaking away from my former sponsor was challenging and exhilarating--extreme sides of the same coin. It was an incredibly freeing feeling, yet, frightening!

Lauren came with me to Nationals in Wisconsin where I racked up another Overall win and then we drove to Crandon for Footstock. We met up with Judy and Casey, who came rolling up in their RV. They both came to provide support and encouragement. After working together so closely for the last two years, they had slipped into the role of my second parents. I frequently turned to them for advice, guidance, and wisdom-- and to this day, they care for me as if I were their son.

The tournament was coming on the heels of a roller coaster year and I wanted to finish the barefooting season with the Footstock title in my name. Three of the top endurance Figure-8 skiers were sponsored by my former sponsor and Peter Fleck was the guy to beat--he had won Footstock four times and he was a tough opponent on the water.

I was decked out in my sleek, black Vortex wetsuit with a matching long-sleeved heater shirt under it. Mary Jo had tweaked my diet in ways that provided me with amazing energy and I was really feeling it. During the first couple of rounds, my opponents were dropping like flies. Halfway through the tournament, the director announced that I would be giving away free cups and autographs. I wanted to make it clear to the footers and the fans that I was now on my own. In between rounds of skiing, I signed autographs and gave away 200 cups with my name and "KSO Barefoot School" plastered on them. I felt as though I was starting my business from scratch again. I had to reestablish myself and I wasn't going to be shy in doing so.

I had worked my way up the ranks and was paired up against Fleck. The two of us had just finished doing a grueling three and one-fourth "eights" against other footers so we were tired when we faced each other. As we kicked off our skis, I settled in for what I figured was going to be another long round. We were halfway through our second "eight" when I caught a toe and fell. I groaned. The fall meant I was now in the loser's bracket and would have to work my way back up to the finals. It also meant that if Peter had no falls, I would have to face him in the final round and beat him not once...but twice. I tried not to think of the incredible amount of work that I had ahead of me. I just wanted the title and I would do whatever I had to do to capture it.

I made it through the grueling head-to-head format and sure enough, in the final round I faced Peter. He had beaten everyone before him and hadn't taken a single fall. I had worked my way up through the loser's bracket and I was tired. Yet, I was also feeling that second wind that comes after a strenuous workout or like the runner's high that comes after a few miles when the muscles adapt to the repetition and abuse. As Peter and I jumped in the water, I took a closer look at his wetsuit. Peter was wearing a black and white wetsuit with a tiger pattern etched into it. I suddenly remembered something about Peter. Long before I got into barefooting, Peter was famous for wearing a wetsuit that looked like Tony, the Tiger. You know the one--the breakfast cereal character famous for saying "They're grrrrrrreat!" As the story went, other footers used to tease Peter before his runs by making references to Tony the Tiger. The teasing inevitably would lead Peter to choke or fall on his runs.

The boat towed the two of us up out of the water and I concocted a plan in my head. I skied up to Peter, extending my hand for the usual "good luck" handshake. "Hey Peter!" I shouted over the roar of the boat engine. "That suit looks like a Tony the Tiger suit. I hope you do grrrrrrrrrrrreat!" I chuckled as I skied away and then glanced back to see if I had gotten a reaction out of him. It was easy to tell that Peter hadn't heard that for years. He seemed a bit rattled as he tried to figure out how the heck I knew about his little bit of history. As we rounded the first bend I was feeling good. We completed the first "eight" and headed back around for the second, then the third. By this time, I was at the point of wanting to let go. My feet were burning as if I was walking on razor blades. *Just stay up--just stay up!* I tried to pump myself up. Mentally, my mind was gone. Physically, I didn't have anything left inside. *I can't hang on much longer! I just can't hang on much longer!* The words kept refraining over and over inside my head. We completed the fourth "eight" and a quarter--a Footstock record! Just as I looked over to check on Peter, he went down. I let go of the handle and sank in the water with a tired sigh. *One more friggin' round to go!*

Exhausted, we both climbed into the boat, hardly speaking to each other. We were both just physically shot after that record round and our feet were hot to the touch. We took a ten-minute break, plunging our feet into a tub of ice to cool them off. "How're your forearms?" I asked Peter. I knew his forearms were hurting him. "They're fine," he said. Peter came right back at me. "How are your feet feeling?" He knew my feet became hot easily on the water, forcing me to lift one foot at a time to cool them off. "Oh, they feel fine," I lied. They actually hurt like hell--and he knew it.

I tried to figure out how I could mentally shake up Peter for the final round. Earlier in the day I had noticed that Peter was hooking his arm in the handle while getting up on the ski. There's a rule at Footstock--you can't hook your arms through the handle when barefoot skiing. The rule is to prevent a skier from falling with a hooked arm which could lead to serious damage and injury. The rule didn't really apply to the take-off while on a ski or at least no one had protested it before. So I decided to play with him a bit as we took off. Peter and I got in the water for our final round and sure enough, he hooked his arm in the handle to save his grip.

"Hey Peter, you can't do that!" I motioned to his arm.

"What do you mean?" He shot me a confused look.

"You can't hook your arm in the handle!" I yelled. "The boat judge was yelling at you not to do that or they will disqualify you!"

"Did they really?" he shouted. I nodded. Peter unhooked his arm and gripped the handle. I laughed inside and I tried not to show it. The boat judges hadn't said a word--I just wanted to level the playing field. We both did not have much left inside of us, but if I was going to have to grip the handle then I wanted to make sure he didn't have an advantage over me by hooking his arm. Fair is fair.

As soon as we kicked off the skis, it was a battle just to stay upright on the water. *Just make it around the corner,* I cajoled myself. *Just around the corner.* As we rounded the corner, I hunkered down as the first set of rollers came up. I rattled over the rollers, staying upright. *Thank God!* I lifted one foot off the water then the other, trying to control the burning feeling in my feet. Every time I put a foot down, I felt as if I was landing on shards of broken glass. I looked over at Peter. Underneath his cool expression, I could feel him grimacing. I was feeling the same way.

Come on, just another 100 feet, I told myself. *Just get through the next 50 feet. Ok, now another 20 feet.* I kept coaxing myself on. The pain was agonizing. I shifted my feet again, lifting one at a time. The muscles in my thighs were screaming and I desperately wanted to let go. *Just make it through another set of rollers. You can do another set!* I looked at Peter. The damn guy was still up.

Ok, just get through ten more feet. Ten feet is nothing. You can do ten feet! Ten feet isn't that far! The burning feeling was torturous. The conversations in my head continued to rattle on. *I hope I don't burn a hole in my foot. This hurts! My God, it hurts! I want to quit now.* Every single muscle in my body was telling me it was time to quit. My back was aching and I shifted my position to try to get some relief. We had just completed the first "eight." I couldn't imagine hanging on for another two, three, four, or God forbid, five "eights." I looked at Peter again. He was hanging on with one hand trying to get some relief for his aching forearms. He re-gripped and then shifted hands again.

I tried to psych myself up. *Get around this bend, come on, just hang on around this bend!* We were rounding the corner, approaching the dock and another thought hit me: *My former sponsor is probably watching. I want to win this.* I gripped the handle even tighter. I was not going to give up now. Out of the corner of my eye, Peter went down in a splash in front of the crowd.

I won! I did it! I threw my arms up in the air and continued to ski a bit. I was the new Footstock champion! I loved every second of that victorious moment! My legs were shaking when I walked up the stairs from the dock, but I was running on an emotional high.

The sweetest moment of all came later... it was the moment that the Footstock committee handed over the winning check. I could hardly walk, but I was on a high when I held up the check and posed for photos. My feet were bruised and extremely sore for two and a half weeks afterwards. The muscles in my forearms were so painfully worn out that I could hardly grip a pen. My thighs were as tight as banjo strings, and every movement brought out pain. But feeling beat up after winning a championship like that was not only worth it--it was priceless!

Lauren and I kept in touch with daily phone calls after I flew back home. With each call, I couldn't get enough. The more I got to know her, the more I wanted this woman in my life, totally and completely. Lauren and I made a point to see each other every month. She often flew to Florida to grab the perfect weather. I made it up to Chicago a couple times but it was difficult to find time away from the ski school.

The first time I met Lauren's parents, I noticed that Lauren was the spitting image of her mom, Virginia. Her dad, Don, wasn't an easy man for me to get to know at first. He stood well over six feet tall, with his dark hair slicked back like a Chicago mob boss. I had some difficulty figuring out his personality. Halfway through our conversations, I never knew if he was serious or joking. I think he did that on purpose--he was screwing with me. As a result, I ended up feeling pretty intimidated and I steered clear from him the few days I was in town. During one of my visits, my dad flew in to join me on a trip up to Wisconsin for a conference. Lauren joined us at the conference and drove us to a Chicago airport afterward. My dad's flight was cancelled so we went out to eat with her parents that evening. Throughout the night, I watched as my dad and Don exchanged friendly banter. My dad was quite the character that night and Don seemed to be thoroughly entertained. The next day, after Dad flew home I could feel a friendly shift occur between Don and me. "Your dad cleared the path for you, Saint! I like him a lot!" he boomed. "Now I know where you came from--and I like you a little more." I breathed a sigh of relief.

Lauren and I had a long distance relationship for one year. The monthly visits weren't enough for me. I knew without a doubt I was in love with her and I wanted the relationship to move to the next level. One night, over the phone, I laid it all out. "For this relationship to last, you are going to have to move to Florida," I said. "We have to be together every day--and actually, in the same town would be nice. I can't move because my business is here and I still have goals to achieve regarding my barefoot water skiing career. I can't really fulfill those dreams in Chicago." I didn't want to put her in a corner but she knew it was coming to this.

"I'm willing to move to Florida, but I'm going to need some time to work this out with my parents, especially my dad," she said. I agreed to give her time to work it out. I was really thrilled at the idea that soon enough, she would be with me every day.

By spring, Swampy and I were having deep discussions about joining forces with David Small. His ski school was just forty-five minutes north of my location. Joining the two schools made so much sense. David had a huge European clientele and I had the U.S. clientele. Having two of the largest regions combined would allow the ski school to expand, sell more equipment, and enable us to give back to the sport in hopes to build some younger skiers for the future. The more I thought about it, the more I realized the brilliance of the partnership. Between the two of us, we held two World Championships, countless records, and we were the number one- and two-ranked skiers in the world. I was getting older and David was six years younger than me. I knew my career on the water would not last forever. Swampy outlined the pros and cons of joining forces. "If you don't go into business with David he'll go somewhere else and always be your competitor," Swampy reminded me. Swamp was a champion at playing "Devil's Advocate" and he figured there were more positives than negatives for both parties. It all came down to me--was I willing to let go of what I had built and share it with someone else? My gut instinct told me it was the right thing to do. I had to reach out and see if David could share the same vision.

The three of us met at a local restaurant to discuss the possibility of going into business together. Swampy was our mediator. "Guys, you both have to check your egos at the door before starting this business. Can you both do that?" We agreed we could, but we also understood it would not change our fierce competitiveness on the water. We conducted several meetings over a month and half before we came up with a solid business plan. David and I shook hands on the deal. My rival on the water was now my partner and the World Barefoot Center was born.

Chapter 20: Learning Forgiveness

I've never met a person who is successful-- who didn't have a lot of bumps, bruises and scars from their failed attempts.

~Dave Ramsey

The call from the Mastercraft representative came out of the blue. "We've got a request for you, Keith. Dave Ramsey would like to contact you regarding a barefoot water ski clinic. We recommended you to him."

Dave Ramsey. The name was vaguely familiar--I knew he was some kind of financial guru. I typed his name into Google to find out more. I was intrigued. Dave's mission and his life's work was to help families get out of debt and learn responsible money management. He was the host of a popular radio show, the Dave Ramsey Show. He penned several best-selling books including *Total Money Makeover, More Than Enough,* and *EntreLeadership,* (all which I highly recommend). Dave was best known for his famous quote: "If you live like no one else, later you can live like no one else."

I called Dave and set up the plans for his clinic. Part of the agreement included some training time for me. I was heading out to the World Games in Taiwan at the end of the week, so I had to make sure I would be able to train in the morning and evenings during Dave's clinic. Dave agreed to pull me. I was looking forward to working with him. Little did I know that by the end of the week Dave was going to have a profound impact on my life.

When I arrived at his lake house in Tennessee, Dave greeted me with a warm smile and a firm handshake. I soon discovered that he was a down-to-earth guy with a great sense of humor. I immediately could tell the week was going to be a fun one. Dave and I quickly hit it off. His amazing son, Daniel, also joined us in the boat. He was a skilled wake boarder and slalom skier so he advanced quickly with his barefooting tricks. Both Dave and Daniel were naturals on the water, displaying good balance. Daniel's friend Dane and Dave's friend, Don also joined us.

263

The first evening I arrived and met everyone, they offered me a chair to join them in the kitchen. Dave and his family and friends drilled me with question after question. *Where are you originally from? How did you get started in barefooting? What titles do you have? What are we going to work on this week?* I could feel their excitement about the barefooting that was going to take place that week.

"Wow, sounds like you had great parents along with this Swampy guy." Dave remarked.

"I couldn't have done it without them. My parents were supportive and Swampy kept me motivated. I'm very lucky to have such great parents and Swampy!"

I realized that most of my answers were about my parents and Swampy, but quite simply, I owed my entire barefooting career to them. As the night grew late, we all agreed get up at 5:30 a.m. to start skiing at 6. We wanted to get the smoothest water possible and beat the heat from the humidity of the Tennessee summer.

I was outside early the next morning at the far side of the lake house when Dave and the others found me warming up. My knees were completely bent, with my shins to the ground and I was lying on my back. I looked like a contortionist.

"What are you doing over there? That looks painful!" Dave laughed.

"This is one of the stretches I do every morning. It keeps me flexible on the water. I'm going to Taiwan to compete in the World Games after this week and trying to keep loose."

"I may pop a knee cap if I try that one-- but how do you do it?"

"Just sit down on your knees and gently push your hips forward, while leaning back. Keep your rear end on the ground. This is one of the best ways to stretch your quads." Dave slowly got himself into the position.

"Youch, I feel that in my ankles!" Dave groaned.

"It took me a year to get where I am and I started in the same position you are in now," I laughed. "I said the same thing the first time I tried it!"

"Where did you learn these stretches?"

"I hurt my back a few years ago and was unable to ski, so my dad gave me a few ideas on what to stretch and he taught me this one."

"So, how did he get into this stuff?"

"He was in an accident many years ago. He was at work, standing behind his bucket truck with orange cones around him cordoning off the space. A milk truck came around the corner--the driver lost control and drove through the cones. My dad ended up pinned between the trucks. He broke his pelvis and as a result, he has had tight muscles for years. He learned various stretches and also began to eat healthier in an attempt to get well."

I soon had everyone stretching before we headed out to the early morning session. Dave learned to barefoot when he was sixteen. He started by kicking off a ski, the way most people started back then. For thirty years, Dave was content to barefoot up and down the river without learning anything new. I started off teaching the basic fundamentals and making minor adjustments to everyone's stance and form. They all learned the deep-water start as well as several tricks. The gang worked hard on the water and we all came back starving. We all relaxed, had lunch, and kicked back by reading a book or going online. We planned to wait out the afternoon heat and do a second set at dinnertime. This would keep the boat traffic off the lake and the sun would be going down. After lunch, Dave began to check his emails because he received so many every day. Most emails he answered quickly, otherwise he would be at his desk for days. He spent close to an hour answering emails.

"It's tough putting up with some people isn't? I said.

"It sure is. How do you deal with some of your tough customers?"

"My dad actually taught me a lesson one day. I was ranting to him about some customers who were getting under my skin--I felt like they were doing it on purpose. So I asked him, 'How should I deal with people like that?' His explanation was simple: 'It is not the other person who is annoying you, it is *you* that has an issue with yourself.' I didn't quite get it, so Dad explained more. He told me that I had to work on understanding and accepting the other individual for who they are--and that I was the one with the problem, not them. Once I learned to look at it that way, I was no longer annoyed."

265

"You have one great father, Keith, and I hope to meet him one day." Dave said. Dave and I developed a friendship from the many talks we had during the week and he helped me find the answers to the many questions I had about God and faith. We said our goodbyes and as I walked down the stairs Dave stopped me. "I'm going to send you a package with some books that I think you'll enjoy," Dave said. "One of the books that I recommend you read is *The Shack*. That one won't be in the package so buy it if you see it. It's a great book. I cried during some parts of it," he said.

I stared at him in surprise. "Dave, it's funny you mention that book. A few months ago a good friend of mine, Murray, another barefooter who is a chiropractor, suggested I read that same book. I'll have to check it out."

At the airport, I decided to stop at the bookstore and browse. As I glanced over the rows and rows of books, I found it sitting on a shelf right in front of me: *The Shack*. *That's a sign!* I thought. *A friend told me to read the book, Dave told me to read the book, and here it is, right in front of me!* Sometimes you have to be hit over the head a couple of times to recognize a sign. I bought the book and once I boarded the plane, I settled in to read it.

During one of my calls home, Dad casually mentioned that he received a two-page letter from Dave. He proceeded to read it to me over the phone. *I want to tell you about a great experience I recently had*, Dave wrote. He went on to share the experience he had in meeting me and what had transpired during the clinic:

The week arrived and our five guys gathered and waited to see what we were going to learn and honestly I was also waiting to see what type of person I would be dealing with. During the next four days we were bruised and battered, coached, and learned more in a few days than we would have muddled through in a lifetime. But I am writing this letter one Dad to another. My most pleasant surprise was the quality of young man that was in my home for four days. I am very impressed with Keith St. Onge, the man. Your son is humble, confident, articulate, a high-quality teacher, and was a pleasure to get to know.

He wrapped up with: *My personal opinion is that Keith's greatest accomplishment (and yours) is the man he has become. The barefooting thing is just a sideline. I see big things for the next phase of his life and have offered to help him as God leads him to what he will be world champion of next.*

I was speechless.

266

The Good Book

I have met people from around the world and like the saying goes in business, "Never talk about religion or politics." That is a sure way to get into an argument and lose business relationships and friends. I try to avoid those topics unless it is something I agree upon with the individual. As far as religion goes, I was brought up Roman Catholic and went to church every Sunday until I was a junior in high school. Once in a while, my parents would allow me to go barefoot waterskiing with Swampy early in the morning as long as we got back in time to go to church afterwards.

Every now and then in the boat, a conversation about religion would pop up. Students asked if I believed in God. One particular student named Murray McKinnen asked me about my faith. I told him my usual spiel on how I was a Roman Catholic and used to go to church every Sunday when I was younger. He then asked if I ever read the Bible. I admitted I had not.

Many months went by and Murray sent me a Bible with a note inside:

Acts 16:30-34 Sirs, what must I do to be saved? Romans 6:23

Keith, this is a book of truth, courage, forgiveness and comfort. Enjoy! Murray

P.S. I look forward to years of footin and your great coaching and friendship. May this be your constant companion, Love, Murray.

It was a nice Bible with gold-lined pages. I checked it out briefly and put it in my nightstand. The Book sat there for several years before I moved it to a new location to make room for magazines. I moved it yet again, to the bottom drawer to make room for other books I had collected. When I began following my faith again, I wanted to learn more about God, so I pulled Murray's bible out. Lauren and I began to read The Book together.

A Lesson on Forgiveness

At the World Games in Kaohsiung, Taiwan the competition was spectacular. The small lake was surrounded by ancient temples and their vibrancy reflected against the water's edge. Just before one of my runs, I took several deep breaths as I floated in the water and simply took in the amazing scenery. The site ended up being one of the many favorite places I've skied. The competition was fierce but I took home the Overall title for the United States.

A few days after the World Games, when I finished *The Shack*, I emailed Dave to tell him I loved the book and to thank him for recommending it to me. *The Shack* covers the story of a man who had a challenging journey through life after losing his daughter. Along the way he learned to understand his deepest misfortune and how to overcome it. Most importantly, he learned how to forgive.

It turned out to be the right time in my life to read the book. My own spirituality was beginning to grow and I was ready and open to learning more. *The Shack* taught me a lesson about forgiveness--and the lesson was a profound one for me. I had a friend who was a businessman whom I had long admired. He was generous with his time and money in many ways. One night, we had a huge misunderstanding that changed the course of our friendship. The accusations he hurled at me were false and he threatened to publicly destroy my reputation. I was in turmoil. Deep in the pit of my stomach, I was flipped upside down. The entire situation left me physically sick. I wasn't in any mental shape to ski in an upcoming tournament. I didn't know what to do. I sat quietly one morning and contemplated what to do. The more I thought about it the more I realized that I had to face the fallout with my friend and just deal with the situation.

My thoughts were spinning out of control when I slipped into the water for my run at the tournament. I pictured my friend wishing a couple of falls on me. I couldn't get it out of my mind and I couldn't shake off the nerves. *Come on, you trained hard for this. It's time to do what you came out to do. Let your skiing take over.* With a deep breath, I got up on the water and concentrated on every trick. It was one of the best trick runs I had ever done--the skiing was clean and every trick flowed. I finished the tournament with another World Record in the tricks event. This was the first time I ever had so much stress put on me that wasn't from a competitor!

My friend and I didn't speak again for two years and I purposely steered clear of him. I wanted nothing to do with him. For a long time, I carried a grudge in my heart. During one of our encounters, I verbally extended forgiveness to him but I was having a hard time forgiving within. I was carrying the heaviness around like a burden.

When I closed the last page of *The Shack,* I came to realize the true meaning of forgiveness--it was not about my friend, it was about me letting go of the grudge I had been holding within. The grudge was weighing me down like a ton of bricks. There was a passage at the end of the book that resonated with me: "Don't let the anger, pain and loss you feel prevent you from removing your hands around his neck." I realized I was actually holding on to my friend's neck in my mind and in the process, I was causing myself to continue to feel angry. I was causing my own turmoil about the situation. Finally...finally, I let go. I was able to move on with my life knowing I had done the right thing. As odd as this may sound, I thank my friend for putting me in that situation. I used to be the person who would hold grudges on others for a long time. Forgiving allowed me to let go of many things in my past. I became a new man.

Challenges in life happen for a reason and we learn our greatest lessons from them. Life lessons are what we make of them. We can choose to be angry or we can let go and move on. Everyone has the freedom to make his or her own choices. Like Andy Andrews said in his book, *The Traveler's Gift*—The Fifth Decision: "I will choose to be happy."

> **"God never promised an explanation, however he promised to be with us on the journey"**
> ~Courageous, the movie

Lauren Moves to Florida

Lauren's dad finally let go of his little girl and grudgingly gave her permission to move to Florida. He made it clear that he wasn't happy with the move, but in the end, Lauren made the final call. I booked a one-way ticket to Chicago. The plan was to visit for a few days and then drive Lauren's car to Florida with her. I was not looking forward to dealing with her father and I was dreading the trip.

On the last evening, we were all sitting around on the couch chatting casually. "Virginia and Lauren, do you mind if I talk to Keith alone?" Don said.

Uh oh... here it comes. The women left the room. I was trapped with the big guy. He began drilling me with questions. When I say drilling, I literally mean *drilling*. For some reason he was holding a half-inch thick, foot-long drill bit in his hand. He slapped it in his hand over and over, like a baseball player smacking a baseball into his glove.

"You understand I do not approve right, Saint?" *Slap*. "My wife and I did not move in together until we were married. You two should do the same." *Slap*.

"That is how they did it back then, but it's not so easy to do that nowadays." I said carefully. I was walking on eggshells, and I knew it.

"Lauren is the baby and she is very dear to my heart. You understand that right?" The drill continued to slap in his hand.

"Yes." My heart was hammering. I tried not to let him see me staring at the drill bit. I knew I would have to bite my tongue and just let him get it off his chest. I was not going to give in and say she could stay, but I wasn't about to have a debate either. I was smart enough to listen.

> There is a reason God gave us two ears and one mouth. So we could listen twice as much as we talk. Too many people talk too much and do not listen enough.
>
> ~Edgar St.Onge (my grandfather)

"I really do not want her moving to Florida with you, Keith," he continued. "She should be staying here." *Slap*.

Out of the corner of my eye I saw Lauren walk towards the room to save me from the torture. *Come here. Help me out!* I silently pleaded. Don's voice stopped her abruptly in her path, demanding to leave us alone. She followed orders and turned away. I was helpless once again.

Don turned to me once again with a grim look on his face. "You better watch over her like a hawk and don't screw this up. She is so precious to me!"

"No sir, I will not screw this up."

Don put the drill bit down. I could finally breathe again.

On the way down to Florida, we stopped in to see Dave Ramsey at his Nashville office. We spent the day meeting his staff and getting educated on finances. He invited us to his house for dinner that night. Lauren and I showed up at Dave's house and we were joined by his wife, Sharon, and their friends, Don and Joy. He gave us a tour and brought us downstairs to one of his favorite rooms. Dave beautifully refurbished a few dozen antique water skis and they were displayed on the walls. We talked about the history of water skiing and how he came across some of these relics. "Come here," he motioned. We walked through a hallway dotted with pictures on both sides. "I call this my *Hall of Fame*," he chuckled. I recognized celebrity after celebrity-- Oprah, Shawn Rich, Sean Hannity--all standing with Dave in every shot. About three-quarters of the way down the hall, I could not believe what I saw.

Me.

It was a shot of Dave and me barefoot water skiing side-by-side. I looked at him and laughed. "You have us on the wall!" I pointed to the frame. "I'm surprised you would put a skiing picture up here."

"Everyone likes this picture best because it is nothing like the others on the wall," Dave said. "It's an action shot and nobody knows what barefoot water skiing is so they love it."

"Too cool!" I shook my head with a smile. I followed him back to the dining room and we sat down for dinner. We bowed our heads, giving thanks and grace to the good Lord. The food was amazing and we were all enjoying each other's company.

Suddenly, there was an awkward silence. I could have heard a pin drop. I looked over at Dave--he slowly put his napkin down. I could feel a question coming on. Everyone stopped eating for a brief moment and looked up. Dave looked directly at me. I felt like a kid in a classroom hoping the teacher would not pick me. It was like the teacher was looking right at me and I knew I did not complete my homework the night before. If he called on me I would not know the answer and would be embarrassed in front of the whole class.

"So... Keith, why don't you tell us about *The Shack*."

271

My heart completely stopped beating and my mind went blank. In a brief second, I had a million thoughts running through my head. A sense of déjà vu washed over me--*I've been here before and I'm afraid because I don't know the answer.*

The teacher got me this time! I knew both Dave and Don read the book and there was no getting out of this one! But wait... I read the entire book too and it changed my life. I learned valuable lessons from it and those lessons helped me through one of the toughest times of my life dealing with a friend. It taught me to forgive. I took a breath and knew exactly what to say.

I began sharing my thoughts of the book with everyone as they listened with patience. I was able to take my time and explain things in detail. The listeners did not know what had happened to me in my life prior to or after I read this book, but I explained how the book became a small Bible to me. It was like it was written for me. The author had put several life lessons into words and they resonated deeply within me. I leaned back in my chair with a satisfied feeling. I spoke straight from the heart. I noticed Don sitting directly across from me nodding his head as he agreed. Before the dessert arrived on the table, I had the nagging feeling I left something out. I did not know what exactly, but it was important and I was kicking myself for not remembering. As we continued to converse, the window of opportunity to share *The Shack* faded away. When dessert was served there was a lull in conversation and then it hit me...I had more to say about the book. I could not hold it in.

"Do you remember the part about the garden?" Everyone looked up in surprise. "I loved the analogy they used in the book or at least this is what I got out of it: The garden is like our memories, our actions, and even our thoughts. There are beautiful flowers that smell sensational, vegetables that taste superb, and shrubbery that make a yard look like perfection. The soil is damp, fertile, and perfect for cultivation. The vegetation has room for growth and the garden overflows in abundance. But the occasional weed, vine, or roots tend to set in over time, especially if you do not clean it out. We must do our own gardening within ourselves and clean out the unwanted feelings that cause us to feel down or hurt. We must stop the roots and veins from choking the luscious green plants. If we do not cut them away, we hold onto horrible memories and thoughts that we no longer want. We have to clean out our garden to allow fresh air, sun, and rain to penetrate. Without this daily, weekly, or monthly cleanse the garden will never be able to flourish again."

Dave folded his arms, sat back and nodded. Satisfied, I dug into dessert with zeal.

Inspiring Others

Back at the ski school, the phone rang. It was Judy. "I've got some news," she said. "I'm flying to New York to be on the Today Show!" It wasn't the first time Judy was in the news. She was featured in "MORE" magazine and "WaterSki" magazine as the oldest female competitive barefooter. Subway, the sandwich franchise, came to the ski school to film her on the water for a "Fit to Boom" Internet special. Judy was an inspiration to many of my students and she brought in people from all over. Several skiers who watched her on the Today Show were inspired to get back on the water. She inspired Karen Putz, the co-author of this book, to get back on the water after a 20-year absence. If a 66-year-old could barefoot, then anyone could!

Reflections from Dave Ramsey

I work with a lot of world-class people and when I met Keith, I was surprised to find a humble, confident guy. He's a World Champion, but very down-to earth. During the first clinic, Keith talked often about his parents and credited them for his success. He explained that it would have been impossible for him to succeed without their support. I was impressed by this and thought it would be good for his parents to know this, so I wrote them a letter.

I read lots of books every year and I like to try new things. I could see that Keith was in the middle of a lot of personal growth, so I shared some books with him. There are five books that I require my staff to read:

The Legend of Monk and the Merchant, by Terry Felber
The Go Getter, by Peter Kyne
QBQ-- The Question Behind the Question, by John Miller
Rhinoceros Success, by Scott Alexander
Who Moved My Cheese, by Spencer Johnson

At different times in my life there were books that made an impact on me. When I first started the business, it was "Roaring Lambs" that made an impact--how you can bring Christianity into business. I love the "Legend of the Monk and the Merchant." Two or three years later, I came upon "Thou Shall Prosper," which taught how to put God into your money. It's not just pastors who have a ministry, we all have a ministry, Keith has a ministry, you have a ministry--we are all here to serve.

Passion is an intensity mixed with a love for something. What I'm doing now is more than a passion--it is a calling. It is what God meant me to do. I help people with money. My wife and I, we had the pain of losing everything and we want to help others

274

avoid that. We use our experience to teach others and we know it is God's plan.

I've shared my barefoot lessons in my sermons and my talks. For thirty years, I did the exact same thing: I barefoot skied the same way over and over by kicking off a ski and going up and down the river. I ended up with the same result every time: straight barefooting up and down the river. That's the definition of insanity: doing something over and over and expecting different results. I had to get out of my comfort zone to try something new and get different results. And one other thing I learned from barefooting--I learned to be SORE! I often share a quote from Hebrews 12:11: "No discipline seems pleasant at the time, but painful. Later on, however, it produces a harvest of righteousness and peace for those who have been trained by it." After the clinic with Keith, I came away with a sense of pride--of trying something new and accomplishing it.

When I think of success, the Earl Nightingale quote comes to mind: "Success is the progressive realization of a worthy goal or ideal." I like this quote because it can apply to anyone or anything. Take learning to barefoot water ski backwards--I didn't have that as a goal at first, but everyone else was trying it. Learning backward barefoot skiing was a test of perseverance-- a test of not giving up. I fell over and over and I had to keep at it to learn it. The week we worked with Keith, everyone got up backwards except me. I kept trying. A few weeks later, I got up backwards and I was happy to finally catch up! As for success, I've never met a person who is successful that didn't have a lot of bumps, bruises, and scars from their failed attempts. You don't become successful unless you try and fail--and learn from it.

Chapter 21: Living the Dream

A pessimist sees the difficulty in every opportunity; an optimist sees the opportunity in every difficulty.

~Winston Churchill

Right after the holidays we hit a cold snap in Florida and the water temperature dropped to the low 50's. After the long holiday break I was ready to get back on the water and start my training for the 2010 Worlds. The chilly weather lingered that week. One morning, Swampy and I walked out on the dock and couldn't believe what we saw: dead, bloated tilapia floating everywhere. There was no way to ski at that point. The fish would have been land mines in the water. For several days in a row, all we did was scoop out dead fish and bag them. The smell was horrendous.

Swampy and I finally started pulling students again later that week and we had to be careful to steer our way around the few remaining fish. During one of my practice runs, I noticed a fish floating nearby. The wind was blowing across the lake, so the fish were being blown to the other side. The side we were skiing on had no fish.

"Hey, Swampy, keep an eye out for fish," I warned him. "I think I saw one back there on that last run." It was tough for Swampy to keep his eyes peeled ahead while he juggled the speed and watched me at the same time. With the boat going 45 mph, it was all too easy to zip by a floating object. I got up again for a trick run and halfway through my routine, I smacked into something heavy and it felt like a wet kitchen sponge. The minute I heard the soft, fleshy "slap" against my foot, I knew I ran over a fish. Letting go of the handle, I sank into the water.

A quick inspection showed a tiny trickle of blood that ran down my heel. There was no pain. *Oh, that's not too bad, it's probably just a scrape from the fish scales.* The blood continued to trickle down, so I climbed into the boat to take a closer look. I saw another cut a little further down my heel. *Damn!* A large cut meant I would be off the water for a week or two, and I had just started my training. I asked Lauren to investigate the cut closely. "It looks like something is under your skin," she said. She pushed on it and I nearly jumped out of my skin. I stifled a yell. The pain was searing. Swampy came over to take a look, and we discovered several other small cuts as well. At this point, the blood began flowing freely. "You're going to have to go to the hospital and get that taken care of," Swampy said. I let out a stream of profanity as I peeled off my wetsuit. We arrived back to shore and I hobbled up on the dock. Swampy tossed me over his shoulder and carried me to the car. On the way to the hospital, I called a friend who worked there and asked if he could get me in quickly and take a look at my foot.

"Do you want me to come out and take it out for you?" he offered.

"I would feel better doing it at the hospital," I said. "My career depends on my feet and whatever is in there, I gotta get it out without damaging my feet."

Like a surgeon who values their hands, my feet were my livelihood and I was concerned about getting good care. The x-ray showed a fish spine jammed up the heel of my foot. The point of the spine was only millimeters away from my heel bone. After the local anesthetic took hold, the nurse grabbed a pair of needle-nosed surgical pliers and began to create a wider hole around the spine. Moving it in a circular motion allowed the hole of the wound to open up. She was trying to figure out the direction the spine had entered my foot so she could pull it out safely. Her goal was to retrieve it in one piece; otherwise it would mean surgery to remove the rest of it.

"How the heck did you get a fish spine up your foot," she inquired. I explained my profession and how I barefoot water ski for a living. "Oh, it looks so bad that you might not be able to ski again," she said. My heart stopped for a second and I stared at her. I couldn't tell if she was joking because she had a dead serious look on her face. "I don't know if you're joking or not, but you have to understand, my feet are my livelihood--this is how I make my living," I snapped. "Please don't joke about it."

"Oh, I'm just kidding you," she smiled. I let out a sigh of relief and sank back on the hospital bed. The nurse continued to dig deeply into my heel. "Here it is!" The nurse held up a bloodied fish spine. No wonder it was painful--the spine was 3/4 of an inch long. The nurse dropped the spine into a jar of alcohol and twisted the lid shut. "Here you go, a little souvenir for you! Do you want me to stitch this up?" she asked.

278

I took a look at the damage and made a quick decision. "No thanks, I'm going to let this heal on its own. I don't want a scar from the stitches. I'll keep a close eye on it and hope it can heal cleanly." It took almost a month for the cuts to heal and for me to be able to walk around normally again. Yet, there was one small part of my foot that continued to feel as if something was still stuck inside.

"I'm going to open it up and take a look," I told Lauren.

"Are you sure that's a good idea?"

"I really think there is something in there still. Every time I take a step it feels like there's a small pin poking my heel," I said. "If there is something in there, I've got to get it out. I can't ski on this--I won't be able to stand the pain-- especially when I go off the jump." I sterilized a pin and tweezers and cleaned my foot. After 45 minutes of digging through skin, I came across a hollow cavity that was sensitive to the touch. Probing a bit further, I finally connected with a small piece of bone. I slowly extracted it--and exhaled. It turned out to be a fish scale. I took it easy once again and gave it time to heal.

Out of the blue, I received a Facebook message from Dusty. I had never forgotten his generosity that first year in Florida but we had lost touch over the years. He had been married for over eight years with two children. He was successful in his career and owned his own air conditioning business. "I'm still a Keith St. Onge fan," he wrote.

A few weeks went by and his wife contacted me through Facebook. "Dusty has cancer," she wrote. After I heard the news, I wanted to visit him but was too late. Dusty passed away. I paid my respects at his funeral and silently thanked the man who helped give me my start in Florida. Through all he did, Dusty helped make my dreams of owning a ski school and becoming a World Champion come true.

> ## Appreciating Others:
>
> The valuable lesson here has been to let people know my appreciation of them. I've made it an ongoing goal to let my friends get too distant without a call or visit once in a while. If I could go back and do it over, I would have been there for Dusty and his family more often. Dusty went out of his way to help me at a time when I needed it most. To this day, my biggest regret is not keeping in touch with him more often. He did so much for me. Life gets busy, but there's always time to make a quick phone call or visit. I get choked up just thinking about it. I miss that man and wish I could have been closer to him during our years of distant friendship.

Two months later, I was back on the water training for the Worlds. Judy flew in to begin working at the ski school. She took care of the paperwork, scheduling, and served lunches for the students. She brought the ski school up to a whole other level with her expertise.

At the age of 67, Judy's goal was to go to Germany and ski in the Worlds. She had to score 500 points in a tournament to qualify so Swampy started working with her every day. He was selected as the World's Junior Team coach and had won an award as "Developmental Coach of the Year." He wasn't afraid to push her.

Lauren joined her in the boat and Swampy came up with the idea of Lauren training as well. "You're going to the World Championship with Keith, right? You might as well qualify and compete while you're there," he said. Lauren had never competed in a tournament before so it was a long shot. She had just nine months to learn several new skills. Swampy and I figured out what she had to do to qualify and Lauren began skiing almost every day. She was completely committed to qualifying and worked hard on the water. By mid-summer, she qualified for the World Championships in both slalom and tricks.

A.J. was flourishing under Swampy's coaching but he was struggling to produce consistent results on the water. His jumping ability was starting to mirror my own; some days he would land his jumps and other days he would endure crash after crash. After a particularly rough day on the water, Swampy sat down with A.J. in the living room and started one of his famous "powwows."

"We've set some ambitious goals for you," he said. "I know you've hit a rough spot lately. You're feeling down and you're struggling. There was a time I was going through my own tough time. I lost everything I worked for. I literally came here with nothing but my dogs." He reached into his pocket and took the card out of his wallet.

If you can imagine it, you can achieve it. If you can dream it, you can become it.

"Keith got this card from another barefooter during a low point in his career," he continued. "He passed it on to me after he achieved his goals. When he gave it to me, I was at my own low point but I've found my calling again as a coach. I'm passing this card on to you. Hold on to it, read the words on it, and believe in yourself. When you achieve your goals--to get on the elite team, to go open pro in all three events, and to become the National champion—then you can pass this card on to someone who needs it." A.J. put the card in his pocket. The inspiration that had passed through the hands of five people continued to ripple on.

Dave Ramsey Becomes a Mentor

I went back to Tennessee to do another clinic for Dave Ramsey. This time, we worked on tumble turns and barefooting backwards. It took two days for Dave to accomplish the tumble turn--something he had wanted to do for thirty years. Everyone was whooping and hollering in the boat when he spun on the water and got back up on his feet. He had a smile that I can hardly explain; it was a smile that showed his inner soul. For those few seconds, I could see true happiness as if he were a child once again. He was just taking in the "now" and celebrating it.

One evening, after a great day on the water, we gathered on the patio and the men broke out cigars. I politely declined. Most of the conversation was about cigars, which I knew nothing about. I quietly listened while being educated on how the cigars are made, how they taste and where they are from. One of Dave's friends mentioned he was reading the book *Thou Shall Prosper.*

"I'm reading that too!" I jumped in. "Dave, you sent me that book and I've highlighted a lot of lessons from it. You know...I have that book with me, let me get it." I scurried off to the bedroom to grab my copy and ran back. I opened the book and almost didn't know where to start. I had copied down the most important lessons, highlighted many passages from the book, and jotted my own thoughts in the margins. "Ok, let me share my first note on what I learned: You must take what you want to learn, understand and practice it over and over again. This will lead to confidence."

"Very true." The guys nodded.

"If you feel good about your profession, you sweep others along with you on the waves of your enthusiasm," I continued. "This was one of the quotes from the book that I liked." I continued to rattle off the various lessons and they nodded along in agreement with my perspective. Of all the books that Dave shared with me, this was the one book which stood out the most because it was filled with so many life lessons.

I felt even more comfortable this time around, for Dave and I had become friends and I looked to him as a mentor. One afternoon in the middle of the week, Dave returned from a Jet Ski ride and joined me on the wooden swing on the dock. We talked about life and our discussion turned to God. I knew Dave was a man of strong faith and I was filled with questions regarding this topic. I knew his answers would be straightforward and that's what I was looking for. I grew up attending the Catholic Church but I had not followed my faith for several years. I began exploring my faith in recent years but I had too many unanswered questions to make sense of it all. I felt comfortable asking Dave question after question and I learned a lot from his answers. Dave explained we are here on earth to serve one another and that everyone has a purpose. I nodded. "How do you explain to someone who does not believe in God, that there is a God?" I asked.

"It comes down to faith," Dave said. What I got out of our discussion was this: God does not want us to try and figure it all out nor understand what he is and why we are here. The only answer to understanding God is to have "Faith in him." Believe, and live life as honestly as possible. If we can do this, all of our questions will be answered.

In the middle of our discussion, I told Dave about the biggest lesson that I learned from *The Shack*: forgiveness. I told him about my friend who had accused me of something I did not do. For a long time, I let that incident eat at my insides. I felt that my character, my integrity, and my career had all been attacked. For a long time, I held on to a grudge and didn't want to let it go.

"There's a difference between forgiveness and reconciliation," Dave explained. "Forgiveness means letting go. It's about you, not him. You don't need a relationship with him to move on. Christians get confused about this all the time--we sometimes think that if you forgive someone that you have to have a relationship with them and that's not true. It's like a dog that bites you--you don't play with the dog again. You don't invite that dog into your home."

> Forgiveness means to release, to let go, any sense of obligation to make something right again. You don't have to wait for the other person to act to be okay--you'll be okay without action from them.
>
> ~Dave Ramsey

"Yeah, that's what I learned from *The Shack,*" I said. "After reading the book, I came to realize that forgiveness was not about getting back on good terms with my friend. Instead, it was about me letting go, forgiving, and moving on. I was finally in a place where I had accomplished that. I'm so thankful you recommended *The Shack* when you did, Dave. It came into play when I needed it most!"

Aiming for Another Title

There was one thing I knew going into the 2010 World Championship--I wanted the Overall title under my name again. Despite being an older athlete, I was skiing better than ever before and I wanted to continue to make my mark on the sport. I had worked long hours and trained hard in the weeks leading up to the tournament and I felt confident I would perform well.

Lauren and I arrived along with the U.S. Team in Brandenburg an der Havel, Germany jet-lagged but excited. Our faces quickly turned to dismay when we saw the tournament site. The course was covered in whitecaps. It was clear that we were not going to get in any barefooting practice that day. We returned to the hotel to rest and outlined our practice plans for the next day.

The tournament site was great for spectators though, with a large grandstand and food vendors. It was a popular sporting site which hosted rowing and water skiing competitions. A large Jumbotron TV was set up on the water to display the events from both courses via a split screen. Every run was filmed from the boat and displayed so the spectators could see each run from start to finish. We streamed the runs live on the World Barefoot Center site. This was the first time that a Worlds tournament could be viewed all over the world via Internet.

The next morning, we arrived at the site only to find the water was still too rough for barefooting. The flags on the grandstand flapped in the wind. Without a doubt, this was the roughest water I had ever encountered at a tournament. I quickly met with the team and we decided to take a run and test it out. David took a hard fall and rammed his knee into his nose. He emerged from the water with blood running down his face. Not only did we encounter whitecaps, but also we had to deal with rolling water all over the course. The site sat on a public waterway with boats passing through every few hours. The wake from the boats bounced off of the parked boats at the marina and come right back at us. Skiers were falling left and right during their practice runs and many could not even stand up on the choppy water.

I started out my first round with a bang, scoring high enough on tricks and slalom to put me in the lead. I was happy with my scores considering the rough conditions. During the first round of jump, I had a distance that was my personal best of 86.3 feet and I had surpassed my goal. This gave me a big enough lead to put me in a perfect position to win the Overall title. With those first round scores, David would have to produce a massive jump and a trick score close to mine.

There were many problems with the jump ramp during the first round. The officials had difficulty keeping it level as it was extremely unstable whenever rollers would hit it. During some jumps, it would flip over sideways after a skier took off in the air and it had to be righted again. David didn't jump much further than I did and he was close to maxing out. I was sitting pretty after the first round!

My joy was short-lived. Things began to change. The tournament officials decided to change the jump ramp for the second round. They no longer wanted the hassle of keeping it level every so often. An antsy feeling began to come over me just before the second round. I couldn't shake off the feeling. My mind was jumpy and I just couldn't settle down. My skiing turned defensive because of the rolling water and from trick to trick I struggled to maintain control. The next thing I knew, my foot bounced out from under me and I took a tumble. I was so angry inside--mad about the rough water and mad at myself. I had to turn it around, and get myself psyched for the next event. *All right, there's nothing you can do about this. It's finished. Move on and improve in the next round.*

Many of the skiers were landing jumps much farther than usual with the new ramp. The officials thought the video measuring system was off but after extensive double-checking they concluded that everything was being measured properly. The only explanation for the difference was the ramp itself. When I hit the jump in the second round, the feel was quite different from any ramp I had experienced before. The ramp was solid on the water and there wasn't the usual "give" that was typical for other jumps. I only jumped a tenth of a foot further so unfortunately, it didn't help me much. A few minutes later, David sprang off the jump and landed a World record jump: 97.7 feet. The crowd went crazy.

Our attention turned to the female jumpers. "Keep your eye on that girl, Ashleigh Stebbeings, from Australia," our team coach said. "She's one of two girls who can jump inverted and she can keep the U.S. team from winning the Overall." We sat transfixed as Ashleigh rocketed off the ramp. The girl had some solid barefooting skills and she was a force to be reckoned with on the water. However, we had one ace of our own, Elaine Heller, a young twenty-year-old who was also jumping inverted.

Later that evening, Lauren and I sat across the table from Ashleigh and her mom, Fran. In the past, we never had much of a chance to talk being on separate teams from different countries, but I enjoyed getting to know them better that night. I quickly discovered that Ashleigh was personable and pleasant. Ashleigh began barefooting at the age of eight and a year later, she was skiing competitively. She worked her way up the ranks to become one of the top female barefooters in the world. At the end of the evening we said our goodbyes and headed back to the hotel.

Back in the hotel room I ran through the same tricks again, going through the motions of each one and committing them to memory. The next day, my run was going well and I wanted to squeeze the last trick in to stay well ahead of David. As I turned, I felt a sharp pain in my hip as I caught my foot sideways and I fell. It was a simple trick and something I should not have fallen on. Despite the fall, I was pretty sure I was home free on my scores as I had completed all the tricks in time. I needed 11,450 points to beat David and take the Overall. Inside, I was ecstatic!

Swampy and I went to review the judge's sheet to confirm the points. I stood there stunned. A cold feeling washed over me. The judges had cut my run back to around 9,000 points. "Something is not adding up." Swampy said. We went over the scores again. "Two out of the three judges have credited my score properly, but I'm not getting credit for all four tricks," I said. "And they're still inside reviewing the video."

"I think you need to submit a protest," said Swampy. "You did all four tricks and they need to credit you for them, especially since two out of the three judges paid you. Those four tricks will give you the Overall title. Without the four tricks, you will be in third place. If they give you two out of the four tricks, you will take second." I followed Swampy's advice and submitted a protest against the scores. When the results came back, the judges gave me credit for just two of the four tricks.

"I heard they reviewed the video with people who were not judging in the boat," Swampy fumed. "They're watching it far more times than they've done with other skiers. Plus, we have some people that should not be a part of the decision-making process--they're viewing it and voicing their opinions. As a result we have improper scoring. This isn't fair!" Swampy walked over and got into it with the Chief Judge. He protested the unfairness of the judging but the Chief Judge held firm. The final decision remained the same: two out of the four tricks would be credited and I would receive second place. I was not happy with the decision because I completed all four tricks and should have been credited for them. I did not want to push the issue any further. I wasn't one to complain, even though I felt I should have won.

The loss was a hard one to swallow. Yet, I had made tremendous personal growth over the last few years so I was able to look at it in a positive way. David took the Overall title and it was a win for the business. That was one of my main goals--to grow the business and gain worldwide recognition for the World Barefoot Center. David and I were in this together so it was a win - win scenario. Plus, we had a lot to celebrate as I won the Trick and Slalom titles while David won the Jump and Overall titles. We had a clean sweep at the 2010 Worlds!

The Proposal

I was planning to propose to Lauren in the fall but I wasn't exactly sure when. A week before we took off for Chetek, I toyed with the idea of popping the question while we were there. After all, that was the exact place where we met two years and three months prior. Lauren and I were slated to ski in the last show of the season. There was another sign which indicated the time was right to propose: the theme for the show that summer was "My Big Fat Wisconsin Wedding." It would be perfect for me to propose during the intermission--on the same stage we met. What better place than that to propose? I enlisted the help of Rick Meskers, one of the show skiers before we left. "Can you keep a secret?" I asked. I outlined my plan: I would barefoot during the intermission, slide into the dock, and ask for the announcer's microphone. I would then speak to the crowd and thank them for showing up. Following that, I would call Lauren up on stage. Rick's job was to make sure Lauren stayed near the stage and she didn't wander off somewhere.

Lauren's mom, Virginia, threw a monkey wrench in my plans because a few days before the show she decided to head home. It was a six-hour drive and there was no way I could get her to come back to Wisconsin without giving away the plan. To make matters worse, Lauren's dad had plans to head home that morning. I had to come up with a quick reason to convince Don to stay without arousing suspicion. "I really want you to stay and see the show," I told him. "This is the first time I'm going to ski in a pyramid and I've always wanted to do that. You may get a good laugh if I fall too!"

Lauren shot me a strange look. "What's the big deal? It's just a ski show."

"Well, it's a big deal for me, I've never done a pyramid before," I explained. Don grudgingly agreed to stay for the show.

I tried to stay calm as the show began. As the intermission drew near, I could feel the nerves build up. I was more nervous and flustered than any other time in my life. I did two runs in front of the crowd. As I got ready for my final run, I felt like jelly inside. I had to commit to this and there was no backing out now. I needed to have a clean entrance at the least. Nothing would be worse than falling in front of the whole crowd just before I made my proposal. I signaled the driver to take off and then a crazy thing happened. I hit a few bumps and the very thing I was afraid of... happened. I fell on my start. It had been years and years since I fell on a start.

"What was that all about?" Rob, the boat driver inquired as he idled back. "I've pulled you for the last five years and you've *never* fallen on your start!" I just shrugged. "Was it my driving?" he chuckled. "Or are you nervous?"

Hell, yeah I'm nervous! I wanted to shout. He had no clue what I was about to do.

"It had nothing to do with your driving skills, buddy," I retorted. "It was all me. But come on, I'm not nervous...uh, just a bit unlucky with the start." Rob took off for the second time and I managed to complete my run. I slid in perfectly and hopped on stage. I casually grabbed the microphone, cleared my throat, and waited for the applause to die down. "I'd like to thank everyone for attending the show tonight and hope you enjoyed it." The crowd clapped again. "I would like to thank the Chetek Hydroflites Water Ski team for hosting the clinic and supporting me. This club has several young kids that are becoming accomplished barefoot skiers and everyone should be proud of that! Chetek has been like home to me and I've been coming here for over five years. They even let me put on a pair of skis now and again and that is a little difficult for me...I'm not used to those big things on my feet. I'd like to ask my girlfriend, Lauren, to come down to the stage." The crowd clapped again.

I tried to make everything look low key. I told the crowd how Lauren had skied in Chetek for fifteen years and she qualified for the World Barefoot Water Ski Championship this past summer. I paused. "During one of my trips to Chetek I met Lauren and since that moment, we have always been with one another. We trained for tournaments together and traveled the world. I can honestly say I have not just fallen in love with Lauren but she's become my best friend as well." My voice started to waver and my eyes began to water. "So, I'm going to take this time now," I knelt down on one knee. "Lauren Lindeman...will you marry me?" The crowd went wild with applause. Her answer was muffled under the din so I yelled into the microphone, "She said yes!"

In the middle of the crowd, Don sat on the bleachers taking it all in. A friend managed to witness my soon-to-be-father-in-law shedding some tears while snapping pictures. I had to laugh because this tough, burly man did not fit the mold of a crybaby.

We set the date: 11-11-11. There would be no way for me to forget our anniversary in the future.

Be Careful What You Wish For

Shortly after the World Championship I came home to train for the Texas Jump Jam, a tournament held at the Barefoot Ski Ranch in Waco, Texas. I was still feeling a little burned out with barefooting and my enthusiasm for jumping was at an all-time low.

Man, I wish I could take a break from footing for while.

It had been three weeks since I was on the water, but I knew I had to do some jumping to get ready for the tournament. The first day of practice went well. My jumps were pretty consistent and I was landing them with ease. The next day, the weather wasn't great and the water conditions were not ideal. I took an early morning jump set which went well but I was only able to get two jumps in before the wind tore up the water. Later that day I debated skipping the afternoon set. That little voice inside spoke up: *You jumped well this morning. Leave for Texas with a positive head.* Instead of listening to that little voice inside of me, I got in the water.

"Swamp, let's try to get one more set in. I'll try three jumps and that's it." I changed my timing on the first jump and had a nice pop off the ramp. "I'm going to do the same thing again." I flew off the ramp again with a much higher pop in the air. When I came down for the landing, I was a bit off-balance--and I could tell I was going to be a little late. I caught my foot sideways, twisted my knee, and the handle popped out from my hands. In an instant, I knew I wasn't going to be competing in the Jump Jam. I lay in the water in excruciating pain. Swampy raced the boat back.

"It's bad," I said as the boat came up next to me. "Give me a few minutes. I need to let the pain go down." Slowly, I climbed into the boat and tried to put some weight on my leg. I had trouble walking and my knee felt loose. We headed back to the dock and I walked up and down to assess the damage. From my knee to my ankle, I had no control. I could feel my knee acting as a ball and joint instead of a hinge. A horrible feeling washed over me--how long would this take to heal? An MRI later revealed a grade-one tear to the MCL and ACL. The tears were minor enough to heal without surgery, which was great news. My wish for time off certainly came true as I didn't train for the next five and a half months. It all turned out to be a blessing in disguise--a blessing that brought me something precious: time.

During the summer, Swampy received a phone call from a brand new customer. "Glen Plake called and he said he knows you. He wants to come down in October with his wife, Kimberly. He asked me to give you his number so you can call him back. Do you know this guy?" My heart skipped a beat. "Glen Plake! He was my childhood idol!" As a teen, I followed his freestyle and extreme snow skiing career with great interest and I strived to ski like him on the mountain slopes. Years ago at a Water Ski Expo in Orlando, I spotted the 15-inch high Mohawk walking around. I decided to go up to Glen and introduce myself.

"Hi! I'm Keith St. Onge. I'm a fan of yours. You were a childhood idol of mine and it's an honor to meet you." He introduced his wife, we all shook hands and then I walked off.

"Wait, what's your last name?" Glen called out. I walked back nervously.

"St. Onge," I said.

"Hey--I know you! You're a barefoot water skier--I've seen your name in the water ski magazines!" My eyes grew wide and I was floored. Plake knew who I was!

"My wife and I are barefoot water skiers," he continued.

"It's cool that you barefoot! That's awesome. I can't believe it! I thought you only snow skied?"

"I love all sports on the snow and water! I would love to come to your school some day and hang out." Glen said. We talked a bit more and I explained I was from New Hampshire and grew up snow skiing on Wild Cat Mountain. He also skied there too. We shook hands and I walked away on a complete high. Here was an athlete I idolized as a kid and he knew who I was! I was completely blown away.

Ten years later, I had the opportunity to barefoot water ski with him. This experience ranked right up there with the time I trained Gary Unger, the hockey great from the St. Louis Blues. Watching Glen on the water the first day, I could see he was definitely a skilled barefooter but the lack of formal instruction showed. After several runs, I motioned for him to come in the boat. "This is going to kill me, but we're going to have to take this back to basics," I explained. "We're going to go back and build a brand new foundation to your skiing." Like most people who have barefooted for years, Glen wasn't too thrilled about starting over from scratch, but he was game. He cleaned up his stance and polished his tricks. Kimberly worked on the same basics as well. Both of them quickly advanced on the water.

After a couple of hard falls, Glen had enough for one day. "Let's do something fun!" he suggested. "I'm getting mentally fatigued!" So we changed gears and I taught him how to ski on his hands and knees. As one day turned into another, I began to realize I was learning more from Glen than he was learning from me. The guy showed an incredible zest for life--laughing through each day and really getting into every moment. He didn't have a care about what was going on around him. He was stress-free and loving every minute on the water. It was almost distracting for me. I had a hard time with it and I couldn't figure out why. But then it dawned on me--I was the opposite of Glen. I'm the one who's always looking ahead, thinking about the future, worrying about what's next, and how to organize life. Here was Glen on the water, taking it all in and laughing, yet totally focused on what he was doing and *totally into the moment* he was experiencing. I was taken aback. It was a lesson for me: life is about more moments like that. I was thankful to Glen for teaching me that.

> You must live in the present, launch yourself on every wave, and find your eternity in each moment.
>
> ~Henry David Thoreau

A New Student Arrives... And Stays.

"World Barefoot Center, how may I help you?" Swampy couldn't recognize the rapid-fire accent on the other end. "Please slow down. I can hardly understand you," said Swampy.

"My name is Ben Groen and I would like to come to your ski school for two weeks in September. Do you have any openings? I've been working at a camp all summer and have organized a trip to Florida to work for a barefoot ski school. They don't open until October first and I arrive on September first. I have no place to stay or to ski and I was hoping to visit the World Barefoot Center. I am willing to work and help out as well. Can you work out a good deal for me?"

"Dave and Keith are gone until September 15th, but I'll be here. I think we can arrange something," said Swampy. "Call me back with your flight information and dates you want to ski. I'm going to contact Keith and Dave and see what kind of deal they want to work out since you will be here over two weeks. How old are you and what kind of summer camp are you working at?"

"I just turned eighteen and I'm working for a kids' summer camp in New York as a camp counselor and teaching water skiing. I love water sports and I have the time to travel a bit." Swampy promised to get back to him.

My phone rang. "Keith, this is Swampy and the young fella, Ben Groen from New Zealand is coming in. He's going to work for our competition but wants to ski here first. What do you think?"

I paused and mulled it over. "It's a conflict of interest, of course, but if the kid wants to come and ski with us then our doors are open to him," I replied. "We can't say no and he's a good kid. I know the Groens well and I've done a few clinics with them years ago. In fact, I taught Ben years ago and from what I remember, he didn't like barefooting much. Maybe he found a love for it again?"

Ben and Swampy worked out a deal and when I arrived home from my traveling clinics I met with Ben. He was a bit taller than me, and sported a shock of blond hair and piercing blue eyes. He was quite stout for his age with broad shoulders. He always wore a half smile on his face--like he was ready to laugh at any moment. The first few times I worked with Ben I could see his passion for the sport. His talent level wasn't there yet, mostly because his knowledge for the sport had not been developed. We worked through all of his basic skills and he executed them well. When it came to surface turns, he was literally a fish out of water. I could not believe how awkward he looked when he attempted each turn. I shook my head. "Hop in the boat, Ben." I sat him down and showed him what to do step-by-step. He was eager to learn and I put my own passion into teaching him. Toward the end of the week, Ben and I met with Swampy and I outlined the improvements Ben needed to work on. I wanted Swampy to work with him before he left for the other ski school. Swampy hesitated.

"Come on, Swampy, he needs you! He knows what to do but his head is playing mind games with him. He is scared to fall and his turns are not consistent. Can you take him out a few times and work him through it?"

"All right. Darn right, I will!" he boomed. "I'll take him out and whip his butt. If he can't do what I tell him to do, he can swim back from the other side of the lake." Ben shot Swampy a nervous look. He wasn't sure what to make of Swampy's deep voice. "If he cannot do the turns, we'll take him out behind the shed and shoot him!" Swampy continued. "Do you know why we would do that, Ben?"

"No, um, no--I'm not completely sure. Why is this?" His New Zealand accent quivered.

"Back in the day if a horse broke his leg, he couldn't run the same as before. So, they take the horse out back and shoot him because the horse is of no use anymore." Ben's eyes grew wide. I was laughing inside because I heard those little mind games a million times. He was getting the upper hand, and instead of Ben worrying about his turns, he would have to worry instead about Swampy. Swamp was a mastermind when working with kids and he brought out the best in them. The kids work hard on the water as not to disappoint Swampy--he is an authority figure and he gives them a swift kick in the butt when they most need it. Not everyone can handle a Swampy in their life, but the ones who accept him are the ones that progress and excel! Just as he did with me, Swampy broke Ben like a wild stallion. At the end of the week, Ben did not want to leave and go to work for the other ski school. We made an agreement with Ben to stay several more months and he began working for us.

What separates an average skier from an amazing skier is often the passion they have inside of them for the sport. A passionate student doesn't let a fall or a setback affect them mentally. They are not afraid to make mistakes and fail. They get back up and try again. Someone without a passion for the sport will let a fall get to them. They may give up too quickly or forget the focus of their goal. A passionate barefooter will ski even harder the next time, coming back with more determination and with laser focus on the goal.

Swampy often tells his students, "Don't be afraid to fail! Not trying, now that is failure!"

Chapter 22: It's All About the Journey

To know the road ahead, ask those who are coming back.

~Chinese proverb

One of the fondest memories I have is from the time Lauren and I took a "Spontaneous Vacation," as she called it. I needed some time off from the ski school and Swampy agreed to take things over. As a guy who thrives on structure, I like to have a plan when going somewhere, but Lauren often adds a twist to things just to throw me off. I was game for an adventure, so we decided to put a mattress in the back of my Avalanche truck and live out of it for four days. I came up with a plan I thought Lauren would like. "OK, you know how an atlas has numbers down the side and letters across the top?" I explained to her. "When we pull out of the driveway, we will open the atlas up to Florida. We will start with my first initial 'K' and the month I was born, which is '12' and go wherever that is on the map. Then the next day, we will take the first letter of your name 'L' and your birthday month, '10' and go there. What do you think of that?"

"I love the idea!" she smiled. Lauren spread the map open and searched for "K-12."
"What does it say?" I asked. I felt like a kid on Christmas morning.
"Vero Beach!" she laughed.
"Okay, that's where we are going!" I laughed. "How do I get there?"

It was a lazy, scenic drive to Vero Beach. For all of her spontaneity, Lauren couldn't contain herself by waiting for the next day to see where we were going to go next. "I want to see where my first initial and birth month are going to take us," she said. We talked back and forth about checking or not. "I can't wait. I want to look!" She opened the map and looked for "L-10." Her face fell. "There is nothing there." She pointed to a green spot on the map.

"Sorry babe, looks like an orange grove or something!" I grinned. "Maybe you should try the second letter in your name." We laughed and conjured up a new route. The next day, we came up with another new plan. "Since we're near Daytona, let's go see the sunrise!" I suggested. Lauren wasn't too enthusiastic.

She was not much of a morning person. "I'll drive and you can sleep along the way," I cajoled her. She reluctantly agreed to the plan. We parked ourselves on the beach and watched as God painted a brilliant masterpiece across the sky. Getting up early was worth it. "Let's go to the natural springs next," I suggested as we walked back to the truck. "That will be a good place to swim and wash up."

"Well, I've got an idea. Since we are driving west, let's head to the coast afterwards and watch the sun go down," Lauren said. "That way, we will see the sunrise and the sunset in the same day!" I liked the plan. We visited three springs on the way across central Florida, booked the last hotel room on Cedar Island, and settled down on the beach to end the day. I held her in my arms as we watched the colors dancing across the sky for the second time that day. I reflected on how our lives unfolded over the last year. Lauren always seemed to calm me down when I most needed it. She knew I was working too much and needed the break. The "Spontaneous Weekend" was exactly what I needed.

Back at the World Barefoot Center, we were growing by leaps and bounds. We were far ahead of our business projections and expanding at a rapid rate. In any business, it takes many spokes to make the wheel go around and we needed everyone to handle the growth. The boats were filling up daily. There were some days we were running two or three full boats all day long and sometimes into the evenings. One week alone, we had skiers from seven different countries.

Judy and Swampy were booking students left and right and it was a struggle to keep up with the paperwork. Swampy was delegating and managing everything, along with training the junior skiers. Judy coordinated an annual Women's Barefoot Week and it was featured in both The Water Skier and WaterSki magazines.

Ben was making countless trips to the gas station to keep the boats fueled. A.J., Lynn Johnson, our web developer, and Jay McCarthy, our art designer, teamed up to make changes to our website. We added a blog and began sharing skier stories with the world. Lauren was the "Everything Gal." She did whatever we needed. When Judy wasn't there, Lauren handled lunches for the students and crew. The orders for KSO Wetsuits were piling up. Lauren was right beside me every step of the way, taking inventory, and making hundreds of trips to the Post Office to ship out orders. "We'll look back someday and laugh at this," Lauren told me. Sweat was pouring off our faces as we counted the wetsuits stored in the attic.

Dave and I were exhausted, but elated. In the midst of running the business we managed to squeeze in training time. The World Barefoot Center was growing at a rate beyond our imagination. During the first two years of our partnership, we were still working out the bugs in the business and getting to know each other. By the time the third year rolled around, we became a strong team. We had each other's back and we worked well together. I could honestly say that there was never any jealousy between us.

When Swampy and I first explored the idea of Dave and me becoming partners we encountered a lot of concern from other people advising us not to do it. "Do not ever form a partnership because a large percentage of partnerships fail!" We heard this over and over and it's often true. However, we both knew the business of barefoot waterskiing was very different from the average business. It's a narrow niche and we knew we would be competing for business. Joining forces to build a business together sounded like a good plan and continues to be the best choice yet.

In our business, we both know that one compliments the other and we share the same vision for the business. On the water, we're still intense rivals. We have similar accomplishments in our careers and if anything, we motivate one another to be better because we both want to win!

Shaping Another Life

The phone rang on an ordinary day. It was Fran Stebbeings, Ashleigh's mom, calling from Australia. She inquired about the possibility of Ashleigh coming to the World Barefoot Center for some training. Fran poured out Ashleigh's story to Swampy. Ashleigh took up barefooting when she was just eight years old and began competing a year later. She rose quickly through the ranks and became the top female skier in the world. But now her daughter was burned out and close to quitting the sport. Her heart wasn't in it any more. She was tired of being the sole female on the water and the long drive to the lake was taking a toll on her. The sport she had once loved dearly was no longer fun. Fran didn't want to see Ashleigh toss away her talent and all the effort she put forth. She was hoping a trip to America would turn things around. We arranged for Ashleigh to train with us.

297

Ashleigh was shy and a bit unnerved when she arrived. Short and muscular, Ashleigh soon learned to hold her own on the water with A.J. and Ben. Before long the three were inseparable both on and off the water. The two boys adopted Ashleigh as a sister. There's a contagious atmosphere at the World Barefoot Center where the skiers feed off of each other, and Ashleigh picked up the boys' enthusiasm. She also enjoyed the short walk down to the dock, which was a big change from the long haul to her usual practice site.

Swampy took Ashleigh right under his wing and employed his psychology skills from the get go. He sat her down and talked about her past and her barefooting journey. Little by little, she opened up and talked about how she had lost the passion for the sport. Day by day, Ashleigh began to find that passion again out on the water. Swampy also addressed her fears. Over the years, Ashleigh had taken some brutal falls. There were two things that struck fear in her: multiple turns and inverted jumping. Swampy went back to the basics and began to teach her a whole new way to approach her skiing. He helped her change her thought process and work through the fears. "Trust the system, Ashleigh, and you'll take your skiing to a whole new level," he said.

Ashleigh's skill level began to grow and her enthusiasm for the sport returned. Swampy set up challenges for the three teens and they began to push themselves each day with multiple turns on the water, egging each other on. There were days when nothing worked but they all learned to put it behind them and approach the next day with renewed energy. "You're only as good as your last set, and there's another one around the corner," Swampy reminded them. Then one day, everything came together and Ashleigh had a breakthrough: she did her first 720-degree multiple turn. No other female barefooter in the world had ever accomplished that.

Nine weeks later, it was time to say goodbye. "Remember, quitters never win and winners never quit," Swampy reminded her before she left. Ashleigh went back to Australia and set a new World Record at the very next tournament. She was doing tricks that no other female could do. She continued to set record after record and at the last count she was on her tenth "pending" World Record.

Before long, the phone rang again. It was Ashleigh. "I'm coming back, this time for five months!" Soon, Ashleigh became part of our staff and she began training students.

> **"Many of life's failures are people who did not realize how close they were to success when they gave up."**
>
> ~Thomas Edison
>
> Just think how close Ashleigh came to quitting the sport. Had she walked away from barefooting, she would have never experienced the many pending World Records she set.
>
> What would this world be like if people gave up when it became tough?
>
> Christopher Columbus was one who faced a difficult decision-- whether to turn around and head back home or continue on to find land. He had a vision and a strong feeling that land was ahead. What if he had given up?
>
> Michael Jordan didn't make the cut for the varsity basketball team in high school. If he resigned himself to the idea that he wasn't made for basketball and walked away, the world would have missed a highly talented player.

Lauren and I were finding it increasingly difficult to have privacy and quiet time at the ski school. Students were coming in from all over the world and the bunkhouse was full from day to day. Summer was coming up and I didn't want to be separated from her as I traveled from clinic to clinic. I tried to come up with a solution.

"Either we have to rent or buy a house, but we really don't have enough money to buy just yet," I mused. "I've always dreamed of buying an RV and doing a tour. Why don't we look into that? Would you be up for it?" I asked her.

"I would love to do that, but how long would we be living in the RV?"

"Well, if we purchase an RV this fall and move out of the ski school after the holidays then that would be about eight months." I calculated.

"Eight months? Gosh, that's a little longer than I had imagined but I'm always up for an adventure and traveling," she said.

We put an offer in on a few cheap, foreclosed homes, but did not have any luck. We had to make a decision quickly. Buying a house was taking too long, and we didn't want to throw away money by renting, so we scoured Craigslist and several RV sites and started researching RV's. I would not typically recommend the purchase of an RV, but since it would be a business tax write off and we planned to use it as a marketing tool, I was okay with the decision. We did not plan to buy a new one because as soon as you drive something off the sales lot the value immediately plummets. We also didn't want to have a loan on the new vehicle. Most of the time RVs can end up being a money pit. However, as a business decision the advantages were many: it would be a great way to market my name, we could move out of the ski school, we would have it for several more years for future tours and best of all, it would be an adventure!

The next thing I knew, the plans were in place to do a "Barefooting Across America" tour. We purchased a used RV and set out to find sponsors for the trip. Our biggest sponsor came from Anytime Fitness, a franchise of fitness centers. Mike and Natalie Betts, the owners of eight Anytime Fitness franchises, were avid barefoot water skiers and students at the World Barefoot Center. The RV was wrapped with the Anytime Fitness logo and a bigger-than-life photo of Lauren and me barefooting together. We began planning our route during the months of November and December because we needed to know well in advance who was interested in hosting a barefoot water ski clinic. This would determine our route through the U.S. We planned to go up the East coast first, then across towards the Midwest, and then straight down the middle ending at Waco, Texas for the 2011 U.S. National tournament. The logistics were complicated and it took us all of two months to get deposits and our path planned out. Our first stop was Tennessee, followed by West Virginia, Pennsylvania, Connecticut, Massachusetts, New York, Indiana, Michigan, Illinois, Iowa, Minnesota, Wisconsin, Missouri, Kansas, Texas, Louisiana, and finally bringing us back to where we started in Florida. We covered a total of 15,000 miles by the end of the tour. Several news stations provided TV coverage and we landed in newspapers as well.

During a visit with Mike and Natalie Betts I told them I was writing a book and expressed an interest in speaking one day. "You're interested in speaking?" Mike said. "We are having a well-known keynote speaker in Chicago this weekend after your clinic. I hired Andy Andrews to speak to the customers I do business with. You and Lauren should come and listen in." I wasn't sure who Andy Andrews was but I was up for learning and listening in. I learned that Andy lost his parents as a teenager, became homeless, and lived under a bridge for a while. He turned his life around and became a New York Times bestselling author. He was a well-known speaker who gave speeches at the request of four U.S. Presidents. Mike invited us to dinner with Andy and Andy's ten-year old son, Austin. We had a wonderful dinner with them. I was captivated watching Austin interact with the adults. He responded to questions with a wonderful touch of Southern politeness, "Yes, Sir" and "Yes, Ma'am." I made a mental note to raise my future kids the same way.

Andy talked about his upcoming book and later asked me questions about my barefooting career. Suddenly, he stopped and peered at me. "My friend Dave Ramsey loves to barefoot water ski and hired a professional to teach him and his family, would that happen to be you?"

"It sure was." I smiled. "He was telling me about your clinic last time I saw him and he is not going to believe I'm sitting here with you!" Andy said. We both laughed. The evening was a wonderful one and I was looking forward to hearing him speak. The next day, Andy truly engaged his audience and was extremely funny. I discovered he used to be a stand-up comedian and it was easy to see why he was so skilled with humor. Andy signed books afterwards and I autographed a few posters for him and Austin as well as several other people in the banquet room. We took a picture together and sent it to Dave.

"I'd like to send you a few books in a week or so," Andy said. A large box showed up one week later. Andy sent me every book he had written. Now, here's the thing--before I met Dave and Andy I had not picked up a book to read since high school. After the two of them started sending me books, I became hooked on reading. I have read more books in the last two years than I have throughout my entire career. With every book, I found myself stretching my mind and growing in more ways than I could have ever imagined.

Surround Yourself With Those You Can Learn From

I often have some wild conversations in the boat while instructing my students. After all, I have to discuss something while being cooped up in the boat with five students all day. The boat has been a great place for conversations and for me to learn from those who have achieved success. Many people live fascinating lives or do amazing things and I am always curious as to how they achieved their goals. Many times I find their journey follows the exact path I took in my barefoot waterskiing career. The students took some falls along the way, they got back up and tried again, they changed their approach and technical position, and then they finally experienced success. Every little success along the way gave them just enough motivation to do it again. The fact of knowing it is possible to achieve a dream is enough to persevere. Another way of looking at this is not being afraid to fail. Work as hard as you can to achieve your dream or goal. After failing many times, there will be so much you learn along the way. That is exactly how life works in almost all areas.

With barefoot waterskiing or any other sport for that matter; an athlete can progress more quickly by playing their sport with others who are better than them. We see it time and time again: skiers who obtain instruction from skilled athletes progress and succeed quickly. If these athletes had to clear their own paths and ski on their own, their learning curve would be several times slower. Both Dave and I have advanced from the instruction of those who were better than us as we climbed the ranks in the sport. Some people are intimidated to be around World Champions in the boat while others thrive off of us, but surrounding yourself with others who are better than you will always accelerate your learning curve.

Life Unfolds

At the Barefoot Ski Ranch in Waco, Texas, Lauren and I were wrapping up our tour and competing at the 2011 Nationals. I slid into the water. Sweat dripped from my forehead. The tepid lake water offered no relief, the result of daily 100-degree heat. The wind was steady but the air felt like a heavy, wet blanket settling in around me. I studied the lake. The water was rippling something fierce halfway down near the jump. I contemplated my options. Should I adjust my trick routines? Should I play it safe, hold back, and guarantee a 12th National title? Should I go all out and aim for the 13,000-plus points--a risky move with the unstable water conditions? Ben and Dave had struggled on their trick runs but A.J. had nailed his. It was now my turn. I thought about the card that Swampy gave A.J. awhile back. The card had started with John, then to Patrick, to me, to Swampy, and now to A.J. The card had changed so many lives.

If you can imagine it, you can achieve it; if you can dream it, you can become it.

A.J. was on the elite team, he was skiing as an Open Pro skier and he was ranked among the best in the world. The kid had come so far. His training with Swampy had paid off and he racked up 11,000 points on the water. He was gunning for the gold and determined to swipe it from me. The pressure was on and the rivalry was out in full force. If I had one little bobble on the water or a few missed tricks, then A.J. would be the new, shining star at the Nationals.

David came in off the water. "The far end is so rough I couldn't do my first trick," he said.

I contemplated what to do. Setting a new record over 13,000 points was a goal on my vision board. Both David and I were gunning for that record. It was just a matter of who could ski the fastest and cleanest to rack up the points. Swampy had put together my trick runs and both runs would generate 13,300 points if I could execute them perfectly. In practice, I was able to score it in time, just once.

> Once a dream is fulfilled, more keep coming in. That's what keeps us going!
>
> ~Keith St. Onge

At the PGA tournament in Port St. Lucie earlier in the year, I went all out in both passes, pouring my heart and soul into every turn. With the exception of a hand touching the water, I skied it clean and completed all of my turns. Pumping my fist in the air, I knew it was a run that broke the 13,000-point barrier. The celebration was short-lived. The judges tossed out the 13,100 score and downgraded it under 12,000. I was furious. I had been putting up with erratic scoring for years. The process was testing my patience time and time again, with World Records continually being denied. Today's barefoot athletes possess skills that far surpass the judging. It would only be a matter of time before the judging would change to reflect the proper scoring, but I was running out of patience.

I tried to tune out the voices chattering away on the dock behind me. "In gear," I called out. The rope slowly uncoiled in the water to a straight, taut line. I took another look down the lake. The wind was still roughing it up. *Maybe I should eliminate the one-foot 360?* I fell twice on that trick in practice and I wasn't confident that I could execute it.

I wish I had more time on the water this summer. I didn't get enough practice time. The summer tour had really taken a lot out of me. Eight-hour days in the boat with students, a quick dinner at night, and then setting up and breaking down the RV between each stop--all of that had cut into my training time. I tried to throw in a run here and there but sometimes I would be stuck with a boat that barely went 40 mph. There was no quality training time for me this summer and I was about to ski the Nationals with very little practice behind me.

I thought back to the whole *Barefooting Across America* trip. The entire experience was a fun one. In the past, Lauren and I were often separated as I went from one clinic to another. This summer was so different from all the previous summers because I was spending every day with Lauren. Every night, we sat down to dinner and gave thanks for the remarkable life that was unfolding for us. The summer was about hard work and long hours in the sun and on the road, but it was also about fun. We explored the states that we drove through and met so many new friends along the way.

I made up my mind. I was not going to go for the 13,000 run. The rough water, the lack of training, and the falls during practice made the decision an easy one. *It's been a wonderful summer despite little training; I'm going to go out there, ski my heart out and enjoy it. Whatever happens, happens and it's meant to be.* No pressure. This was going to be fun.

"Okay!" I hollered. One last, quick breath and the boat took off. Fifteen seconds usually pass by in a flash in most people's minds but in barefoot water skiing, fifteen seconds seems like an eternity. There was no thinking, just executing. All of the years of practice rolled out on the water at once. The moment I stood up, instinct took over. The run felt solid and clean. I slid on the water and tossed the handle away. One more pass to go. I was going all out again. I wanted that "in the zone" feeling a second time. Another fifteen seconds later, I tossed the handle aside once more and slid to a stop.

Over the loudspeaker, I could hear Swampy adding up the tricks. "It looks like we have a preliminary score of 13,200!" I laughed. I knew it didn't add up, as I had taken out one of my tricks. I knew it would only take Swampy a few seconds to recalculate the run. I headed to shore, swimming with slow strokes, reviewing the runs in my mind. I knew the gold medal was once again mine. A.J. would have to wait yet another year to try again. I climbed up the bank. The wind was picking up more speed and the water was starting to ripple all around me. *Wait a minute. I thought the guys said the water was rough?* Slowly it dawned on me--the water was calm during my runs. Lauren came walking up. She had noticed it too. She smiled. "God was watching out for you, Keith."

Years ago, I would have scoffed at the idea, believing that I earned every run on my own merit. I believed I was the master of my own fate and every outcome was the result of my hard work and effort. In fact, shortly after arriving on shore I learned that the final score of 12,950 was downgraded to 12,850. It still remained to be seen if it would pass as a World Record. Years ago, I would have been frustrated and upset at the slow progression toward success. Today, I've learned to enjoy the journey and watch how my life unfolds--learning new lessons along the way.

I may have been a late bloomer in my relationship with God, but over the last few years my faith journey has taken on a whole new path. I'm living my life as He taught us to live. I've learned that He is always waiting patiently with an open hand. I've learned that it's never too late to reach out and ask for forgiveness just as I have learned to forgive others. With God in my life, walking on water is something I no longer do alone.

> Each man's life represents a road toward himself.
>
> ~Herman Hesse

It's All About the Journey

I'm facing another birthday and for an athlete birthdays signal a ticking clock. There's a "shelf life" that we talk about in the sport and the older I become the more I realize I've gone well past the halfway mark. I never thought the end of my career would be more important than the beginning, but I'm now realizing just that. These last years are going to be the benchmark of my career and I have to take what I have learned and apply it to many different avenues of my life. I've been truly fortunate to cross paths with people from all over the world and they each have taught me something along the journey. I think the journey is what matters--not the goals, not the results, but the journey. I can't stay on top forever as a professional barefoot water skier. Teaching others, motivating others, helping others, and finding my faith in God, all are part of this new path on my journey.

Way back in sixth grade, the teacher called on me to answer a question. I gave the wrong answer. After class, two students came up to me and called me "stupid." That kind of stuff hurts when you're a kid. They continued to put me down throughout the day. I tried not to show the tears in my eyes as I walked away. *Maybe I am stupid*, I thought to myself. At the end of the day they continued to taunt me as we walked outside. I turned and got in their face. "I'm not stupid! Don't ever call me that again!"

> When you judge another, you do not define them, you define yourself.
>
> ~Wayne Dyer

I made up my mind right then and there I would never call people names. It's not up to me to criticize someone else. Later on in life, I learned not to judge people. It isn't up to me to be the judge in others lives. I know God will give them a fair shake and be the deciding factor.

At different times in my life I went through periods of doubting myself. In high school, I was an average student and I couldn't keep up with my smart friends. I never went to college. When I first moved to Florida, I signed up for classes at the community college but I was already filled with doubts. I didn't think I was smart enough. The tests I took for placement showed I had to take basic math all over again before I could qualify for college courses.

In the early years of running a business I knew I had a lot of common sense but I felt I was lacking in intelligence. I would hold back in silence rather than speak up and have people think I was an idiot. Over the years, Swampy tried to convince me that I possessed intelligence. "People don't understand how smart you are," he would say from time to time. Swampy was right, it just took me many years to understand this.

Over time on the journey I began to discover hidden talents. I think this is true for all of us. As we learn and gain experience in life, along the way we unwrap our abilities. For a long time, my writing skills were weak, but I started writing articles for water ski magazines and began to realize, "Hey, I can do this." The shy, quiet part of me was terrified of public speaking, but more and more I began to hone the ability to speak in front of crowds of people. Along the way, I discovered I wasn't too bad in math after all. I don't have the talent of figuring out quick math in my head like Swampy does—I just need a calculator!

Talent comes with confidence and sometimes it takes years to understand what you can and cannot do. Over time you will learn what you're capable of. In some situations you won't overcome obstacles, but in other situations you will. We all have our talents and we spend our lives learning what those talents are. In areas where we may lack talent, sometimes it's simply a matter of accepting this and moving on.

Everyone has to find out what their own passion is. Get into it, learn about it, research it, understand it, gain confidence with it, love it, and enjoy it. Everyone has something they love to do whether it's Frisbee golf, playing guitar, or football, everyone will have one thing that puts a smile on their face. With passion we can accomplish anything!

Epilogue

After I returned from my honeymoon, Swampy met me at the ski school. "I have a new trick run for you, Keith. Remember what we said? Training starts after the honeymoon for the World Championship. Let's go!" With a sigh, I grabbed my wetsuit and followed him down the dock to the boat.

Swampy idled the boat through the channel toward the lake. I zipped up my wetsuit, cranked down on my cinch straps and prepared the rope. Swampy did a rundown of the new trick run and I mentally ran through it in my head. Near the shore, an osprey swooped down to grab a fish out of the water with a wavering squeal. I turned to look at Swampy. "Someday, this is all going to end for me. You know that shelf life we've been talking about Swamp?"

"I sure do, KSO."

"How much longer do you think I can do this? You know it's in my blood, but even I know there's an end at some point."

"Well, you are skiing better than you ever have at the age of 34 and as long as you want to keep it going, you can." I sat down on the edge of the boat and took a swig out of my water bottle. "Do you ever look back, Swamp, and think we would still be doing this today?" Swampy shifted in his seat and turned to look at me. "I never thought it would go this far, but we set these goals since the very beginning, I guess, and look where we are."

I nodded. "We have accomplished everything we wanted to and now it's time to build this ski school so others have the opportunity to become the best. I would have loved being a part of something like this when I was a teenager. I feel good about this. It's our way of giving back to a sport that has done so much for us." I paused. "Now that we're devoting so much time to the kids who come here, I get a better sense of all the time, money, and sacrifices you made for me. I wouldn't be here today...if it wasn't for you. Do you ever regret giving up so much of your life for me back then?"

"I don't have any regrets." He shook his head. "I'd do it all over again. You're very special to me. You're...like a son."

I could feel a lump form in my throat. "I appreciate everything you've done for me, Swamp."

"Okay, you're going to make me cry, Keith!" He turned away and gripped the wheel. "Get your butt moving. Do you remember your trick run?"

"I got it, but...do you think you could scale it down a little bit and make it easier?" I teased.

"Nobody said it was going to be easy," he barked. "Our job isn't done yet! Jump in the water. You've got some training to do."

A Note from Karen Putz

The story of how this book came about is a story itself. In the fall of 2009, my husband sent me a link to a Today Show segment featuring Judy Myers, a 66-year-old barefoot water skier. I sat at my desk watching "The Old Lady" skim across the water with two-time World Barefoot Champion Keith St. Onge at the helm of the boat. It had been 26 years since I tripped over a wake while barefooting and I crashed headfirst into the water. In an instant, I went from hard of hearing to deaf, thanks to a weak hearing gene in my family. After watching the video, I had a burning desire to get back on the water again. I got in touch with Judy and she invited me to come to the World Barefoot Center to receive instruction with Keith.

In March 2010, I found myself in a boat on Lake Conine in Winter Haven, decked out in a wetsuit and getting instructions from Keith on barefooting. I was 44 years old, overweight, and very much out of shape, but the moment I put my bare feet on the water the old passion for the sport came flooding back.

Two weeks later I was back in the boat, hungry for more instruction. During a break from skiing, Keith and I started to talk. "You've done it all as a World champ, what's next for you?" I asked. "What do you want to do five years from now?"

"I want to write a book and do some speaking," he said.

Back home in Chicago, Keith and I continued to keep in touch. One day, I was on my way to work when I was startled by a voice. As clear as day, I heard the words: "Write Keith's book." For a minute there, I was puzzled. Did I really *hear* those words, or did I just think them? The voice was so real; it was as if someone was sitting in the passenger seat talking to me. That night, I was on Twitter when a link popped up: "How to Write a Book Proposal." Just for fun, I played around with writing a proposal for Keith's book. The words just flowed. I debated whether or not to send it to him; after all, I barely knew the guy.

"Call me crazy..." I wrote in the subject line. I attached the proposal and hit Send.

"Call me crazy...yes I will," Keith wrote back. A few more emails flew back and forth, discussing how to proceed. I offered to write the book with him. No contract. No strings attached.

Keith was in a quandary: He had started the book with his cousin. He called his mother to get some input. His cousin had discontinued working on the book and Keith wanted to know if this deaf barefooting student of his was the right one to move on with the book. He didn't blink twice when she told him to work with the gal he just met. He trusted his mother's guidance.

There were challenges at first. In the dance of getting to know each other, I discovered Keith craved structure and a map for guidance. He learned to deal with me--a free spirit who was guided by an unpredictable muse. During hours and hours of phone conversations with a team of interpreters signing everything, we crafted a book compiled of some amazing stories and life lessons. During those hours of phone conversations, there was one memorable conversation which stood out:

I was watching the interpreter on the screen of my videophone when suddenly a puzzled look crossed her face. "It sounds like water," she signed. She furrowed her brow. She continued to interpret Keith's conversation as I took notes.

There was a long pause. "He's, um, flushing the toilet," she signed. I threw my head back and laughed.

"Keith, are you in the bathroom?" I asked.

"How—how did you know??" he stammered. "I thought you were deaf!" Keith quickly learned a lesson of his own: interpreters sign everything they hear!

In all the hours of conversation over the phone, in the boat and at the local Crispers restaurant, I came to know a humble teacher with rich life lessons. Keith knew what he wanted to do from the time he was 13; he wanted to make a career out of walking on water. The journey wasn't an easy one in a sport that traditionally has little money tied to it. On his life journey, Keith learned the lessons of success, both on the water and off.

In the two years of writing this book, Keith became a brother, mentor, and friend. He taught me more about life and success than I had ever learned from anyone else. There is a saying, "When the student is ready, the teacher will appear." Keith's book, *Gliding Soles,* became that teacher.

A Note of Thanks from Keith

I would like to thank my parents, Claude & Jackie St. Onge, for such a positive and supportive upbringing. A special thanks to my sister, Kendra, for her love and support.

To all four grandparents, thank you for being my biggest fans every step of the way.

Huge thanks goes out to Swampy for being my second father, while keeping me motivated and pushing me to always achieve more!

Thanks to Judy Myers for being like a second mother to me and for all of your help in bringing the ski school to the next level.

Thanks, Spray Danny, for being such a great skiing partner and wonderful friend in my early years of training.

A big thank you goes to all of my friends and family for your support and encouragement throughout the years. Thank you for sharing your stories in the countless interviews which were done for the book.

To Patrick Wehner, thank you for giving me support at one of the lowest points of my career. The card you gave me started a ripple of inspiration beyond anything we could have imagined. Even after your recent diagnosis of Lou Gehrig's disease, you continue to inspire others with your positive outlook on life.

A special recognition goes to the backbone of the World Barefoot Center ski school for all of their help and support they've given me. Thank you, David Small, A.J . Porreca, Ben Groen, and Ashleigh Stebbeings.

Thank you Dave Ramsey, Dan Miller, Tom Ziglar, Bill Graham, Matt St. Onge, Dave Tombers, Kevin St. Onge, Jess Albright, and Cheri Hanners for your input while this book was in the final stages.

Thanks, Karen Putz, for putting up with all my stories and listening to my whole life over the phone, even though you couldn't hear me. Thank you for all your patience and motivation to continue until the book was complete.

314

Another thank you goes to the ZVRS interpreters who translated hours and hours of our conversations.

The biggest thank you of all goes to my wife, Lauren, for encouraging me to put countless hours into working on this book to help benefit others which was my first goal and priority.

The Ripple of Inspiration Goes On

The card which Patrick Wehner gave me in 2002 became part of a ripple of inspiration which continues to this day.

I would like to share this inspiration with you. I invite you to cut out the inspiring words of William Arthur Ward below and begin working on your dreams. Once you have achieved progress or accomplished something meaningful, take a moment to pass it on to someone who can benefit from these words of encouragement. Continue the ripple of inspiration and make a difference in someone's life.

I would love to hear your stories of how your card has inspired you and others. Please share your story at www.keithstonge.com or email me at keith@keithstonge.com and let me know how this card has traveled from you to others in your life.

Keith St. Onge and Patrick Wehner

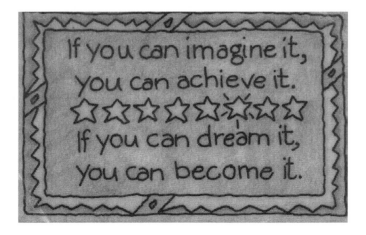

If you can imagine it, you can achieve it. If you can dream it, you can become it.

316

Made in the USA
San Bernardino, CA
08 April 2015